CW00820233

WALTER MACKEN

DREAMS ON PAPER

WALTER MACKEN

DREAMS ON PAPER

ULTAN MACKEN

MERCIER PRESS
IRISH PUBLISHER – IRISH STORY

MERCIER PRESS
Cork
www.mercierpress.ie

Trade enquiries to CMD BookSource,
55a Spruce Avenue, Stillorgan Industrial Park,
Blackrock, County Dublin

© Ultan Macken, 2009

ISBN: 978 1 85635 630 5

A CIP record for this title is available from the British Library

10 9 8 7 6 5 4 3 2 1

This book is sold subject to the condition that it shall not, by way of trade or otherwise, be lent, resold, hired out or otherwise circulated without the publisher's prior consent in any form of binding or cover other than that in which it is published and without a similar condition including this condition being imposed on the subsequent purchaser.

No part of this publication may be reproduced or transmitted in any form or by any means, electronic or mechanical, including photocopying, recording or any information or retrieval system, without the prior permission of the publisher in writing.

Printed and bound in the EU.

CONTENTS

INTRODUCTION

I first planned to write a biography of my father over twenty years ago. I remember writing about forty pages of a first draft and reading it to my mother in the kitchen of our house in Menlo. She listened very carefully and expressed her concern about how personal it was. I taped a series of interviews with my mother which included some valuable insights and I talked to her constantly about him. Her husband was her favourite subject and she loved to talk about him.

One of the cornerstones of my research work was the papers and manuscript material he left in his filing cabinet. Unfortunately in the late 1970s, my mother decided to sell his papers to a German university – Wuppertal. They bought 6,000 pages of documents for £12,500. I was disappointed at the time, as I had hoped to draw on them in writing the biography, but I visited Wuppertal in the early 1980s and photocopied 800 pages of material from these documents, trying to focus on personal matters.

I began training regularly for marathons in 1980 and in the autumn of 1981, I got pneumonia. The doctors insisted I was to stay indoors for six weeks, so I gathered all my father's letters and the photocopies from Wuppertal and I catalogued them in five folders. Among these papers were the love letters my mother and father wrote to each other and I thought that my mother was very generous to allow me to read these intimate letters.

Another obstacle to my writing the biography, was the traumatic experience of my marriage of nineteen years, which ended in 1990 when my wife and I decided to separate. That summer I also decided to leave my staff job at RTÉ and search for alternative employment. In the years since 1990, I spent the first few months in America and then returned to live in Galway with my mother. I went back to teaching and worked as a substitute teacher and a freelance journalist until I joined the Irish Civil Service in 2006 as a clerical officer. I worked for the Department of the Environment and then came to Dublin to work in the National Council for Curriculum and Assessment. I left that job in the summer of 2009 and now work as a freelance journalist and writer.

Meanwhile I kept researching and trying to understand the life of the extraordinary man who was my father. I published an open letter in the national newspapers asking for people's memories of my father. I received some great replies, and have been able to draw on some of them for this book. I have also talked about him quite a bit on the radio. When I went home to live in Menlo with my mother, for the two years that remained of her life, we became very close and she talked for hours about my father and about their life together. I think that I gained a greater insight into his life from those years at home with my mother than from anything else I did. After she died in April 1992, I felt I had the freedom to write this biography.

My father was born on 3 May 1915, the youngest child of Walter Macken and Agnes Brady. He had two sisters, Eileen born in 1912 and Birdie born in 1913. Less than two months after Walter Jnr was born, his father, becoming suddenly unemployed, volunteered to join the British army and went to Dover to train as a member of the Royal Fusiliers. In 1960, my grandmother Agnes gave my father the letters her husband had written to her and I have quoted extensively from them in Chapter One.

My grandfather was killed in the trenches of France on 28 March 1916 and so my father grew up without a father and in poor circumstances. He seems to have wanted to write since he was very young; my mother told me that he began writing when he was eight. On leaving school, apart from a brief period working as a clerical officer with Galway Corporation, he went straight to work at the Taibhdhearc theatre in Galway. There he met my mother, Peggy Kenny, and after they eloped to marry in Dublin in 1937, they moved to London where he worked as a life insurance salesman for a little over two years. When the resident producer at the Taibhdhearc, Frank Dermody, decided to leave, they asked my father to return to Galway to work as their producer. He returned in the spring of 1939 and he worked there until the end of 1947. He then moved to Dublin to work in the Abbey Theatre, where he stayed for three years. By that stage, he had two plays and two novels published, and was working on his third novel, *Rain on the Wind*, while living in Dublin.

The successful production of M.J. Molloy's play, *The King of Friday's Men*, in which he played the leading role, resulted in his being offered a chance to act on Broadway, so he resigned from his job with the Abbey. While he was in the USA, *Rain on the Wind* was published and its success meant that he was able to earn a living as a full-time writer. He bought a house on the shores of Lough Corrib near Oughterard and we moved there in the summer of 1951. He was to spend most of his life in Galway and wrote novels, plays and short stories. In September 1966, he moved from Oughterard to the small Gaeltacht village of Menlo, some three miles from Galway city, where he had a small bungalow with two bedrooms built. *Brown Lord of the Mountain* (his last adult novel) had just been published and he was working on his second children's novel, *Flight of the Doves*.

In January 19767, he was approached by an English songwriter, Peter Hart, to write a stage musical based on the life of Fr James McDyer; he called it *God's Own Country*. In mid-April, he was having some stomach trouble so he was admitted to hospital and had a battery of tests. He continued working on the musical while in hospital and was allowed home on Friday 21 April. My parents went for their usual walk on the prom that afternoon and that night they watched television for a while. They retired to bed at around 11 p.m. My father could not sleep, so at about 2.30 a.m. he told my mother that he was going into the sitting-room, to see if he could get to sleep on the couch. Half an hour later, my mother heard him making a noise and she went to the sitting-room to check on him, but found him dead. The doctors said afterwards that he died of a massive heart attack. He was only fifty-one.

In writing this book, I am drawing not only on the memories of my mother about my father, but also my own memories and especially my brother's memories and the letters my father wrote to him. I'm also drawing on memories of my cousin, Tom Kenny, and on many close friends of my father.

Since my brother left home when he was only seventeen and I was twelve, I was at home alone with both of my parents for the rest of my teenage years. I was very close to my father and spent many days fishing and walking with him. I absorbed a lot of what he was saying and, while writing this book, I recalled many of our conversations.

I gave theatre audiences an introduction to my father's life and times when I presented my one-man show *My Father, My Son* in 2001 and again in 2004. I first presented that show at the Studio in the Town Hall in Galway in May 2001. From there, I took it to Andrew's Lane in Dublin and also brought it to a number of schools. I took it to Boston in June 2001 as part of the Boston Irish Cultural Festival. When I returned to Ireland, I took it to Belfast and to Inisheer on the Aran Islands. I revived the show in 2004 and staged it at the Taibhdhearc in Galway. I also took it back to Belfast. In writing this book I wanted to create a more permanent record of my memories of my father's life.

Dreams on Paper is a culmination of all the research, reading and listening I have done over the years, and I hope that readers will get some idea of the man who was Walter Macken.

Ultan Macken

FAMILY TREE

Walter Macken married Mary Jane Rodgers
(Born 1837)   (Born 1850)

Walter	Tom	John	Michael	Mary	Nannie	Pat	Hannah
b.1888	b.1889	b.1890	b.1891	b.1892	b.1893	b.1894	b.1895

In 1911 Walter Stephen married Agnes Brady who was born 1880, one of fifteen children from Eyrecourt near Ballinasloe, County Galway. They had three children: Eileen born 1912, Noreen born 1913 and Walter Augustine born 1915. Walter Stephen Macken died at St Eloi, France on 30 March 1916.

Walter Augustine Macken married Peggy Kenny (b. 1909) on 9 February 1937 at Fairview church, Dublin. They had two children: Walter Óg born 10 April 1938 in London and Ultan born on 10 September 1943 in Galway.

1

GRANDFATHER MACKEN – HIS LIFE AND TIMES

The 3 May 1915 was an important day in the life of a young Galway couple as their son, Walter Augustine, was born. They already had two daughters, Eileen born in 1912 and Noreen (later given the nickname Birdie) born in 1913. The young couple must have looked forward to a reasonable future together, as the father of the house was a skilled carpenter and was in full-time employment. He was Walter Stephen Macken, born in Cong, County Mayo on St Stephen's Day, 26 December 1888. Walter Stephen was the eldest of a family of four boys, Walter, Tom, John and Michael and six girls, Mary, Nannie, Pat, Hannah, Kate and Margaret. Their father, whose name was also Walter, was the chief forester on the Ashford Castle estate. The job supplied the family with a house and his wife, Mary, worked as a cook at the castle. But tragedy struck when Walter died suddenly. We do not know if it was an infectious disease, such as pneumonia, that killed him or quite possibly, he may have died from a heart attack. His death was devastating for the family, as the landlord evicted them from their estate house and for a few years they lived locally in poverty-stricken circumstances.

My father had planned to research his family history and write about it. I'm sure that he had gathered facts about his family when he visited the Macken aunts in the United States in the 1950s. I remember visiting Cong with him in the mid-1960s and his attempts there to find out something about his father, Walter Stephen's, family. I learned from my father that my grandfather and his brothers ended up at Letterfrack Reformatory School near Clifden, but I had no idea of how they actually came to be there. Having been told stories about their time at Letterfrack, I wondered if these were true, as I was shocked to hear they had been sent to an industrial school. I looked up the census of population for 1902 and found the names of my grandfather and his three brothers as residents of Letterfrack Reformatory School. Even when I was growing up in Galway in the 1950s, it was a mark of shame for anyone to be sent to such a school and it was clearly a matter of shame for the brothers in later life.

To clarify the details of my grandfather and his brothers' time at Letterfrack, I contacted the Congregation of the Christian Brothers in Ireland who were able to check their records and give me details of the exact times and years that the four brothers spent there:

> Walter and Michael arrived in Letterfrack aged nine and eight on 1 March 1897. Their parents' names were given as Walter and Mary. At the time of their arrival, their father was dead. Begging is given as the reason for the committal. The other two boys, Thomas and John arrived on 9 August 1899 aged eight and seven, the reason given for their committal is that they were receiving alms and did not have a proper guardianship.

What these records reveal was that because the two older boys were begging, they had been brought before a court and sentenced to a period of detention at Letterfrack, which was of course thing of terrible shame for them. The records also revealed:

> Walter was discharged on 11 February 1904. He had been employed in the school as an assistant carpenter. By May 1905, the school authorities had been told that Walter was doing well in Galway. Michael was officially discharged on 1 February 1905, although he stayed on in the school for a short period. In May 1905, he left the school and emigrated to the United States. The school was informed in March 1907 that he was doing well. Thomas was officially discharged on 1 August 1907 but remained at school while waiting to be placed in employment. Eventually he was sent as an apprentice to a Mr Spellman, a journeyman tailor in Galway. By February 1908, the news from him was that he was doing well.

Their records about John are interesting: 'John was officially discharged on 1 August 1908, kept on in school and then later on in August went to be an apprentice tailor to a Mr Patrick Conroy of Carna in the Connemara Gaeltacht.' However, their records also indicate that John went to America, that they heard from him in 1910 and he was doing well. I'm almost certain that this information is incorrect, as all the references to Uncle John in my grandfather's letters clearly indicate that he was living and working in England. From my own research, I believe both he and Tom lived most of their lives in South Shields in the north of England. However, in their letter to me, the Christian Brothers further add to the confusion by making another reference to John being in America. 'John paid a visit to the school with his wife in 1959, we would regard him as a credit to the school, took a look around the school, home from holidays in America, he gave £1 to the boys to buy sweets.'

In all my grandfather's letters, he talks about his brother John having joined the British army as he had. Auntie Birdie also told me about Tom and John living in the north of England. The account of him coming back to visit the school was I think the year he visited us in Oughterard. I can remember clearly his visit to us at our home and he brought his second wife, Lorna, with him. I was only thirteen at the time, but my impression was of someone who was very English, with a strong northern English accent.

When I began my research work for this biography in 1981, I discovered from my father's American first cousin, Sabina Walsh, that my father's uncles, John and Tom were still alive, and she sent me their addresses. Without thinking, I wrote and asked them if I could come over to talk to them about their childhood. With hindsight, I should have gone over to my Auntie Birdie's house in Sunderland and then arranged to go to visit them with her. Instead, by writing to them and telling them I knew that they had been in Letterfrack, I destroyed any hope that they would talk to me. Uncle John wrote back first, saying that he would have to contact Tom about talking to me. The following week he wrote again and told me that he and Tom had talked, and they had decided that they were not interested in speaking to me. They referred to the fact that our American cousin, Sabina, like other Americans, seemed obsessed with finding out about her roots, but they did not think that I would be like that and were disappointed in my desire to find out about both their experiences and the experiences of their brothers and sisters. They would prefer it if I left them in peace. John said that when he met me, he found me to be a reserved person who he thought would respect other people's privacy and not a brash person like their American cousin seemed to be. So I don't know what happened to them as they grew up, and I also don't know what exactly happened to their mother or indeed to their sisters. I believe it is quite likely that the sisters could have been sent to a girls' industrial school. There was one run by the Sisters of Mercy in Clifden at that time. There is also the possibility that they were sent to the orphanage in Galway city. I do know that my great-grandmother, Mary Macken, came to live in Eyre Street, because it was from that address that my grandfather wrote the first letter we have from him to my grandmother, Agnes Brady.

When my grandfather, Walter Stephen came to Galway in February 1904, he was sixteen, and because he had experience and qualifications he had no problem finding a job. Emerson Builders employed him as a carpenter, a job he held for the next eleven years. From his photographs, you can see that he was a strikingly handsome man. As well as working hard as a carpenter, he was also a very talented actor, singer and performer and soon after he came to Galway, he joined a drama group and appeared on stage regularly. Apparently, he was a wonderful actor. When I worked for a period on the docks in Galway, the dockers told me stories of how when they were children they used to go to see Walter Macken on stage. My grandfather always played the lead role in the melodramas they watched and they would come out of the plays and imitate what they had seen.

The drama group staged their plays in a place called the Father Crotty Hall in Middle Street, right in the heart of Galway beside the Augustinian church. Beside the Father Crotty Hall there was a pub come dance-hall called the Racquet Court. Each night when the plays were over, the actors used to go in there for a drink and it was there my grandfather met my grandmother, Agnes Brady, a striking-looking woman who originally came from Ballinasloe. Her family were farmers from East Galway, near Eyrecourt. There were fifteen children in the family: five boys and ten girls. Agnes was one of the youngest. As each one grew up, they emigrated to the United States and I think most of the Brady boys and girls ended up in the Boston area.

Mr and Mrs O'Shaughnessy, the owners of the Racquet Court, visited the Brady home (they may have been relations or from the area) and when Mrs O'Shaughnessy discovered that Agnes (fourteen) was to be sent to America, she persuaded them to allow her to take Agnes to Galway. When Agnes came to work in the Racquet Court, she was too young to serve in the bar, so for the first few years she cared for the O'Shaughnessy children. When she reached eighteen, she began to work in the bar and, as she was a beautiful woman, all the young men enjoyed chatting to her.

One of her best friends was a woman called Mrs Spellman (possibly the wife of the tailor Spellman to whom Tom Macken had been apprenticed when he came in from Letterfrack). Mrs Spellman became a life-long friend and told me how they always went around together. Mrs Spellman worked in the Great Southern Hotel and she and Agnes would meet up and go for long walks out to Salthill.

Walter Macken asked her out many times before she agreed to go out with him. There was an age difference of six years between them, with Agnes being the elder, and this probably explained her reluctance to go out with him. However, once they began to go out their romance flourished and they were married in May 1911 when Walter was twenty-two and Agnes was twenty-eight. My grandmother was an extraordinary woman. She was a wonderful storyteller and there is little doubt that her story-telling ability was passed on to my father, who spent a lot of his early life listening to her every day. My grandfather, Walter Stephen, also had talents which were obviously passed down through the genes: his ability to sing, to act and to write. This is one of the reasons why I have included substantial extracts from his letters to my grandmother, as they seem to me to demonstrate his writing ability.

Before my grandmother died in 1964 at the age of seventy-five, she sent my father the letters her husband had written to her from the beginning of their marriage, with the comment: 'They include the letter that broke my heart.' These letters are a wonderful resource and give us a real insight into what my grandfather was like. They also give us an idea of what their life together was like before he joined the British army in 1915. The first letter was written shortly after they married in 1911, when Agnes had gone to Ballinasloe to spend Christmas with her father and brother. The address given is Eyre Street, where the couple obviously lived with Walter's mother:

Eyre Street.
Xmas Eve

My dearest Agnes,

Your letter and Xmas present arrived today, many thanks for your kind thoughts and wishes. You are looking forward to a long letter no doubt but I fear that I'm going to sadly disappoint you, owing to lack of news or something to say, for as you well know, I'm a man of few words. I would, however, say something of what's in my mind only that I'm afraid you would laugh at me for saying what you call silly things, for as you know *we agreed to put no love in our letters* [*Author's italics*].

I'm sorry and thankful at the same time. I'm sorry that you dearest are or rather feel a bit lonely but remember Aggie what I told you before you went, that yours is a labour of love and charity. I think I can safely classify it as one of the eight beatitudes. Only think to yourself what would these two poor men do without someone to care for and bring some small bit of joy and comfort to their poor hearts this blessed Xmas. I only wish my pet that the time was come when I had someone to work for and comfort but please God that time is not too distant. I'm thankful at least that you have someone like Flossie [*a friend of Agnes*] to keep you company.

And now Aggie, I think it's time to bring this nonsensical scrawl to a close, as I'm lost for anything more to say. Don't be in a hurry back, make your dear father and brother as happy as you can, give them my best wishes, let you all enjoy yourselves as well as you can and that God and His Holy Mother may watch over, protect and send you all blessings this Xmas, the prayer of one who is yours Aggie until death.

Walter xxxx

My grandfather's desire for children 'to work for and comfort' was soon satisfied: Eileen was born in September 1912, Noreen was born a year later in December 1913 and Walter Augustine arrived in May of 1915. During those years, my grandfather earned his living as a carpenter working for Emersons. Something of the flavour of his work pattern is given in this the second letter from the collection. Walter was sent to Labane, beside Ardrahan, about fifteen miles from Galway with other men from the company to repair a house. They travelled to and from Galway by train – the train line ran from Galway to Athenry and from Athenry to Ennis and then to Limerick. At this stage the couple had two children so the letter was probably written in 1914 or 1915:

Labane,
Ardrahan.

Dearest Aggie,

Your letter received this morning. I was more than delighted to receive it, you made me feel very lonely telling me about Eileen and darkie [*Noreen*], the poor little kids, isn't it a blessing they are so good, for God's sake Aggie, don't let them run too much about in the street, it would drive me mad if they caught the fever, you cannot be too careful in a case of this kind of thing.

Well Aggie, I hope that Joe Lydon went to you early yesterday with the few shillings. I hope you will not be too vexed with me for not sending you the £1. I had a day off last week because of the rain. The weather is something fierce. I daresay we'll have broken time for the next month or so; there is not the least bit of shelter where we are working.

Indeed I had made up my mind to go straight home last Friday, if it didn't stop raining before 12 o'clock struck.

Working on the roof last Wednesday and I can tell you, it would take a cat all his time to hang on, so Aggie, if you do not get the £1 for a while, don't be too upset, I'll send you all I can. I told Dick Emerson yesterday to give Jack Connelly 15/- for you, early Saturday, so you can be sure to have it by two o'clock. I will send you whatever I can then on Sunday. The nights here are terribly lonely, the only comfort we have is Joe Dolan, the mason, and he has an old fiddle so we generally manage to have a dance or two nearly every night. I went to Gort yesterday evening to get my light boots repaired.

The first person I met at the station [*railway station*] was Maisie Cooke. She nearly dropped; I was the last person she expected to see. I left the boots with her father. Birdie is as big a devil as ever. They all thought you were sick or something when you hadn't written. I was annoyed with them asking me – how is Aggie? I told Birdie that her shift [*her dress*] was all right and that I would be getting you to send it on at once.

I'm afraid before I leave here, I'll have to get a pair of hob-nailed boots as the roads are in a terrible state. Well Aggie, I haven't much more to say to you, only that you'll scarcely know me when you see me; the food in the house is better than I could almost afford in Galway. Soup three or four times a week, mutton, pork and plenty of eggs; so even if we are paying high itself, we are getting the worth of it.

I don't know yet when I'll take a run home. I don't think I'll go home before Saturday week at the earliest; because I don't think it's worthwhile. So until then, Aggie, goodbye, take care of yourself and the children, don't let Eileen run out into the street too much. Kiss them for me and keep a big one for yourself.

Your fond husband,
Walter

NB. Tell Paddy Naughton that I'll send home the plane next Saturday by Jim Dolan.

Life can change dramatically in a short period of time and in my grandfather's case it certainly did. My father was born on 3 May 1915 and only weeks later, in June 1915, my grandfather's employer, Dick Emerson told him that he had no further work for him. At that time the British army had launched recruiting campaigns all over Ireland. (My father gives a very good description of the kind of campaign in his historical novel – *The Scorching Wind*.) For someone like my grandfather, who was now suddenly out of work, with a wife and three children to support, there was little choice – he joined the British army for economic reasons, to earn money to support his family. Moreover, British propaganda was so powerful it convinced thousands of young Irish men that by joining the British army and fighting the Germans, they were helping to stop men, women and children in the smaller countries being raped and pillaged. So he went to Renmore Barracks and joined the infantry regiment, the Royal Fusiliers.

Within a month, he was sent to Dover to begin his training for trench warfare. Like many other Galway women, Agnes accepted that her husband had to go. Just three weeks after he signed to join up, his employer offered him his job back, but by then it was too late, Walter's future was sealed. It is from the training camp in Dover that many of his surviving letters were sent home to Galway. The first letter was sent to a family friend called Ivy. She seems to have been a close friend of both Agnes and Walter:

Duke of York School 18092, 8th Company, 6th Battalion,
Dover Royal Fusiliers.
10th August 1915

Dearest Ivy,

Forgive me for not acknowledging your kind letter and parcel sooner. I partly guessed you would be a bit busy last week between the work in the bar and looking after some nice fellows. I dare say you were pretty well kept on your feet. I suppose the Bazaar was a great success. I had a letter from Agnes on Saturday; she didn't say anything about it; she said she would be writing on Monday, you can tell her I will not answer until I next hear from her, tell her also she forgot to mention anything about the kiddies.

I'm afraid Ivy that my furlough that I was looking forward to about the middle or the end of September is to be put off for a longer period, all through a crowd of crabs of Home Service men who they want to send off to Africa or India to relieve soldiers for active service.

My squad were due to go on firing next week as we had passed our test for drill and gym but a new order came out that those old crabs who had done next to no drill were to be taken on the rifle range immediately and go through a course of firing. That means we will have to remain at our daily drilling for a few weeks longer and get into trained quarters about the end of September, unless something turns up to take them out of our way.

October is a bad month for the Irish channel crossing, but I don't mind that so much as we are pretty decently clothed. It is having to wait for those old cripples to get out of our way that gets on my nerves. There was a rumour last week that we were to be sent to a station just outside London but I have heard nothing further about it.

I felt terribly homesick all last week, it was the first touch of homesickness I felt since coming here. I suppose thinking of the Bazaar and the Races made me feel that way. So I went out to Jerry's son-in-law's house on Tuesday and spent a few hours with them.

But the feeling of homesickness returned again on Wednesday and to make matters worse, I had no letter from anyone until Aggie's came on Saturday. Then again, my chum went home again, you couldn't imagine how I put in Sunday fooling about all day. I could not get myself to write a letter.

Now thank goodness, a new week has come, I have left my loneliness behind me and I feel all right again. I daresay that you feel a bit disappointed that Johnny [*Walter's brother*] did not get to Galway before going to France but cheer up we may all be there for good before Xmas is over.

Bye, bye for the present, dear Ivy,
Give my best to all at the Racquet,
Kiss the kiddies and Aggie for me,
Yours as ever,
Walter

There are often references in the letters home remembering his friends at the Racquet Court, where Agnes was still working.

The next letter I have is a fragment of a letter he wrote to my grandmother, probably in or around the same time as the one he wrote to Ivy:

Dearest Aggie,

Your welcome letter came this morning, also the two stamps and many thanks for those. My reason, Aggie for not saying anything about my homecoming is simply I'm not sure when I can get my furlough, you see we have to wait until we get off the drill square and get into training quarters, it's while we are in training quarters, we get our furlough, we only stay in these training quarters for about a month, before going to the front, the soldiers here call it, their last home.

From what I can see, we may be going there sooner than we expect, as in about three weeks time, there is a whole battalion going from here in the rush I told you about in my last letter. If I have passed my musketry tests by that time, you can expect me about the middle of September. I believe they are only giving four days furlough on account of all the fellows that are overstaying their leave. The four days furlough would only give me one day with you Aggie, if they do not consider my case and allow me three clear days at home, I'll risk a week's confinement to the barracks.

In the following letter there are some very interesting details about his life as a British army soldier:

Dearest Aggie,

Your most welcome letter and postal order arrived yesterday. It was like being back with you to read your letter, why don't you always let yourself go like that?

Well Aggie, as to the rocking chair, we better not make arrange-ments in that direction until later on, everything is now in God's hands and as you say when the war's over, we'll think it out. You ask me about Warsaw. I don't know what the Irish papers say about it, but when you come to consider that before leaving, the Russians removed all pillar boxes off the street, they took down all the church bells, took away all cooking utensils that were any good, and took all the wheels and axles off every car and cart in the place, you may be sure that the Russians did not mean to defend it. The Germans did not even have a square feed to get in it, and the Russian army is still unbroken, you can take it for certain that they have some deeper game going on.

About my getting home next month, do not place too much hope in it. Did Ivy show you my last letter to her? I explained in it why I'm or rather was inclined to think I could get home before October. But Thank God, things seem to be going all right again as we are detailed off for firing tomorrow week and if nothing turns up to affect our orders, I don't see why I can't get my furlough before the end of September. But then as I say, a person is never sure what will happen.

Talking of Dover, Aggie, taken altogether it is not too much; there is nothing really to be seen in it. Khaki is in the majority everywhere, I'm sure between all there are at least 20,000 soldiers stationed here. Our barracks is about two miles from Dover, about 300 feet above it on the right, on top of the cliffs.

With the exception of Chrissie Baldwin I have not spoken to a woman since I came here and I do not feel inclined in that direction so far.

The inoculation we get after coming here takes the harm out of us for three months at least. I am not a bit surprised with John Sam Gough [*another local man who had joined up*] being fed up with the army, he is not the only one, every day, I'm almost sickened to death listening to fellows grousing, the damn asses. I suppose they thought they had nothing else to do but get a rifle in their hands, learn to shoot, then to knock about and do what they liked for five or six months before going to the front.

John Sam may thank his lucky stars he didn't join my regiment or any English regiment for that matter, he'd be dead by this. They are not half as strict in Irish regiments as they are in the English ones, as every little thing is punished in the English regiments.

All day long we are kept on the move from five in the morning until three in the afternoon, with only an hour or so for our breakfast and another for our dinner, and even then we are not sure of being left alone, we may have to turn out and get into our trenches.

The furlough did not come as soon as my grandfather hoped, which he reveals in the next letter, as well as talking about the news from home and what was happening with their neighbours:

Dover.
22nd September 1915

Dearest Aggie,

Your very welcome letter came this morning, many thanks for the PO. Aggie love, don't worry your head about sending the money for my photos, as on consideration, it would be better to wait until I get home, when we can all be taken together. When you come to consider it, that I am three months from home, six weeks will not be long in passing. It would take a clever man to tell you where I will be sent. I'm inclined to think it will be France. I hope it will be as if I have the good fortune to be wounded, I'll have a good chance of getting a furlough for a few days, if I'm sent to the Dardanelles, I'm afraid I won't get home until the finish.

Yes, Aggie, the war does not look as rosy as it did a month or two back, I'm inclined to think it will last almost into next summer, if not longer, there are hundreds of young men, laughing up their sleeves at us, the only recruits I see coming down here for the past two months are almost cripples or old men, but it's not want of men that is prolonging the war. You might have seen the papers a few weeks back about those Russian factories that through treachery were blown up. Well Aggie, we are supplying the Russians with ammunition for the past four months, were it not for that, the Germans would be well driven out of France by then. I've no idea why mother isn't writing and I've no intention of asking, I mean to pay her back. Although it may seem hard to do so, I'm fully intended not to see her when I get home on furlough.

The remainder of my upright relatives can sniff as they like; sooner or later they might find out the truth, not that I'm so anxious that she [*his mother*] should visit my family or write to me, but if she had any heart or conscience, which I'm afraid she has not, she could swallow her spite, once in a while. Is it not lovely for poor Maggie, going to bring another baby in to the world? Tell her I wish her every happiness. I was sorry to learn of poor Ursula, she is unfortunate poor thing, is she in hospital? You never speak of Mrs Griffin or Mrs Bruce; remember me to them when you meet them. Mike has not answered my letter up to this. Aggie, love there is nothing else of any importance I could tell you, only that I'm enjoying the best of good health. I'm having a pretty easy time this week and next week will be still easier, remember me to all at the Racquet.

Bye, bye for the present,
Kiss my darlings for me,
As ever,
Your devoted husband,
Walter

In his next letter, Grandfather Macken refers to a very nice gesture being organised on behalf of all soldiers by the YMCA:

Dear Aggie,

The YMCA has organised a special league which is setting out to have photographs taken of the families of the soldiers who are too poor to pay to have them taken themselves. There will not be any cost on the families at all. The amateur photographers have volunteered their services free. I think it is one of the nicest acts that has been performed during the war.

It doesn't matter where the soldier's relatives live, in the smallest back street or village in the British Isles, these photographers will reach them. So you can be prepared for a visit within the next fortnight, don't forget to send one or two to me. If you wish, I think, but I'm not sure, you can have Ivy taken with you, you could say she was my sister, I have put family on the form, I had to fill in. I had a letter from Flossie and Ivy; I will answer them next week.

You know that Zeppelin that I told you about in my last letter, well it was our guns that hit her, the devil. I bet no more of them will visit Dover, if they can help it; it is the best fortified place in England. I had a beautiful letter from Nannie today that I enclose; you can see that mother is still putting on the poor mouth. I think I'll ask her to write to you, it can do no harm, besides as she says we can still think of our young days. If you are writing to her say nothing about mother, just treat her doings as a matter not worth noticing.

Bye for the present,
How are all the chicks?
Kiss them for me,
Your beloved husband,
Walter

Later he again refers to his hopes of getting home, although it is clear he had no set date for this. The letter was sent on 29 September and these are some extracts from it:

Dearest Aggie,

I suppose by now you have seen the report of the great advance in France and Belgium. This is what I told you about in some of my letters. The newspapers have not been given the full story. We landed 20,000 troops in Ostend over the past eight days. If things go all right, we will have no trench work for the winter, it would do your heart good to hear the guns hammering Ostend like hell for the past three weeks. We can hear them quite plainly.

Talking of the war, Aggie, I may as well tell you not to be surprised if you see me come home after three weeks, there is a draft of five to six hundred soldiers to be sent to the front next month.

I had a letter from Nannie asking me if mother could go back along with me from Galway to England. I had a letter from Mary a few days afterwards wanting to know if I'd accompany Mother as far as Manchester, but unfortunately my journey does not take me anywhere near Manchester, so I suggested too, that Mary should meet us at Holyhead. Mary told me in her letter that the Pink Form man is after Thomas, wanting to know why he has not joined the Army; she thinks he is going to volunteer. She also told me that Michael has joined the Canadian contingent, that will mean that the whole Macken family will be in the fun.

It was five months since my grandfather had left home and he was still hopeful of getting to Galway for his furlough when he wrote the following letter on 7 October 1915:

Well Aggie,

Things looked very blue for my six days leave last Sunday as all leave was stopped until further notice and I half expected to be warned for [*sent to*] the front before a fortnight. But Thank God that cloud has rolled by and I won't be a bit surprised if I am home in a fortnight from next Monday.

We sent a draft from here to France on Tuesday morning. I pitied some of the poor fellows; nearly half of them had their six days leave cancelled and a crowd of them who had gone off for two days were recalled.

I thought there would be a strike on Sunday as every one of them went before the Colonel but all he said to them was that they were unlucky, the poor devils went off singing and shouting just as if nothing has happened. I think there were over seven hundred of them, altogether. There was not a great number left here who are able for the front, so I shouldn't be surprised if I'm there in about six weeks time.

You will be glad to know that I got on splendid with my shooting last week. We finished our recruit's firing on Monday and on Wednesday we started our duty man's course, which means we have to fire for our pay, or rather for an increase in our pay as they tell us but we never get it, I believe until we have served two years with the colours. We finish our duty man's course tomorrow (Friday) and even without tomorrow's firing, I have taken first class points. I only need thirty more points to qualify as a marksman, but I'm afraid I'll remain as a duty man's class as my sight is no good at six hundred yards. However, if I remain in the army for two years (which I hope not), I'll have my pay increased by 6d per day.

I had a letter at long last from John today, he has gone up very close to the firing line, he wants to know when I'm getting my furlough as he is going to try and be home with me. God, Aggie, wouldn't it be beautiful.

I wish to heaven if it were only true and he is going to have himself attached to the field ambulance to which I'll belong when I get over there, I'm sure Aggie that piece of news will please you. So Aggie, pray your best that he and I meet out there. It would give me heart to fight like the devil if Jack [*John's nickname*] were anywhere near.

He is still talking about getting home in his next letter send on 13 October 1915:

My dearest Agnes,

Your very welcome letter arrived here today. I would have received it yesterday only I was on guard from 3 o'clock yesterday until 3 o'clock today. Being on guard is a nice job, Aggie, only at night they are very strict here. Dover at present is a hard place to either get in or out of. In the past week, something had to be done as the whole place swarmed with spies, you can imagine what it was like last night with me being on my first night of guard duty too. I suppose I shall catch it pretty often while I am still here.

Aggie, I got to my new company last Saturday (3rd Company instead of 8th) and you will be glad to know I'm far happier in it than I have been since I left Galway, the men in my room have all been to the front, some of them have been there twice and expect to get there anytime again.

Of course they have all been wounded, they are better now, one of them got wounded the same day as poor Pat Power was killed. It would surprise you to hear them talk, much the same as if they were at a football match.

I have not heard from John since, but I'm expecting to be told off for my furlough anytime next week, and if not it will surely not pass the week following, so Aggie love, I'm all nerves until next week is here. God if you only knew how I look forward to seeing my loved ones and my little cabin again. I have lived and hoped for nothing else for four months. Aggie, I do not give a thought to what happens when I'm leaving you again and I want you Aggie dearest to do the same, it's time enough to think of that when it comes, let us think of nothing else for the present but my homecoming.

Did Nannie write to you yet? She threatened to do so in her last letter, I'm not sure if I told you. I had a beautiful cake from her today, poor thing; she's the only one outside of you, who writes to me, Mrs Macken [*his mother*] or Miss Brady [*a sister-in-law*] has not written so far, but never mind, I shall not turn grey with worry.

I will say no more for the present love. I hope to have definite news next week as to my homecoming so I'll conclude with love and kisses to you and the kiddies.

Your devoted and affectionate husband,
Walter

P.S. Send me on your photos as soon as you lay your hands on them.

The next letter, also written in October, also came from Dover:

Dearest Aggie,

Your letter, fags and parcels arrived, many thanks. I was just out of fags and money when yours arrived. I would have answered your letter sooner but I had no stamps. I hope you are not too vexed with me. But in any case, Aggie, even though I didn't get sent yet, I believe that if all turns out well, I will never fire a shot at the Huns. Everyone here is absolutely certain that the war will be over before the end of October. We were out all night on Friday on trench work and during one of our lectures, the sergeant (he is not long back from the front) told us that the most we'd have to do would be to go out and let all the soldiers there back, he said that in a month's time or six weeks at the latest, the great movement that we have been waiting for since spring was coming off. The English will have two million soldiers out there for the final push.

So, Aggie, old pal, keep your heart up, yesterday we sent a batch off to fight the Turks and an order came last night, there were to be no more drafts, the next drafts were being put back for another week or two. Fortunately we were put on trench-digging this week and we go to the training company in a fortnight's time, so someone must be praying hard for us. Trench-digging, Aggie is blooming hard work. We have breakfast at seven in the morning, start at a quarter to eight and dig away with only one quarter of an hour's rest until one o'clock, we then come back for dinner and then have to turn out marching until four. About these photos Aggie, I have just sent my pal over to the YMCA to enquire about them.

He hasn't come back yet; I'll see him before I post this.

By the way, Aggie, I have found a shop in Dover, where I can have three photos, something about the size of a cabinet, taken for four shillings. If you can spare the money, I'll have them taken but on no account, Aggie, leave yourself short.

Aggie, excuse me finishing this scribble,
I feel awfully tired,
Kiss my kiddies for me,
Your devoted husband,
Walter

I have read these letters many times over the years and one of the fascinating insights that they provide is the way these British

soldiers in training seemed to have no money – Walter has to ask
his wife to supply him with four shillings to pay for photos and
there is a reference to the fact that he does not have any stamps.
Another aspect of my grandfather's war experience that is not
that clear from his letters, is whether he actually did get home for
a furlough. My father's own memory suggested that he did. He
told me he remembered seeing his father dressed in British army
uniform. When I told my mother how my father had told me of
his clear memory of this, she doubted whether it was possible that
a baby of five months old could remember something like that.
However, Winnie Kelly, a next-door neighbour, told me that she
believed my father's memory of this was accurate, as her mother
had told her about my grandfather visiting home in his uniform.

The following letter also appears to confirm that he did get to
spend his furlough in Galway with his family, probably towards
the end of October 1915, as it explicitly states 'a week or two
before I went home'. He also talks about friends and neighbours,
such as Pat Healy, Mrs Griffin and Mrs Flaherty, as if he has just
seen them:

Dover.
Friday

My dearest Aggie,

Your welcome letter received this morning; also paper, I'm sorry to
hear that yourself and Wally are sick. I trust in God that you are
all right by the time this reaches you. I am not for the front this
week, Aggie, in all probability; I will not go there before Christmas.
Although we were told yesterday to stand by for a draft to be picked,
nothing came of it and last night I was in the quartermaster's office

and I was told there will not be a draft here for at least three months. But it is as well to take all these kind of rumours with reserve; one never knows in the army what is going to happen next. The War Office controls all these kind of matters; whatever they say must be done.

For my part, Aggie, I'm not much particular about when it comes, I'm ready and with God's help, I feel that nothing will happen to me and we shall be happy together again.

Poor Eileen, God help her, she is surely fond of her Daddy. Aggie when the train left the platform that evening, I felt proud of you, knowing how you felt, you were so calm and brave, I assure you it makes my heart light, something told me I will see you all again, and although I felt awful homesick after coming back to Dover, the thought of you on the railway platform made me forget my loneliness.

I had a letter this week from John about his leave. In fact I believe that all leave from the front has been temporarily stopped. Poor fellow he is unfortunate in his leave. I'm thinking that there will be some big fighting in France shortly from what I read between the lines. I would not be surprised if it came off in four or five weeks time and this is my reason for doubting, whether I shall be here after Xmas.

Mary [*his sister*] is becoming good to me lately, a week or two before I went home, she sent me a dozen stamps and this week I had a half-crown postal order from her to buy cigarettes. Talking of cigarettes, I didn't have to buy a single one since I left Galway thanks to Pat Healy, Miko and Ivy. I'm just on my last packet of woodbines today.

I haven't written to thank any of them yet and can't do it now until Sunday as I'm on guard duty today. I don't come off guard duty until four or five o'clock tomorrow. I may tell you, none of us are in humour for writing letters after coming off guard duty.

No more at present, Aggie, give my love to all at the Racquet, remember me to K. and Mrs Griffin and Mrs Flaherty. Trusting you and my pets are well and looking forward to your next letter.

Your devoted husband,

Walter

The next letter is just a fragment of one written not long before he was sent to France. He is worried about his wife and family, as he had not heard from them for three weeks:

Thursday

Dearest Aggie,

Is there anything the matter with you or any of my darlings? You have my heart nearly worn out worrying. If there was anything wrong, you had right to let me know, just fancy three weeks without even a postcard from you. Whether there is anything wrong or not, write immediately, if you have not already written and don't be afraid to tell me everything.

In addressing your next letter leave out the 8th Entrenching Battalion as I have just been ordered to join my unit so by the time, you receive this I will have had a taste of what war is like. Address your letter to 4th Battalion, RFBEF (Royal Fusiliers, British Expeditionary Force) and for God's sake Aggie love, do not leave me much longer without a letter.

Grandfather Macken wrote the next letter I have on Christmas Day 1915. By this stage he had been sent to France, although he had not yet been to the front line:

25th December 1915

A few lines I'm writing to you, to wish you and my darlings all the blessings of the season. I feel very lonely all this week. I have not received one letter from anyone belonging to me. Did you answer my last letter? In any case I cannot blame anyone in particular as I did not give you sufficient address. I thought when I was sent to Rouen that I would be sent up to the firing line a few days or at most a week afterwards. But I'm still here and although we were sent out to join the 4th Battalion, I believe we are to be sent to a different battalion, so I'm afraid if any of you wrote to me, it will be some time before I get the letters, if I ever get them.

If you have not written before this, do not do so until you hear from me again, I expect to be in the trenches in about three days time. You will be glad to know, I'm sure that I was at Confession and Holy Communion this morning. We had a midnight mass here last night. I lay awake all night thinking of you and the mites. I tell you I prayed more than ever I did in my life that God would bring me back to you all again, yes the longing to see you, was very strong. Please God, I'll see you all again.

So in about three of four days time, you can start your prayers in earnest as I shall be having my first tussle with those dogs of Germans. But for God's sake Aggie, do not worry yourself; it will do neither yourself or our darlings any good.

How is Mrs O and all at the Racquet? I hope they are all well. Did poor Ursula come out of hospital yet? Remember me to them all. I have not written to or heard from John since I came out. I don't want to write to him yet as I'm not sure which part of the line I will be sent to. And now Aggie, I have no more to say at present until I get to my destination. When I get that [*sic*], I will write to you immediately. Give my love to all at home. Kiss my little pets for me. God bless and keep my darlings safe until I return.

Goodbye,

Your devoted husband,

Walter

P.S. If you have not yet got my photos, write to Mrs Baldwin, 19 Lawn Road, Dover.

My grandfather's next letter was posted in January 1916. There is one thing that comes out very clearly in all my grandfather's letters – his absolute belief that he would survive the trenches and return home to his family, something his two brothers, John and

Tom did, of course. This letter is interesting in that he appears still not to have gone to the front:

Tuesday 18th January 1916

My dearest Aggie,

Your most welcome letter received yesterday. I would have answered it by return but I was working a bit late. I was more than delighted to know that you and the kiddies are well, may God keep you well for me. Poor little Birdie, I'm glad the poor mite wasn't forgotten on her birthday. Sometimes at night, I lie awake or rather I'm kept awake, no chance of going to sleep, while guns and pretty big ones at that are greeting each other all the time. While lying there wide awake, I think of you and the kiddies and wonder what you may be doing, but isn't it strange Aggie, I never feel homesick. I only think of when I'll get home to you all again. I'm glad you were pleased with the card I sent to K. Griffin. Don't you think she deserved something? I would have sent her a far better and nicer one if I could have got up to the shop where they sell some beauties. However, I may be able to send her something better as a small token of my gratitude. My mother has written me one letter, an answer to the one I wrote her. I acknowledged it and on the face of what you've said, it's the last she'll hear from me. I feel fairly fed up in that direction, though I might tell you, Aggie, I'm just as well pleased she keeps away. You need not worry about sending me anything, Aggie, if I want anything, I will ask for it, who else would I ask?

I can buy fags here or anything I want on the line. I may as well spend my money, the little I get, otherwise it could get lost before I get home. There are many ways of losing money here, so I may as well spend it. Aggie, go to Leaper (is it he that is doing the photos?) and haunt him until he does them for you and tell him I have you annoyed over them, tell him anything so long as you get them from him. I will have a pain in my heart until I get them. I hope you get them. I hope you get them before you write again. I receive the 'C. Bell' all right [*the local Galway newspaper of that time*], also the 'Galway Express'. I see that Kathleen [*a neighbour*] is doing secretary for you.

Tell Ursula, I'm glad she is out of hospital and getting well. Give my regards to all the Racquet Court. How are the pictures going? [*The Racquet Court was probably showing silent movies.*] Excuse the short note, Aggie, there is very little to say since I last wrote. Good-bye for the present, Aggie, heaps of love and kisses to your dear self and the kiddies. God bless all four of you and keep you safe for me.

Your devoted husband,
Walter

The next letter, dated February 1916, contains his first account of his experience of the trenches:

Dearest Aggie,

A line to let you know, I'm still all right. I had a letter from Ivy while I was in the trenches. I will answer it by this post if I can. It was so good of her to write to me. I thought I might have a letter from you. I need not tell you how it would have cheered me up, however, Aggie, I'm not vexed. I thought you might be waiting to send those photos. I hope I'll have a letter from you before going to the trenches again.

Your devoted husband,
Wally

The next letter was directly about his experiences in the trenches:

Well Aggie,

I have had my first taste of trench work. I knew it was hard and heard a lot about it but no one can realise what's it's like until they experience it. I have had mine. The Germans did not give us much trouble while we were there, but the weather I never experienced anything like it. It started to snow one morning at six o'clock and did not leave off even for five minutes, until ten o'clock the next day, then it started to freeze. The snow came back the following day and this kind of weather went on for four days.

The trenches we were in, had been lately taken from the enemy, they were in a terrible state, in some places we were above our knees in mud although we had rubber boots up to our thighs. We prayed a few times that the Germans might make an attack so that we could warm ourselves. We could not light any fires and it was sudden and sure death to put your head above the parapet, their snipers are splendid shots, we were just beginning to have our own back with our snipers though when we were relieved.

I am sending you some souvenirs I found on a German that I had to bury. I found an illuminated watch, a purse of German notes, a penknife, a wallet, with photographs, and some letters and a diary. I gave up the wallet with the exception of one photograph; the chap whom I buried is sitting. I have his grave marked. I believe the officer and some of the men are prisoners of war. I want you Aggie, to keep those things for me. I think if you ask Arthur Clark, he would frame the photograph and the notes all in one frame, the photograph in the centre, he will know, but he will do it if you tell him I asked.

I will register the watch. I was offered a pound for it but I refused. Let me know immediately when you get these things. Did John get his leave yet? I have not heard from him at all, I wonder why doesn't he write? When I was going up to the trenches, I passed within a short distance of where he was stationed, but could not get to see him unfortunately.

How are Mrs O and all at the Racquet getting on, remember me back to them. Are the pictures doing well? I wish the war was over and I was back home again, however, please God, I think it will not last that many months longer, something will have to break shortly. I think we have the better of the Germans now, but the devils will make a terrible fight of it before they give up. You want to hear our artillery when we start at them, it would do your heart good to see the wire fences and parapets going up in the air. The beggars begin to roar and squeal like rabbits, they get into a terrible state. I pity them when our fellows start a general bombardment.

Well Aggie dearest, I will now conclude, how are the children? I sincerely trust the little darlings are not catching cold. God protect you all and bring me back safely to you.

Goodbye, write immediately when you get this,

Your affectionate husband,

Walter

There are only two letters left in the collection of letters my grandmother kept. This, the first one, was written on Thursday 1 March 1916:

Dearest Aggie,

Your very welcome letter received a few days ago. I would have answered it sooner but I thought I would wait to see if I got those photos. I daresay that if you sent them on, I will hardly get them for a few days yet. I'm delighted to see by your letter that you are keeping your heart up.

As for me Aggie, I have nearly got used to the noise, at least I had, as I was not very long in the trenches. At present we are having a rest but I daresay we'll be back there again and if I'm not greatly mistaken, there will be some lively doings, however, Aggie love do not fear, I will keep my heart up, I only hope we will be able to shift them out of France before the summer.

All the boys are in the best of spirits, one would think to look at them, that there was no such thing as a war on. All last week we had snow and frost out there. I have never felt colder in my life. I hope we are done with the frost for now.

In case I forget, my full address here is 18092 4th Battalion R.F.X Company, 7th Platoon, BE7 France. Put this address somewhere safe so that you won't lose it, as if you forget to include the company and platoon numbers, letters are always delayed and I need not tell you how I fret when I don't hear from you.

Yes, I think, Delia [*Aggie's sister*] is more than good, God will bless her for it, I wish I had her letter, I will be only too glad to write to her. Sister Anthony [*Walter's aunt*] is a very bad correspondent; I only had one letter from her since Xmas. I had a letter from Uncle Michael in Spiddal and he told me he sent on cigarettes and stockings. I'm afraid I haven't received them as yet; perhaps like all my other parcels they will have gone astray altogether.

I wonder if John got his leave yet? I haven't heard from him for a considerable time. It's hard luck as where we are resting is only about 10 to 12 miles from where he is stationed. I might be able to manage a pass to go to see him, but not having heard from him for so long, I'm afraid I'll be disappointed if I get a pass and go to visit him only to find he is gone on leave.

I'll conclude this scribble for the present hoping your dear self and kiddies are all well. Goodbye for the present, write soon again and don't forget to put the full address on your letter.

Your affectionate husband,
Walter

The next fragment is from a letter to my grandmother posted on 22 March 1916. This was the last letter my grandmother received from her husband:

My dearest Aggie,

Your welcome letter received yesterday with the photographs. They are lovely; the boys say that Eileen is the image of me. I received your other letter a few days back when I was in the trenches. I would have answered it straight away only I guessed you would send on the photos immediately you got them. I received Arthur's [*a friend*] letter at the same time and answered it. I need not tell you how glad I was to hear from him.

I thought he was never going to write again. I have not received your shamrock yet. I had some from Uncle Michael a few days before St Patrick's Day and I wore it in the trenches. I'm more than delighted he called to see you. He speaks well of little Wally. I daresay Mother has not called …

Of course, my grandfather was on her mind all the time and one night she had a particularly vivid dream, which my mother told me about. She saw her husband walking along the trenches, there was the sound of gunfire and a starburst over his head and he fell down dead. The morning after that dream, she went to work in the Racquet Court. She went there most mornings to clean up and make it ready for business. It was very early in the morning and she was completely on her own. She heard a sound behind her and when she turned she saw her husband standing in his full Royal Fusiliers uniform: 'Oh Wally,' she said to him, 'why didn't you warn me you were coming home, I would be wearing my best clothes to meet you, will you look at me, I'm a mess.'

The figure said nothing and she knew then that he was dead – when she got the official letter, it didn't come as such a shock to her:

My dear Mrs Macken,

I am writing to tell you that your husband, 18092, Pt W. Macken of this regiment was almost certainly killed on March 28th, though his name will appear as missing, I cannot give you any particulars. He met his death doing his duty and now his work is finished here but we can pray that he will rest in peace and I am sure that for a man who does his duty, well truly death is a passing to higher things.

  With all sympathy,
  Yours sincerely,
  Noel Mellish, Chaplain, Royal Fusiliers

This was the letter that broke my grandmother's heart.

2

WALTER MACKEN – CHILDHOOD AND SCHOOL DAYS

Agnes Brady had to face a future without a husband and raise three children in 1920s Galway. Although my grandmother had very limited resources, she seems to have provided well for her children. She was in receipt of a soldier's pension, and did various jobs: sewing, mending and laying out the dead. In my father's book, *Cockle and Mustard*, the details appear to me to be almost identical to his actual life experience, although neither my father nor my mother ever told me whether the book was autobiographical or not. Despite this, I will draw on some of the material in that book, as I feel it provides an understanding of my father's experiences as a child. The book was submitted to Macmillan & Co. for publishing, but was rejected – to date, it has not been published.

My grandmother was very keen on education and as the two girls were attending the Presentation Convent National School, which was about one hundred yards from his home, young Wally was also sent there at about the age of three or four. It was common for young boys to attend the first few years of their schooling at a girls' national school. So my father was sent to the 'Pres' as it was called.

Early on in his school life, my father had an interesting experience, which he wrote about in an article for the Presentation Convent Annual celebrating their centenary in 1965. At that time, in all national schools in Ireland, children sat at desks that had a white inkwell containing blue or black ink on the right-hand side. Every child, with a simple wooden pen with a nib, used this ink. Every morning the teacher filled all the inkwells with ink from a large bottle. This was still the practice when I went to national school.

Imagine the scene: it is 1921 and my father is six years old, he is in Middle Babies. He has graduated from Infants and he is sitting in a classroom with thirty to forty other six year olds, most of whom are girls. There was at least one other boy, Jo Jo Keenan, and probably a neighbour, Danny Griffin:

> It isn't every male who can boast he was convent educated. I am one of them. In the 1920s there were quite a few boys in Galway who spent three years in the Presentation Convent School. Then it didn't have such a high flowing title, it was just called 'The Pres'. The Pres was up near Canon Davis' house and frankly the canon was a bit of a hazard.
>
> As you raced from St Joseph's Avenue, up the back of St John's Terrace, across the canal bridge, down New Road and around the corner like an aeroplane, you would often bump into the canon, and shifting from foot to foot explain to him why you were a bit late, receive his rebuke, and then when you got into your classroom, almost breathless, use him as an excuse, saying, 'the canon kept me'.
>
> You made three changes in the Pres, from Infants to Middle Babies and then into First Class, which seemed to be the goal of all desire, almost the same as striving for heaven, although the bliss was

tempered by the fact that Sister Ursula was reputed to have an eagle eye, so that some of our higher informants told us that First Class wasn't really heaven, it was more like purgatory, a sort of anteroom to heaven, or the next best thing.

My memory of Infants is all about chalk. I remember trying to eat chalk, and somehow I still have the taste in my mouth. Also I remember building blocks, coloured ones with the letters of the alphabet on them, and I remember those coloured beads on wire frames that taught you how to count.

I seem to remember there was a partition between Infants and Middle Babies that could be folded back against the wall but already when you were in Middle Babies, you were feeling a sense of superiority over those poor kids in Infants. Middle Babies meant only one thing to me, ink. I sat at desks with a white ink-bottle stuck in a hole and one day, I drank the contents.

This action I remember brought me into the limelight. My sister was sent for from upstairs and she came down and had to wash out my mouth with the tap in the concrete yard outside the glass door. I think she took a dim view of my action as she was the one to suffer because of my actions. What a stupid thing to have a brother lunatic enough to drink ink! I often wonder if I got ink in my veins that day in Middle Babies and I'm still trying to use it up. It's very difficult to give a logical explanation of why you should drink ink otherwise.

First Class meant Sister Ursula, who could wither a class with a look, and yet impress her personality on you so that you would never forget her and think of her in fondness. It meant that the rattling of the beads of Sister Magdalene as she came down from the room upstairs if we were unruly and under the care of a daunted pupil teacher. The sound of the big beads was enough to induce peace and apprehension, without the (to us from our small desks) enormously tall commanding no-nonsense presence of the Sister herself.

While my father wrote about his childhood, he rarely talks about deprivation, but they must have been very poor. Two of the young fellows he hung around with talked to me about him: the late Jo Jo Keenan told me how they spent their free time: 'We played endless games in the street. You could take a simple thing like an old car tyre and we would roll it all up St Mary's Road round by Nilodge and then around by the Crescent and back by Sea Road home again.'

As young fellows they always kept their ears open for the possibility of earning a few bob: 'At that time,' Jo said, 'there were a whole range of small shops all around Lower and Upper Dominick Street. We used to deliver messages for them. One day the shop man asked your father to deliver something to Lower Salthill. When he came back, he offered your father some fresh grapes, but your father said no, he wanted money so he paid him 1/– (one shilling). With this your father was able to buy us five Woodbines and bring us both to the pictures in the Racquet Court.'

Danny Griffin was another neighbour and lived in a house right opposite my father in St Joseph's Avenue. He told me how he and his family ended up living there. They grew up in the Gaeltacht area between Barna and Spiddal. His father was the second son and he was running the farm as the eldest son had emigrated to seek his fortune in England. However, the eldest son returned and Danny's grandfather then insisted that his father leave the farm as it was the eldest son who would inherit the property, so the family moved into Galway: 'We were much poorer than your father's family. We kept chickens and even had a pig in our back garden.' Danny had great memories of playing games with my father and all the children in the street.

Cockle and Mustard gives us further insight into life as a youngster growing up in Galway in the early part of the twentieth-century:

The boy learned to read, Sister Ursula insisted on that. Sister Ursula's main purpose in life was to instil the penny catechism into his thick irreligious head. There were some shocking big words in the catechism. He'd want two tongues to get around some of them but eventually he was able to gabble them off, so that he was ready to face his First Confession. He had to learn how to examine his conscience and see what he had done wrong according to the Ten Commandments.

Had he been stealing? When his Mammy sends him to get a message at the shop and there is three half pennies left and the boy keeps them instead of returning them to his Mammy, is that stealing?

So he waits with the others, trembling as his time comes to go into the Confessional Box. He is all alone in there entirely, for the first time in his life. It is dark and the shutter is closed. He can hear the priest whispering to the client on the other side of him. It is very dark. He hopes that the grill on his side will never open but it does and he is so terrified that the priest has to prompt him and then he starts telling him about his sins in a run.

He starts off with the formula Sister Ursula has taught him and that he has learned: 'Bless me father, for I have sinned'. And he goes on from that. He tells the priest about his sins and wonder of wonders the priest doesn't faint, he listens and absolves him from his sins using the Latin words, while the boy says his act of contrition. Then he gives the boy his penance and he tells him to say three Hail Marys and an Our Father. He doesn't really understand what is going on but he feels different when he comes out of the box.

The First Holy Communion is the climax of all the preparation that he has been doing with Sister Ursula. His whole class is in school on that Sunday morning before they go to mass and they are being inspected.

The boy passes the inspection by Sister Ursula and the other nuns, as his mother has rubbed the face off him last night. The boy is dressed in a grey flannel suit, white socks and new shoes that creak like hinges on a door that needs oil, and he has a white rosette in his lapel and a Holy Communion medal hanging from it, and a little white prayer book and a pair of white rosary beads.

The boy knows that he is going to receive God, which is an overwhelming thought; it makes you feel awed really. How is it to happen? He has to take the wafer on his tongue and on no account must he bite it. It mustn't even touch his teeth while it dissolves and he then must swallow it. He will then have God inside him and he will be near the angels. It's a mystical experience that he doesn't really understand. But it's awesome! What is the reality? The wafer is very big for his mouth.

He goes back to his seat, hardly daring to breathe, his mouth open with his lips closed. It takes a long time for the wafer to soften. But then it does and he swallows it and he says the simple prayers that he has been taught. He says his prayers and he looks up and sees how the others are doing around him.

My father wrote a very interesting description of his experiences of First Communion in the article in the Presentation Convent Annual in 1965:

Then a day came when the classroom ceased to be a place of confinement and became instead a feasting hall. It was the day we made our First Communion and we came back afterwards to the classroom for the feast. The desks were transformed into tables holding sweets and fruits and biscuits, leaving you with the thought that if only the classroom was like this all the time, what a pleasant place school would be.

In the same article he describes how he learned about girls as a primary school boy:

Afterwards came the most testing of all times when you were made tragically aware that there were two races on earth, not just a lot of children, but Girls and Boys and you had to make your choice. This is the way it happened. Once a month, I think it was on a Saturday, all the children who had made their First Communion, had to march out to St Joseph's Church from the school for Confession before the Children's Sodality on the following Sunday.

This was a terrible time for boys. At the time there were only two of us qualified for this, myself and Jo Jo Keenan. Listen to what we had to do. It was awful. We had to walk up the stairs, the two of us, to the big room upstairs, where the partitions were back, and sit on a long form in a place that contained hundreds of girls, and wait sweating, until they are ready and we would walk out with them to the Church. We had cause for sweating because as soon as the teacher's back was turned, these girls pelted us with bits of blotting paper, paper arrows, or anything at all to hand. They would make catapults with their fingers and a piece of elastic and whing missiles at us from all sides. It was all rather degrading for two little boys, because we couldn't hit back. The reason we couldn't hit back was because they were about a hundred to one. We just had to suffer it patiently like gentlemen.

That wasn't the end of it. As we walked to the church, there were still only two of us against so many, and we got many a pinch, many a push, many a hair-pulling, but we suffered it all as patiently as possible, because we knew there were only a few more months to go and we would be going to a place where there would be all BOYS. Imagine that, we would say to one another, no GIRLS.

All good things come to an end, like convent education, and time tempers even incipient misogyny. One felt a man going to a school where there was nothing but boys. But all the same those three rooms in the convent school left sort of tender trails of memory which one can always call up.

It was only afterwards you realised that you left there with a most precious acquisition, one that you thought you would never acquire, that seemed almost miraculous – you could read and once you got your tongue between your teeth, you could write, and that after all is the foundation of education, and the world of literature and history, art and drama, was yours for the taking. So you left the convent with these two things in mind and also a strong and uneasy feeling that Girls were the Master Race.

In *Cockle and Mustard*, my father describes the kind of house where he first lived – 18 St Joseph's Avenue, the last house on the street. It now has a plaque on it telling people this was where Walter Macken lived. This is his description:

> The houses they lived in were what was called pre-war houses. The rent was two shillings and ten pence a week, later rising to three shillings and ten pence. The front doors of the houses opened on to the street. At the back of the houses there were concrete yards with high walls around them and these back yards had a wooden door. All these back doors lead out into waste spaces dark and unlit where people threw out cabbage stalks and such like things. These waste places were great for warfare and plotting and for disappearing when your parents wanted you to come in.

As a child, my father lived through turbulent times. These working-class corporation estates were strong supporters of Sinn Féin and the independence movement, and the Royal Irish Constabulary walking through their streets were actively hated. The policemen were mainly Irishmen doing their job, yet in their black uniforms they were objects of hatred and scorn. This is reflected in a passage from *Cockle and Mustard*:

> At the end of the street, on this evening, the light is going out of the sky. The single electricity lamp dimly lights the street. Light from the houses also seeps out from the windows. At the far end of the street, a lot of boys are gathered. The big boys are separated from the small boys. The small boys look at the big boys in awe as the big boys are blowing smoke from their Woodbine butts through their noses. The big boys are Mungo, Christy and Mick. The small boys are listening to what the big boys are saying.
>
> 'I'd shoot them,' Mungo is saying, 'I'd shoot the whole bloody lot of them.'

'Me, too,' says Mick, 'they're a proper shower of bastards.'

'Hey look,' says Christy, 'here's a couple of them coming up the street.'

'Let's give them a buzz,' says Mungo.

He puts his lips together and makes a rude noise. Then all the big boys look up at the sky as if nothing has happened and all the small ones feel fear in their hearts as the two policemen with holstered guns appear in the light of the lamp. They stop there looking towards the group of boys. It's impossible to convey in words the fear engendered in a small boy's heart by the sight of the black uniform of the Royal Irish Constabulary.

Next minute, Mungo shouts: 'Up Dev.'

Great God, you can hear the night holding its breath. The policemen turn and move towards the boys. In an instant they are gone. The small ones, are off running, first around the houses and then down the back alleys, even before the big boys have thrown away their cigarette butts. There is a scattering of running feet in the darkness. The young boys look back and see the policemen standing at the entrance to our alley. The boys sang 'Kevin Barry' and then had to stop as the policemen chased after them.

As well as meeting with the RIC on a daily basis, my father went through the trauma of seeing the infamous Black and Tans come to Galway. They were all veterans of the First World War and were deliberately sent to Ireland to terrify the nationalist population. My father witnessed them coming into his street and told me how they used to jeer at the Black and Tans when they saw them passing by in daylight, they would even sing republican songs, but at night it was different, as *Cockle and Mustard* illustrates:

The young boys hid until they knew that the two policemen had given up their search. Then the young boys came out of their hiding place. They heard their names being called by their mothers. They knew they should be in bed now … But they felt they weren't babies anymore, why should they have to go to bed at 6.30? So they walked back through the alley and reached the street and ignored the calls of their mothers, that was until they heard the sound of the Lancia lorry. It was a special sound, a hard grating sound that you recognised immediately as being that of the Black and Tans. They had often seen it in daylight with its big high bonnet, its high sides and the fellows in it, insolent with their rifles and the black tails of their bonnets laid out in the breeze.

At the sound of the approaching lorry, every front door in the street opens and the mothers call out the names of their children. They ran home with their hearts in their mouths. The mother is at the door waiting for the boy.

'Come in, come in for the love of God! I told you not to be out so late in these times.'

Now he was inside, sitting by the light of the paraffin lamp, it seems almost worse to be inside the house with the lorry driving up the street. The lorry stops in the middle of the street. They hear rough voices shouting: 'Put out those lights.'

Their mother turns down the wick of the lamp. They can picture all the lamps in the street going out. They hear a shot, they run up-stairs, groping about in the dark.

'Get into bed,' they hear their mother telling them. They are in the big bedroom.

There are lodgers in the small bedroom. Packey and his wife live there. His wife is in hospital at the moment so Packey isn't in the house either. Their bedroom has two windows. There is a double bed in the corner near a small iron fireplace. The boy sleeps in that bed with his mother and his two sisters sleep in the double bed in the other side of the room.

The bedroom is a big room and it's a nice room when they are not afraid. They don't talk and the boy's mouth is dry. The girls put on nightdresses. The boy gets into bed in his shirt. He is very frightened and even though he pulls the bedclothes over his head, it doesn't help, He just feels worse.

'Can I get into your bed?' he begs his sisters. They agree and in moments he's snuggling up in their bed.

'What has them out tonight?' he asks his sisters.

'It's the funerals,' they tell him.

There were a lot of tragic funerals in the town at that time. There was Mr Walsh. They took him away in front of his children and they shot him down near the Spanish Arch, people said that they kicked him into the river. Mr Walsh's was a big funeral.

Everybody went to his funeral and then followed the funeral cortege. The RIC and the Black and Tans lined the route watching the crowds closely. Then there was Fr Griffin, who had been taken out of his house on Sea Road and brought up to the Barna Road where they killed him and buried him in a bog.

Fr Griffin's funeral was a very big one too. There was a long queue in St Joseph's church and the boy was there holding his mother's hand. It seemed to take a long time to reach the top of the queue. He was afraid because he had never seen a dead person before. People said that if you were afraid of the dead, all you had to do was put your hand on their cold flesh and your fear would go away. His mother lifted him up to see the dead priest in the coffin. The boy was terrified. He held on tightly to her. Fr Griffin had fair hair, the boy saw, a sort of long nose and his hands were joined and he looked awfully peaceful. But the terrible still-ness in him made him afraid. It was very sad. People were weeping. The boy was just afraid because this was the first dead person, he had seen.

As he lay in the bed, they talked about all these things. It was a pity, they agreed that they had no father. Somehow if you had a father, you wouldn't be as afraid. All the other fellows with fathers had amazing tales to tell.

They told you how their fathers would face up to the police and how if they weren't family men, they would be out in the hills with the IRA. It was sort of frightening to think of their mother down there on her own in the kitchen with only the light from the fire, as she listened to the sounds coming from the street.

Their father was only a picture on the wall. A fair-haired, young man, who people said, looked very like the boy's younger sister, looking down at them, calmly from the wall. The picture was only a head and shoulders, but it was big enough to see he was wearing a British army uniform. He knew that about him.

He knew he had joined the British army when the boy was two months old and that he had died at St Eloi when he was nine months old. He was twenty-six when he died, their mother told him.

He had been a carpenter, the boy knew that, because there was still a table he had made in the yard. There was also an oval sort of basket thing, made of thick straw with two handles that held all kinds of intriguing things such as saws, bit braces, squares, levels and hammers.

The children had asked their mother why their father had joined the British army and she told them it was because he needed a job. But they found it hard to take that he didn't stay at home and fight for Ireland.

It was hard to boast to your friends and tell them that their father died for England. It was a pity that mother had to be alone. It was hard on her. She had to bring them all up on a British army pension of only £2–6–8d a week. The children must have fallen asleep, for the next thing they heard was a thunderous knocking on the front door. They heard Packey going down the stairs, 'All right, I'm coming, can't you hold on a minute?'

In the story, one of the sisters opens the bedroom door, so they can hear what is going on downstairs. They hear the big bolts on the front door being opened and hear voices talking, but they cannot hear what they are saying. Then they hear Packey:

'A fine thing,' Packey is talking to them, 'to be rooting around in the house of a widow of a dead soldier. Was that why the man was sent out to fight for the rest of ye? So that you would be coming into his house and rooting the decent woman out of her bed in the dark of night?' The children waited for Packey to be shot, but there was no shot, just more mumbling and then the sound of heavy boots on their red tiled kitchen floor.

'Yes,' shouts Packey, 'there, he is on the wall.'

They hear them going away after this. They cannot believe it but it's true as they hear the front door being closed again and they are gone.

This is the kind of incident experienced by many in Ireland, including a young Walter Macken, throughout the War of Independence and later the Civil War.

3

WALTER MACKEN – SECONDARY SCHOOL

From records in the Presentation Convent National School, my father probably spent four years there, and when he completed First Class under the watchful eye of Sister Ursula, he transferred to the Patrician Brothers National School (The Bish) in 1922. He went to school there until 1927.

His experiences in the Bish were difficult: corporal punishment was the norm then and the Patrician Brothers practised it widely. The following are some of the descriptions he gives of corporal punishment in *Cockle and Mustard*:

Noseen was his nickname and the boy would have been surprised to hear him called by his real name. He was a small-sized man with a big nose that got very red when he was angry. He usually lost his temper several times a day. When he didn't lose his temper, he could be quite nice and you could even get to like him. He was dressed like all the brothers were dressed. He wore a big black soutane from neck to heel with a black four-cornered biretta and around his waist there was a green belly band that was fastened in the middle and hung down towards the floor. The bellyband was a handy thing to hold the cane.

The boy thought you get to hate canes. When you get a few

slaps with canes across the palm of your hand, it raises up purple welts, which stay on your hands for a few hours. It's not too bad if they hit you with the cane straight across the palm of your hand but sometimes the blow will fall on the first knuckle of your thumb and it hurts like hell. The only thing you can do when you are about to get beaten with a cane is to hold your hand as straight as possible, spreading your fingers and let them hit you. If you are tentative about putting out your hand, you might get the blow from the cane on your fingernails and if you haven't cut them properly, the pain from that is pretty bad too. And if you hesitate, the Brother will get mad at you and hold your hand over the edge of the desk so that he can give you a really good wallop.

Whatever happens, you mustn't cry. Crying always infuriates the person who is giving you the beating. It seems to drive them into paroxysms of anger. You must show a nice balanced sense of fortitude. This is hurting me, but I deserve it and therefore I will put up with it.

He paints a frightening picture of one brother who terrified the Sixth Class and he also writes about how when this particular brother was about to flog someone, the whole school went quiet to listen to the flogging. The brothers ruled by terror, but my father also experienced a different side of this particular brother – each morning, as an altar boy, he saw him at 6.30 mass. My father could not figure out how the brother could attend mass and Holy Communion, then go into a classroom and terrify a class of twelve-year-old boys.

It was not a good time for him, not only because of the constant corporal punishment, but also because he found very little of interest in the subjects he was taught. He wrote two articles about his school-day experiences, and the following, written in the form of a letter, provides a real insight into how he remembered school:

Dear Brother,

You are taking an awesome chance when you ask one of your past boys to write about his memories of the Patrician Brothers and their schools in Galway. Boys spend a lot of time at school, and at that period of their lives when they are most impressionable; when they judge the world by what the world does and says and think about them personally. In those years boys, however tough they may appear on the surface, are sensitive. They are like blank pages on which you set out to inscribe the story of a life and as you ponder over it more than twenty years later, it is still the selfish and self-centred incidents that remain in your memory, not the fact that somehow, and despite your resistance and against your will, you were educated, your mind was trained and you were launched reluctantly on the world, better prepared for the battle than you yourself knew at the time.

So I remember being in First Class in the Presentation Convent, terrified of the eagle eye of Sister Ursula, and being now a man, aged 7, and absolutely loathed being cooped up in a school with girls.

Girls are hard on boys, particularly when there are a couple of hundred of them and only two of us, hair-pulling, pinching, jeering, so it is no wonder that we looked to our freedom and the day we would be going to the Bish as Xenophon's men longed for a glimpse of the sea. I remember distinctly being told how Jack Deacy had been put into second class, and how Jo Jo and myself were simply dying to emulate him.

So the longed for day came and we went to the Bish. It is unfortunate that reality cannot live up to the dreams, but that is a lesson in life that you learn early on; that the attainment of dreams and ambitions are not everything. You get what you desire and all you can say is, 'So what?' until your final ambition which should be the most important one of all, and I imagine the only one where you will never say, 'So what?' when you attain it.

In the Bish primary school, I remember playing crowded football in the concrete yard, lacerated knees and the seagulls over the river beyond the railings where we fed them with our bits of bread while they performed flying gymnastics as they screamed and called. It was hard leaving the seagulls for the classroom. I remember the class being dominated by the thought of Brother Joseph in Sixth Class. We could hear him in the room over our heads each year as we progressed. He believed in noisy punishment, the sounds of which haunted us, but as dreams cannot live up to reality, neither can nightmares. Things were not as bad as they sounded, when we got there. And now our aching ambition was to get into Secondary. You know why? Because they got longer holidays in the summer. What more would the heart desire?

I remember in a higher class, asking to be excused, and Brother Leonard granting the request and asking: 'Do you want a match, Macs?'

I remember Brother Thompson, and Higher Maths. Himself and a couple of Maths geniuses chuckling away companionably over calculus and plane geometry and other monstrous equations just as if they were compiling a joke book. It was all a pure blank to me and a few other characters I won't name in case, in the interim, they have turned into maths geniuses. People's understanding of Higher Maths has always puzzled me, so that's one place where the Patrician Brothers failed, but I find that they gave me many other things instead, like little prayers copied down in the middle of a Latin Grammar class; little prayers which one still says many years afterwards; a lot of advice which one thought unnecessary at the time but which turned out to be good, oh indeed lots of things which one can't put a finger on, because they all go to the making of the man, but one thing I know for sure, that if I hadn't spent twelve years of my life with the Patrician Brothers, I wouldn't be as I am now. For better or worse the mould of a man is shaped and formed when he is a boy and I think that the Patrician Brother possess good mould-making hands.

I remember my father telling me about those maths classes. Among the pupils in that class was a boy called Brod Newell. One day, when the maths teacher could not solve a particular problem,

he sent Brod and a friend up to the university to bring the problem
to a maths' lecturer so that he would get a solution. Brod and his
friend went out to the toilet and solved the problem themselves
and when sufficient time had elapsed, they came back with the
problem solved! Brod Newell went on to become a professional
mathematician and eventually became the president of University
College Galway.

My father found school boring. In those years, the curriculum
was not demanding, there was a lot of rote-learning and subjects
were not taught in an interesting way. He sat the Intermediate
Certificate in 1932 and obtained the following results:

Irish	168 (400)	42%
English	276 (400)	69%
Latin	160 (400)	40%
History	140 (250)	56%
Geography	70 (150)	46%
Mathematics:		
Arithmetic	90 (200)	45%
Maths I	94 (200)	47%
Maths II	80 (200)	40%

It is interesting that the two subjects he did best in were English
and History.

When he was deciding where to send his children to school,
my father told me he would not send any of his sons to school
in the Bish. We went to school with the Jesuits, where we were
beaten almost as much as we would have been in the Bish.

Unlike his friends, my father did not have ambition to be a train driver, a bus conductor or a carpenter; even at this young age, he knew in his heart and soul that he wanted to write. Occasionally he displayed his ability in essays written for his English teacher, Brother Leonard. One of his schoolmates told me something that happened in class one day. Brother Leonard said he would read Wally Macken's essay and read the opening line: "'Contact,' said the pilot to his co-pilot, and the engines roared to life.' One of the pupils put up his hand to criticise this start, but Brother Leonard said no, it was a dramatic start and he liked it.

At home, Walter had already started writing – he told my mother that he began to write at the age of eight. By twelve he had already written quite a lot and decided to submit a short story to *The Daily Telegraph*. He was disgusted when they returned his story to him, having rejected it.

A whole range of different factors in his background and his experiences growing up helped mould him into the writer he became. I remember my mother saying that when she first met him, there was a degree of violence coming out in his writing. It took her many years to help him to remove the violence that kept re-appearing in his writing. This violence may have been a reaction to events from his childhood. The community in which he lived was a small one and his friends would have spent a lot of their time in the streets playing football or taking part in gang fights. I remember my Auntie Birdie telling me how she often had to go out into the street and rescue him when he was being beaten by boys bigger than himself. He also witnessed very violent episodes in childhood. His autobiography has a vivid description of seeing two men fighting over a pitch and putt game – he heard the slap of a fist connecting with a man's nose and the sound of the man's nose breaking.

Then there was a time when it was rumoured all over the street that one of their neighbours was lying dead in her back garden. The boys went over to the wall and found bricks on which they could stand so they could look over the wall to see the dead woman. He could see the red mark around her neck; she had hanged herself. An adult came along then and chased them away. This incident haunted my father and afterwards he had dreams every night filled with bloody images – terrible nightmares that took weeks to go away. His mother had to take him out of bed at night, hug him and hold him until the fear went away. Just down the road, a young couple, apparently happily married, had a row one night and the husband, who was a former British soldier, took out his knife and killed his wife. (I read a report of this in the *Connacht Tribune*). There is little doubt that this murder stayed in his mind and emerged in his first play, *Mungo's Mansion*.

Although school was not a happy experience for him, there were some things he did enjoy about those days. For many years, there was a school trip to Connemara on the Clifden train. He loved those trips, and enjoyed the sandwiches and the lemonade which always tasted better when you were drinking it in a field in Clifden. When CIE closed the Clifden Railway service, the boys' day out became the sports day. (Although my father gave the impression that the Clifden Railway was closed down before he left school, this wasn't true; it didn't close down until 1935.) He also played hurling, Gaelic football and rugby, winning a Connacht Cup with the Bish rugby team.

My grandmother had great difficulty managing on a British

army pension. To overcome her dire economic circumstances she sent her younger daughter Birdie (when she was ten) to live in England with her husband's sister, Mary. Auntie Birdie told me she felt very hurt because she had to spend so much time in England as a child. Agnes sent the two other children to her brother Frank in Ballinasloe for the summers. The Ballinasloe experience was a good one for my father. Up to then his life had been primarily that of a 'townie' and the summers with his Uncle Frank gave him a solid knowledge of life on a farm. His Uncle Frank, who had a childless marriage, was a hard taskmaster. He was an angry man who seemed to suffer from frustration and bitterness, primarily caused, in my father's mind, from being childless. My father found the work on the farm tedious and never forgot having to weed an acre of turnips by hand – he thought it would never end. Reading his novel based in Ballinasloe, *The Bogman*, the principal character's grandfather seems to me to be a portrait of his Uncle Frank. The characters he created in this novel are true to life and are an accurate record of life in the midlands in the 1920s and 1930s. Although it was hard work, my father learned a lot from working on the farm: how to sow and how to reap, harvesting oats and corn and cutting and saving hay. He worked on the bog, cutting and saving the turf, something he made good use of when we moved to Oughterard. He also worked with animals, feeding them, taking care of them and even bringing the cow to the local farm to be serviced by the bull.

At an early stage in his life he had a brief flirtation with the idea of being a priest. A Jesuit priest had told young Walter that he had to study both Latin and Greek to prepare himself for the priesthood. His mother went to a lot of trouble to arrange for him to attend St Mary's diocesan college following this, as Greek was not taught at the Bish. St Mary's college was a diocesan college specially set up to offer the subjects that were required for those going on to the priesthood. Within weeks of his starting to attend St Mary's college and dreaming of what he would do as a young priest, his idea suffered a set-back. Out walking one night with one of his friends at Salthill, he realised his friend had arranged to meet a girl. The girl had a friend with her and of course she began to walk and talk with my father. So they arranged to go on a date the following Sunday and they kissed – my father realised that his dreams of becoming a priest were not going to come to fruition. Then he had a run-in with the priest who taught him Greek. The man was an exacting tyrant and demanded perfection from his students. If they made any mistake in pronunciation or immediate translation, they were in trouble. Any boy who made a mistake had to go to the priest's room where the priest systematically beat him with his leather strap.

One day, my father was tired, worried and conscience-stricken, as he knew now that he didn't want to be a priest. He had not prepared that day's reading material and was making mistakes. The teacher stopped him in mid-flow and told him he must come to see him after class. When the class ended my father followed the priest to his room, where he took out his leather strap and slapped my father eight times without saying a word. When he was finished my father walked out the door and, instead of going back to his classroom, he walked out of school. He took the road out to Silver Strand and sat there looking out at the sea.

Although he was sorry to leave the school because his mother had gone to such trouble to have him enrolled and had bought him a set of books which he had left behind on his desk, he was generally happier. He returned to his home in Henry Street, where they had moved in 1927, walked into the kitchen and announced to his mother that he was not returning to St Mary's college. He left his mother with the problem of getting him back into the Bish, where he started again in first year.

In another article, *Remembrance of Things Past*, about his experiences in the Bish, he wrote:

It is an infallible sign of middle age when one starts by saying: I remember. At that point young people run for cover or groan and remain patiently bored. But I suppose it will be grown-ups who will be reading this, past pupils, and I know they will grunt a little approval, or hum and haw in disagreement, knock the dottle from their pipes, or flick their cigarette butts or kick the coals of the fire or say: He hasn't changed a bit; he's still talking – have another one Mart.

There is one consolation. This is a Centenary Edition. I wasn't there when the Bish was founded. I was on the team that won the Connacht Junior Rugby Cup many years ago and there's a picture in the school to prove it with the year written on the ball.

So what on earth can you say but: I remember? I could pay great tribute to the Brothers and the Bish, but we didn't think like that in those days, and the lives of their past pupils and how they live now; how they benefited from the education they received in the school will have to be the living tribute of their dedication.

In fact – let's face it – we looked on the Brothers with an eye to their health. It is a fact that if a Brother dies you get three days off from school. Not that we wished them any harm. After all they were religious and when they died where could they go but to Heaven? So it was really no harm to wish for a sudden death – say one every term. The trouble was that all the Brothers I knew were very healthy men.

They never seemed to get sick so you would get few exercises off. The Brothers tend to be disgustingly healthy, in fact, and completely impervious to the death-wish. I often think of this when it has been my duty to chide children who say: I wish Sister this or Father that of Brother Such would pass out. Nothing changes.

Different people remember different things. What matters to one is completely forgotten by others.

I remember the railings by the river in the old school and the way we fed the seagulls with the remains of our lunch. These seagulls were very adept.

I remember the terrible scrums on the hard concrete of the old school yard with fifty boys aside or more. Some boys I will not name played at these scrummages with unnecessary vigour. I feel aching ribs, hot ears.

I remember a newspaper in Second Inter, produced on a home printing set, called Sheriff's Weekly. It was a rather libellous rag.

I remember an excursion to Clifden on the train. Even as un-feeling schoolboys, we were awed by the beauty of that trip on the railway. Whenever I see the pitiful remains of the Clifden Railway now I think of that trip, and am glad we rode that train before they tore it up. I remember the field in Clifden and eating the ham sandwiches and drinking the lemonade. It is a strange thing that never since have I tasted sandwiches that were a patch on those and always feel that the lemonade nowadays is not nearly as nice or gassy as that lemonade.

Really we were sad when we started to have sports every year instead of an excursion, but I suppose we did so much damage to the trains and the railways generally that they never recovered and have been in financial difficulties ever since.

I remember the new school. Nice classrooms, central heating, tennis court in the yard, all grand, but there was something about that old school, even if the floors were a bit dangerous … (I must stop using dots. I remember Brother Leonard telling me about dots one time I wrote an exciting composition for his English class. I have never used them since, until now.)

I remember when we were bigger (how we despised the small fry!) sitting on the bridge. That became an occupation before school and at lunch-time and after school. We polished a lot of limestone up there with our trousers. We discussed many things; how the school should be run; what was wrong with the Government and the United States of America; and I'm afraid we wolf-whistled after girls. If any of the girls had paid attention to us I don't know what we would have done. I always thought we were sort of sheep in wolf's clothing; ready to take off the disguise and bolt.

The trouble about [*what*] I remember is that you could go on forever, one thought leading to another. You would even forget that you had remembered one thing already and repeat it and you'd end up boring your grandmother.

So I will stop. I know that my few will set a chain reaction going with other past pupils, so perhaps it will have served some purpose.

It is the home and the schools that mould you. Now after all those years I have come to a favourable conclusion about my school. I am what I am on account of my home and the Brothers and the Bish and if I had my time over again, taking everything into account, I wouldn't really wish to change. May the Bish and the Patrician Brothers flourish forever.

It's hard to know what direction his life would have taken if it was not for an experience he had one day, as he was sitting on what was called the lazy wall with his school friends, on their lunch break. A tall elegant lady passed by. She was from the Taibhdhearc, the Irish language theatre in Galway.

'Somebody [*we don't know who*] told me you were a good singer and a good actor,' she said to him.

He was astonished that anyone like this would be talking to him at all.

'Well,' she told him, 'the Taibhdhearc is looking for people like you. I would like you to go down there and speak to the producer, Frank Dermody. They need talented young men like you.'

So my father met Frank Dermody. Michael MacLiammóir and his partner Hilton Edwards had brought Frank Dermody into the

Taibhdhearc when they helped establish the Taibhdhearc in 1928. Dermody had been a lieutenant in the Irish army at Renmore Barracks and the two theatre men gave him a grounding in the skills of producing and directing in the theatre. Dermody saw potential in my father as an actor, but he realised that his Irish was weak, so he proposed that my father come with him to the Aran Islands for a weekend so that he could improve his Irish. The Taibhdhearc would pay for the trip and for the accommodation.

My father did not realise that, like his mentors Edwards and MacLiammóir, Frank Dermody was a practising homosexual. In his novel, *Cockle and Mustard*, he tells a very disturbing story about a weekend trip where the main character encountered a number of homosexual men and one of them attempted to seduce him, but whether this experience happened to my father or not is unclear.

Either way, my father went to the Taibhdhearc and watched, learned and listened. The theatre's records show that he played a part in a play based on the famous rebel song, 'The Croppy Boy', between 9–11 July 1933, during his school holidays. My father played the part of a priest – Sagart – who was also a captain in the British army. The 'Croppy Boy' comes to the church to have his confession heard before he goes off to join the rebels of 1798. My father, as the priest, having heard his confession, jumps out of the confession box, tears off his clerical clothes and reveals that he is actually a red-coat captain, then arrests the 'Croppy Boy'. It was a one-act play, staged as part of a night's programme, where there was a full-length play staged as well. Both plays were directed by Frank Dermody who also played a part in the main play as indeed did the chairman of the Taibhdhearc committee – Liam Ó Briain.

In the autumn of 1933, on 16 and 17 November, the young Walter made an appearance in an Irish language version of a Eugene O'Neill play, *Where the Cross is Made*. Also that autumn he appeared in another one act play, *The Hunchbacks,* based on a folklore tale adapted from French to Irish by Liam Ó Briain.

The next part my father played was Seán Mattias, in Pádraig Pearse's dramatisation of his short story, *Íosagán*. Fr Eddie Divilly told me that he saw my father playing this part and he would never forget it, as the seventeen-year-old Walter convincingly played a man in his sixties. It was first staged at the Taibhdhearc between 12–14 December 1933. Two one-act plays were also performed, as *Íosagán* was a very short play, and my father also had a part in the other play, *Scaipín na gCleas*, based on Molière's *The Rogueries of Scapin*. *Íosagán* was also staged as part of the end of year prize-giving ceremony for the Jesuit School, so the production was at the Columban Hall.

He learned his theatre craft under the tutelage of Frank Dermody, while he was still at school. Although he learned a lot from Dermody, I do not think he agreed with his style of directing. My father felt that each actor must make a part his own, whereas Dermody wanted each actor to play the part strictly as he told them, without giving them the freedom to find their own interpretation. Frank Dermody acted out the part of the character as he believed the actor should play it and demanded that the actor do what he wanted him to do. He was not able to do this with my father, who was very much his own man and who liked to delve deep into the character he was playing, much like the method actors of later years.

While learning his trade in the theatre, my father was also

finishing his education. I once asked him if he liked the subjects he did at school and he told me he didn't. He was interested in English and History, but found the teaching methods boring. However, he read extensively, novels, plays and biographies from Europe and America, and was secretly harbouring a dream of becoming a writer himself.

As soon as he finished his Leaving Certificate exam, he arranged to go on a holiday to Cleggan. His stay there was to inspire him, and he obviously met people who had survived the famous Cleggan Disaster, where twenty-five local fishermen drowned during a sudden storm only five years previously, in 1927. Meeting the men who had survived and meeting the relatives of those who had died obviously made a huge impression on him, as his first novel, *Quench the Moon*, was set in this area. But another important thing happened, my father fell in love with Connemara, something that inspired him to go back to live there many years later.

When he returned to Galway after his holiday, he received the results of his Leaving Certificate exam:

This Certificate was awarded to Walter Macken who passed the Leaving Certificate Examination with Honours in 1934 in the following subjects: English (Full Course), History and Geography, and passed in the following subjects Irish (Full Course) and Latin.

My father chose not to go to university, as he felt that if he did he would end up indulging his love for research and he would never become a writer. After school, he resumed his career with the Taibhdhearc, but his mother was not convinced that her son should be wasting his life working in a small Irish-speaking theatre. She went up to the city manager and persuaded him to give my father a job as a clerk in the corporation – he only stayed in the corporation for about two months. He completed his tasks quickly and then spent the rest of the day whiling away the time, whistling the latest popular music hits. Eventually the city manager summoned him and they mutually agreed that working as a clerk did not suit him, so he returned to the Taibhdhearc again.

One day in 1935, his life changed when a new young actress came to join the company at the Taibhdhearc – Peggy Kenny, the woman who would win his heart.

4

PEGGY KENNY AND
THE TAIBHDHEARC

Peggy Kenny, who played such a vital role in Walter Macken's life, had an interesting life herself. She was the eldest of the six children of Tom and Catherine Kenny. Tom Kenny was a journalist and was known as Tom Cork Kenny as he had been born in the southern capital. When Tom was a young man, he worked for a time at the famous English newspaper, *The Manchester Guardian*. When he returned to Ireland, he worked for a newspaper in Kilkenny, *The Kilkenny Moderator*. While there, he met his future wife, Catherine Hunt, who came from a rich farming background. Catherine and her sister ran a hat shop in Kilkenny city. Of course, there was a problem: Catherine was a Roman Catholic and Tom Kenny was a Church of Ireland Protestant. To get married, Tom Kenny had to convert to Catholicism first and then sign the *Ne Temere* decree, by which the Catholic Church insisted that all their children would be brought up as Catholics. Tom was happy to comply and so they were married. His wealthy father-in-law suggested that he help Tom to establish himself as a newspaperman. Tom knew that the local paper in Galway was for sale and so with financial help from his father-in-law and other business people in Galway, including

Gus O'Reilly, Tom Cork Kenny bought out the newspaper owner and founded a new paper, the *Connacht Tribune*, in 1909.

That was also the year my mother, Margaret (always known as Peggy), was born. She was the first born of the Kenny family and became the apple of her father's eye. The other children were Mary (shortened to May) just a year or so after my mother, followed by Jack, and then came Desmond, Kitty and Joan. They lived in the centre of town for the first few years and my mother went to an exclusive private school run by a Mrs Spellman. Later she was sent to Taylor's Hill Dominican Convent School at Taylor's Hill. Then tragedy struck, in 1923, when Peggy was only thirteen – her mother contracted breast cancer and died. Her father decided that as a man without a wife, he could not take care of his daughters, so he sent them to a boarding school in Balla, County Mayo, run by the St Louis nuns. Both Peggy and her sister May went there straightaway and the two younger girls went later. It was a culture shock for my mother, as she was used to living in a house where there were staff who did everything for them, but she enjoyed boarding school and made good friends there. About a year later, she received a big shock when her father visited her with a new girlfriend – Lou McGuinness. She was a native of Dublin and had been coming to Tom's office on behalf of a typewriting firm (she was a saleswoman). He told my mother that they planned to marry in August 1925. In later years, whenever my mother talked about her stepmother, it was always full of painful memories. She tried her best to be friendly with her stepmother, but did not succeed. My mother, like many people of her generation, believed that a person should marry only once and that there was an element of betrayal in someone marrying for a second time.

While still in school, she began to write, and wrote articles for her father's paper, including one about a school visit to Lourdes. There was an inevitability about her career path: her father planned that she would take over as the editor of his newspaper, while one of his sons would work as the business manager and another as a photographer. To prepare her for her career, she went to university in Galway and studied for an Arts Degree, eventually graduating with a first class honours degree in her majors, Irish and French (coincidentally under Professor Liam Ó Briain, the Taibhdhearc chairman), and her minor in History.

On graduation in 1929, my mother began working as a reporter and learned from men like Larry Delacey who was the news editor of the newspaper. When she joined the newspaper, her father decided to launch a mid-week paper called the *Connacht Sentinel*. Tom Cork Kenny was an excellent journalist. He built up a group of correspondents all over County Galway and the newspaper he published became known as one of the best provincials in the country. During the First World War, he had travelled to the front in France and sent back excellent reports on how the soldiers were doing. In 1919, one of his correspondents in Clifden phoned him to tell him about an extraordinary incident he had just witnessed. Two American pilots, Alcock and Brown, had crossed the Atlantic and had landed in a bog near Clifden. Tom Cork Kenny told him to tell no one. He jumped into his V8 and drove out directly to the men. The two pilots had spoken to a number of local Clifden men. One local recalled how he had seen the plane flying over his home and crashing into the bog. He ran towards the plane and the pilots opened the cockpit and shouted at him – 'Here's a fresh orange from Newfoundland.' He never forgot that. Tom Kenny picked the two airmen up and brought them to a hotel in Galway, where he hid them from all other newspapermen. Once he had compiled the material to write their story, he arranged for them to travel to Dublin by train, and he had a scoop that was published all over the world.

Another world scoop came through his trusty correspondent in Clifden. In October 1927 the correspondent rang my grandfather to tell him there had been a terrible accident at sea. Local fishermen at Cleggan and Inish Boffin had gone out herring fishing on the night of 28 October and the fleet was struck by a fierce storm. Twenty-five men from Rossadilisk, Cleggan and Inish Boffin died. My grandfather travelled to Rossadilisk and heard first-hand the stories of the survivors and what had happened to them at sea. He wrote a heart-rending report in the *Connacht Tribune*. There had been men drowned in Mayo, Donegal and Kerry during the same storm, but the Cleggan Disaster, as it became known, attracted the most attention. My father talked to the survivors when he visited Cleggan in 1934.

In 1968, I visited Cleggan myself and recorded some of the survivors' experiences. Four years later, I returned with a camera crew and we made a fifteen-minute documentary for the Tangents magazine programme which was broadcast on the anniversary of the disaster, 30 October 1972. While researching material for that programme, I met many of the relatives of the survivors. The local curate brought me to the house of one of the survivors who he wanted me to meet. As we approached the house, the man came stamping out of his house and said: 'When that journalist [*my grandfather*] came to write the story for the newspapers, he never talked to me and since he didn't talk to me then, I'm not talking to any journalist now.' His story was the most dramatic of all, as he had succeeded in bringing his boat back safely to the shore and, having landed at the base of the cliffs, he managed to climb the cliffs and get help to save his crew.

Over the years, Tom Kenny built a reputation as an outstanding newspaperman, but he was also a shrewd businessman and he wanted to create employment in Galway. He was one of the first businessmen to come up with the idea of establishing a state body to promote tourism and became the first chairman of the Irish Tourist Board as it was called then. He was also involved in aviation and Peggy flew on one of the first cross-country flights to Dublin. Tom had all the latest gadgets, new radio and new cars. He witnessed Marconi's experts sending the first telegraph messages from their station in Clifden to Newfoundland and Massachusetts.

Tom also had his problems. He did not drink alcohol until he was in his late thirties and began then by simply drinking wine at dinner, but from this he progressed to the hard stuff. My mother was horrified to see her father spending so much of his time in bars and drinking with his friends. He used the excuse that he heard about great stories in the bars, but my mother did not accept this. His heavy drinking made her totally opposed to alcohol, as she saw the way it ruined her father's life.

Within two years of Peggy joining the newspaper, the news editor, Larry Delacey was offered a job with the Dublin newspaper, the *Irish Times*. Her father was going to appoint an older, experienced journalist to the post, but Larry persuaded him to give Peggy the chance to prove herself, so at the age of twenty-three or twenty-four, she was running the newspaper. But this didn't stop her living a very full life. She had a job she loved and a good social life. She moved in the upper circles of Galway society and never in the course of her ordinary day would she have had the opportunity to meet someone like my father, as they moved in very different social settings. The only downside was the way her stepmother treated her and she found it extremely difficult to establish any kind of friendly relationship with her. However, her godmother, Esso (I think her surname was Spellman), was a substitute and my mother could open her heart and talk about all her troubles to her. Her troubles increased when her father began to drink heavily. He came to rely on her more and more, stopped turning up at the office and left the job of writing the editorials for both newspapers to her. She found it increasingly difficult to cope and worried constantly about her father's drinking.

One day when she went into work, her father summoned her into his office: 'Your French Professor, Liam Ó Briain talked to me the other day. They have launched this Irish language theatre, the Taibhdhearc, in Galway. They really need people who are fluent in Irish and those who know French to work on the plays down there. So he asked me to ask you would you be willing to go down there and work with them, probably as an actress. It would only be for a few evenings a week.'

Peggy was reluctant to go – she liked her work at the paper and she enjoyed playing tennis, badminton and swimming and dancing. She didn't know where she could fit in a few evenings a week at the Taibhdhearc. She told me that, 'Although, I really was not that interested in the theatre, in those days, daughters did what they were told to do by their fathers. I was a good obedient daughter and I obeyed my father. Thank God I did. Wouldn't it have been terrible if I had not joined the Taibhdhearc? I might never have met your father and that would have been a tragedy.'

My mother went down to the Taibhdhearc in May 1935 and when she walked in, the producer, Frank Dermody, was delighted to see her. Within minutes, she was cast to play the principal male character's mother in their latest production, *The Wonderful Life of Bernard de Menthon*, a play written originally in French. A young Walter Macken was playing the lead role. She also appeared in an original play by Gearóid Ó Lochlainn called *Na Gaduithe* (The Robbers) on 6–7 December 1935. Her next role was as Isolde's mother in *Tristan and Isolde* (16–18 February 1936). The part of Tristan was played by my father and the part of Isolde was played by May Kilmartin. Máirtín Ó Direáin, who later became one of Ireland's most famous Irish language poets, played the part of the King of Ireland. From 1–3 May 1936, she appeared in an Irish translation of a famous French farce by Molière, *Le Bourgeois Gentilhomme*.

There was an instant rapport between Walter Macken and Peggy Kenny. When the rehearsal for that first play, *The Wonderful Life of Bernard de Menthon*, was over, Walter asked if he might walk her home. She agreed and as Peggy lived in the Crescent and Walter lived in Henry Street, they did not live far away from each other. There was an immediate chemistry between them and my mother said: 'Right through my life, I was an avid reader and when I was at college, I studied a lot about writers and writing, and for me, I always hoped that one day I would meet a living writer and get to know him. Here he was, an actor who was primarily a writer.'

My father knew immediately that he had fallen in love with this young woman and that she was the one he was going to marry.

After that first walk home, it became usual whenever they rehearsed that Wally walked her home and then, within a week of meeting, he invited her to come to a dance with him in the Hangar. This famous dance hall venue lasted up to my own time. A tin structure, it had originally been an aeroplane hangar and had a beautiful wooden dance floor. Situated right opposite the promenade, there were dances there in the afternoon as well as at night. My mother noticed that my father was a very good ballroom dancer. When they were on a break from dancing, my father asked my mother to marry him. Her reaction was to laugh. 'Why would I marry you? A young fellow like you is it?'

While my father knew immediately that he had found his soulmate, I do not think my mother was as sure. She was six years older than my father and at that time, that age gap was regarded as substantial. (It is an interesting fact that my father's mother was also a few years older than my father's father.) But my father was determined and he told her that he planned to marry her and he was going to persuade her that this was the right course of action. In many ways it seemed an unlikely pairing, the eldest daughter of one of the richest men in Galway matched with the son of a carpenter. Peggy had completed a university course and was working as a news editor for the local newspaper, and Walter had left school at eighteen and was working as an actor in the Taibhdhearc. In those days, these differences in educational and social background could have resulted in a gulf between them, but for this couple it made no difference.

During the period when they were rehearsing the play, the couple had begun their courtship. Meanwhile my mother was still going out with another boyfriend, farmer/teacher Harry Casey.

He had black hair and wore a lot of brylcream, and I often heard my father joking about how he could smell the brylcream off my mother's lap. Within about two months, my mother realised that Walter was the man for her. So Harry Casey was dismissed and Walter Macken became the steady boyfriend. Reading through the love letters, as you will see, it seems that Harry Casey stayed around for a while, as her family believed he was a much more suitable candidate than my father.

The pattern of their romance meant that Peggy and Walter were spending more and more time together. My mother explained: 'As your father would often have a bigger part in the plays, sometimes I would go down to his house to wait for him to come back from the rehearsals. His dear mother grew very fond of me and one night she asked me if I could do her a favour.' My grandmother brought my mother into a back room and there she showed her a large trunk. She opened the trunk and it was full to the brim with papers covered in writing.

'Would you ever look at these?' my grandmother asked my mother.

She wanted Peggy to read what her son had been writing for many years. In my grandmother's eyes, my mother was a professional journalist and she would value her opinion of this writing.

My mother was astonished when she read the manuscripts. She could see that there were faults in the writing, the style was underdeveloped, but for someone who was still not twenty-one, it was an extraordinary body of work. While my mother was astonished at the extent of the work, she was always very clear, when talking to me, that there was a considerable distinction between the kind of writing she did as a journalist and the creative writing that my father was engaged in. She often emphasised that these were two distinct types of writing. I am not so sure that, with hindsight, I totally agree with her.

When my father came back to the house that night, he was pleased when he found out that she had looked at his work. From that point on, my mother formed a vital audience for his writing and throughout his life, once he began to write regularly each day, the pattern he followed was the same. He would always read the piece he had written that morning to her. Later on, while working in the Taibhdhearc, he decided to burn all his early manuscripts. He described them as part of his apprenticeship and did not see any reason to keep them.

Within two months or so, my mother realised that this was not just an ordinary romance, it was serious. She had such a close relationship with her father that she thought it was time she told him the truth. She was aware too that the maids in the Crescent were gossiping about her romance with Walter. One morning when her father was in his office, she went in to see him. She was very cautious in revealing to him that the man she had met was important to her:

I said to my father, 'I have met a man' and my father asked me the question: 'Well who is he?'

I answered him, 'His name is Walter Macken.'

My father said that he knew him and he knew the family. Then he asked me the crucial question, 'What does he do?'

I answered him by telling him that he worked as an actor in the Taibhdhearc. He then asked me how much did he earn. When I told him, 30/– a week, his response was immediate – 'Well that won't keep you in the comfort you are used to.'

That was it, the conversation was over. 'I knew then that he disapproved and that I couldn't raise the subject again.'

She never spoke to her father again about Walter Macken, although because she was the acting editor, she managed to publish some book reviews that my father wrote for her. This was the beginning of two years of heartbreak for my mother. Here she was, the eldest daughter of Tom Cork Kenny, going out with a man that her father did not approve of.

Whenever she talked to me about those years, it was always with mixed memories. However, there was a lot of joy as my parents discovered each other and in their love letters, which my mother gave me, you can see the depth of feeling between them. Reading those letters it seems to me that my father was more open in talking about his feelings than my mother was.

5

ROMANCE AND
LOVE LETTERS

The Taibhdhearc would send my father to Rosmuc in the Connemara Gaeltacht to improve his Irish and so he became a great letter-writer. The letters bring the reader right into the lives of these two young people. My father always expressed his feelings in a full-blooded manner and spelled out just how important my mother was to him.

As I said earlier, my mother gave me the original love letters which she wrote to my father, and his replies. My father's are not dated, so it is difficult to work out what sequence they should fall in; I have put them in here in the sequence I think most likely. The letters are so numerous they would take up a whole book, so here are some extracts:

The Connacht Tribune.
July 22nd 1935

Wally dear,
I said I'd write to you – first, you will have to put up with the old typewriter – otherwise I'd never have the necessary time. It is now my dreaded Monday morning – elevenish – and I don't feel so bad.

I have been working hard since approximately 9.05, not bad says you – and I am giving myself some relaxation now writing this – or should I be terribly correct and say, typing this … However, I hope you can make some sense out of this.

Even from my office window, I can see a hopeful bit of blue sky, and if I listen very intently I can even hear 'the wandering water ever whispering' – good old Dante Gabriel Rossetti. You know the funny way that the weir whispers in the morning – and yet it keeps on and on – to some destination unknown I suppose.

Wally, there are such a lot of things I would like – I wonder shall I get anything approaching the elusive dream?

Peace is very important, isn't it? Almost the most important, I should think. I'll go back to Rossetti again before I stop – there are a few of his quotations I have on the brain this morning, and this is a nice one, isn't it?

'The sky leans dumb on the sea
Aweary with all its wings,
And oh – the song the sea sings
Is dark everlastingly.'

Don't you like the last line? And the first – marvellous what pictures the man could paint with one short line-stroke of the ever powerful pen. Indeed, there are lovely things in life – sunset glow, changing sea, somnolent summer – applies to me very much I'm afraid [*referring to the fact that the summer made her sleepy*] – and good friends – the later the best of all. Good morning, Wally dear, I must stop pro tem. I hope to return to this again later.

She continues the letter quoting various poets and then she talks about her daily life:

This time tomorrow night DV [*Deo Volante*] we shall be tripping [*this comes from the expression tripping the light fantastic*] at the Hangar, I hope so anyway – I am dying for a dance – it seems ages since we had one – however, there is next week when we shall undoubtedly get a surfeit. I must look up my white frock in the weekend and see if it is still intact – let's hope so anyway. The birds are singing most charmingly just now, and as I look at the old clock – again the slave of time – I discover it is just 9 and I have been writing to you since 8.30.

Jack is hovering around – I think he is waiting for me to give him the necessary adieu – I shall tell him to depart anon. I am sure he wonders what on earth his big sister is writing for so long, and so frantically.

Good night, Wally dear, and I imagine you will be a trifle tired by the time you have waded to the end of this – God bless you.

Peggy

Although the date of this first letter is July 1935, my mother and father met sometime in May 1935 when she joined the Taibhdhearc and they began seeing each other regularly.

My mother, when writing her early letters, was careful not to mention her own feelings and instead quoted famous poets and their views of love. My father, however, did not hold back in his letters:

St Judes,
St Helen Street,
Galway.

My own dear darling Peggy,

I am scheduled for a rehearsal with Sheila Finlay at 1 p.m. so in case I don't get out to the Augey [*Augustinian church beside the Taibhdhearc*] to see you, I am scribbling this note. I got home from the Taibhdhearc at 10.15 p.m. last night. There was a light in the parlour. God, said I, she's there, my ticker ceased to function for many minutes. I crept cautiously in. Mother was kneeling down saying her prayers. Hell, I felt like blue murder.

'She didn't come,' said mother [*meaning Peggy*].

'So I noticed,' said I, freezingly.

It was only a night anyhow and what matter. I had stolen Tommy's bicycle [*Tommy King, the long-serving caretaker of the Taibhdhearc*]; as it being so early, I returned same and walked home again. I wrote that old review for want of something better to do.

I'll send Tommy up with this. I never wanted to see you more than I did last night. I am dying to see you now. Please go to the Augey at once and say a few Hail Marys for me. Just wait five minutes. If I don't turn up, I will be there at ten to four on the dot. We will have the evening anyway and Mother has invited us home for the tea so that is something.

You will have a rehearsal tonight as he is doing 'Sovereign Love'. I am falling in love with you all over again. That's about a hundred times now. I feel like a sick calf. Will you please send me a photograph some time? God knows I want it. I see so little of you lately.

If I don't get some honest labour soon I believe I will lose the equilibrium. One alone would miss me. Wouldn't you darling? I'm horribly lonely, I don't know why but there it is, and here am I. I don't know why I wrote to you today. To get into touch with you, I suppose. I refuse to put that in inverted commas. Besides talking about commas reminds me of coma and who has it or who wants it. Not your obedient lover.

Wally

P.S. Ten to four for sure.

The last paragraph here is revealing – my father felt that by working as a general dogsbody at the Taibhdhearc he was wasting his time, and was hoping to find another job that would give him a salary that would allow him to get married. His letters from this period reflect a general frustration at the situation.

The next letter I have was written by my mother on 5 August 1935:

Wally dear,

Strange – strange there is peace even here – at least there is now the entire editorial staff is at their respective dinners – and I am alone, I shall write this. But I must say, that in spite of all the vicissitudes that I enjoyed Race Week immensely and I loved the dancing – and we certainly had plenty of it.

I am going to try and scoot home early this afternoon, and get a wee sleep if possible at all. And young man you forgot to return to the Lady her keys and most important of all, her rosary, last night or rather this morning. Why is it that we have such a lot to say to each other? Can you explain it?

And sometimes we don't talk so much at all, that is the queer thing. That just reminds me that I should have answered Harry's letter – I am a very rude girl. I am going to finish this scrawley epistle.

Please go and pray for me, and I shall pray hard for you at Lough Derg. I always put you into my prayers these days, but I do feel such a heathen because I was not at mass this week at all. Joan gave me a lovely bunch of carnations this evening which she grew in her own garden at the back – they are wafting lingering perfumes at me just now. Wouldn't I just love a garden full of sweet smelling flowers?

This time next week I expect I shall be in the sunny – I hope – south – far far away Wally, but the same old moon will be looking at me – and I shall picture it casting a faery-like radiance over Galway Bay – and you will think of me too, won't you?

Anyhow, if I discover any memorable milestone on my southward trek, you shall have a full and detailed description of them when I come back, if I don't write them to you.

I'll do my best, I promise, even if I have to sit up in bed when they have all retired, to scrawl them. And don't forget that you are to write to Inchydoney Hotel, Clonakilty, Co. Cork, which will, I understand be our headquarters. These people have a car, you know, and they propose to tour me around a lot.

I hope to get out to you as per arrangement, but one never knows

– anyway tomorrow night at 7.15 DV. Goodnight Wally, don't forget
Saturday and Confession and think lots of me while I am away – I
really think you should consign this to the flames – nice curling fire
all red and rosy with purple tinges – ahem.

Peggy

Here is another letter from my father:

St Judes,
St Helen Street,
Galway.
Monday, 11 a.m.

My darling Peggy,

It seems queer to be writing to you now when I have been so long
writing to you while I have been away. It also seems queer to think
that I'm going away again today and to tell you the truth darling it
is getting me down. Saturday and Sunday were like a dream – what
a beautiful dream – and like a dream they passed in a flash.

They were so beautiful that they have taken on the burden of
being un-scorchable memories – incapable of being burned from
the mind.

Can you realise darling how I hate going to Rosmuc. You don't
realise my own love how lonesome it is. The only joy we have in the
whole thing is the knowledge that on Friday we will be free. How
I long for Friday to come. We really have become so necessary to
one another. Going away for a few days is like an eternal parting.
And you hate the word 'parting' love, it's a beastly word too, I'm
tongue tied this morning. I seem to be able to do nothing but pen
short sentences which sound terrible to my own ear.

I love you, Peggy, love you, love you. I could never stop and
I will love you until I die and much – oh much beyond. It grows
stronger and stronger and has become so strong that it is impossible
to break it now. Keep, loving me, Peggy because it is only in your love

that Salvation lies. Someday we will find the reward of our present sufferings.

Anything worth fighting for is worth the attaining. Anything that makes you fight is the true thing and you must keep fighting until it is yours. We might have a big fight in front of us yet. So let us regard Rosmuc as but another cross, added to our already heavy lot; it will soon be over. I love you Peggy, I love you and I will never cease from thanking God for giving you to me. How empty life would be without you. Say that, and you get hope for the morrow.

I love you. Goodbye darling,

Yours, Wally, always

Being separated from his love clearly sent my father off into torturous sadness. This next letter was written by my mother to my father in November 1935, when he had been sent by the Taibhdhearc to Ballinasloe to do some work for them:

My dear Wally,

As there is a totally unexpected lull in operations this morning, I am seizing my – I was just about to write pen, when I realised that it was good old typewriter – and also that awful telephone rang and I had to seize it (the telephone receiver I mean) and modulate my voice to suit the editor who rings me before going to 11 mass to make all kinds of un-helpful suggestions – all of which I rejected scornfully, and maintained strongly that I wanted to get out the paper early – so there.

With which militant beginning I shall proceed. I am very glad you are going by train. I am going to write a note to May Kilmartin and ask her to meet me on Sunday night after Harry [*Casey*] leaves and we will go to the pictures. I imagine he will leave about 8 or so. In fact I think I will give it to you to deliver today [*the letter for May Kilmartin*]. The sky is actually brightening, Wally, perhaps the rain will stop. Do you know I prayed quite a lot for you at mass this morning – I hope they do some good – one never knows …

I am taking up this letter again at 4 p.m., my dear just after my bath. Unfortunately, this will be rather interrupted because both Daddy and Ivor are parked here with me in the dining-room. Harry has gone up to town with Jack and Ma.

You are in the train by now – I was tempted to write slush – slush – but reformed so now! I shall miss you lots my dear but DV this day week we shall have resumed our peregrinations! Daddy has just said that Ivor and he will go for a walk – they will hesitate for a long time – I have just asked is he going to Dublin and he says not till the week after next, just as well isn't it?

Wally dear, hurry back soon, I shall be looking forward to Thursday. And don't get wet in Ballinasloe. Hoping to hear soon of your safe arrival therein – I shall really have to stop, Cherebeen, here they all come descending on me. The wind howls without and it's family five. Au revoir my dear, I have to stop this time really.

I shall miss you – even so – to remain as ever, my dear, I hate to think of you even 40 miles away. Be good, Wally dear, and write soon to me.

Yours,

Peggy

Ivor and Jack, who Peggy mentions in this letter, are her stepbrother and brother respectively.

My parents hated to be separated and this comes out very clearly in these extracts from my mother's letters written around Christmas 1935:

Wednesday night, Dec. 11th 1935

Wally, old dear, here I am absolutely on my own, and for the moment I have a lapse or lull of whatever you like to call it, and I feel a sinking sensation – it is rather lonely here you know. By now, you are well on your way to Clifden and to the discovery of the nature and origin of that mysterious message. I hope, for your sake, that it means something good. You have become such a part of my life – I nearly said my normal existence – that I cannot imagine it without you. I hope you get a break – it is certainly coming to you. And I do hope, selfishly, that you come back tomorrow – I should hate it if you didn't …

If only something would happen soon – or even the promise of something – one never knows DV.

And now, dear child – I feel more like saying – I must get back to mouldy work – I still haven't thought of an editorial – I'll have to wait until tomorrow and perhaps Daddy would really produce something – but I am so mixed up and mouldy without you that I cannot settle down to write.

Good night, God bless you – and me, my dear,

Peggy

Fri: Wally dear, just got letter from you, but you never said when you were coming back!

Some of the difficulties experienced by the couple are clearly illustrated in the following letter.

Phone Galway 21   5 The Crescent,
Grams: Kenny Journalist   Galway.
Fri. night – at home, 6.35 p.m.

Leaning on my knee, I'm writing this. Wally dear, as the old lady once (or did she?) said – you have my heart broken! Yours was such an un-satisfactory letter. I read frantically to the end to see when were you coming back to me – and lo and behold, not a word about it – just a terse farewell at the end – I want you back with me so badly that I'm prepared to forgive all and do anything you want me to do.

I'll go to Rhodesia and farm – honestly – anything. And I mean it, really I do, and I always keep my word too, even though I have the unfortunate habit of turning up late darling, I'll even go out to Clifden with you to see that awful concert after Christmas if you want me to do that. What more can I do?

I do hope you answer my missive and put me out of my suspense, Wally; oh why didn't you send me a wee message yesterday? If you only knew the miserable day I had, you wouldn't leave me like that. Darling, I have just got your wire and my heart is lifted accordingly – so I'll stop writing rubbish and send this to your house. Your bus gets in, I know at 3.30, so I'll come out to meet you at 6.30 at our usual spot – will that do?

Peggy

The next letter also again highlights how miserable my mother was when she didn't see my father:

Friday 1.15 p.m.

My dear,

I don't know how I am, so prithee forgive in time if I reach even greater heights of incoherency than usual. First of all as I anticipated I have had greater trouble all the morning over that old case I told you about [*a court case brought against the paper*] – admittedly it was my fault to a certain extent but I did not half get it in the neck. Of course, I was feeling so down already that I practically faded out and whisper it easy, I shed many tears of self-pity – I know that is what they were. I wish you could see my face now – my eyes are in a lovely state.

But enough of that gloom. I want to leave here early today and complete my Christmas shopping, but am only just finishing now; alas Pa has gone out, of course, although I did expect something editorial.

But that's the way, and time has taught me to expect no better. I am still in a muddle as to how exactly I am to produce two papers next week. Let's hope they turn out all right. I need hardly repeat that I have started missing you already.

If you could have seen me this morning, I am sure you would have taken me with you on the spot. It is a pity that it is not possible.

I have got so many lectures this morning about that one slip that I have decided that I am incompetent, untrustworthy and unfit for my job etc., etc. I was not exactly told that but I am surmising it myself. Note all the slips, my fingers refuse to behave themselves even moderately well – when, I think of you and me I get several pains, my dear.

And now, I have to do without your cheerful self for a whole week – it seems interminable now – I am full of good resolutions again this morning – to pray for us – and more. I shall be looking forward to your letter tomorrow – TG for that at least – but I shall miss you terribly – I know it now – I knew it yesterday. It is no use my trying to write anymore – I don't feel capable of anything coherent – tomorrow I shall be better perhaps, may you have a happy Christmas, and think lots of Peggy.

In my mother's next letter, she again conveys something of the loneliness she feels, although Harry Casey appears to be still around:

The Connacht Tribune.
21st December 1935

How are you, my own dear – we are snowbound, frost bound here, and everything horrible possible – when I was not killed coming in this morning I never will be! I was so glad to get your letter, it arrived by the first post, but I got a kind of shock when I saw it was so short, but I know you could not help that. TG for this day week anyway – my whole self is focused on that now.

But don't worry, I thought lots about you since – and am still – Wally, you are everywhere with me, so cheer up. I spent a very harassing day yesterday – I told you already about the fracas of the morning, and yesterday afternoon I spent shopping with Ma – expending on the family Christmas presents – with the result that I am practically broke, sad but true. I am glad you liked the pullover, but please tell me if there was anything wrong. And now for yesterday evening. Harry arrived just at 7 after an awful drive over, and I went to the Jesuits choir practice at 7.30 by special request of Fr O'Farrell. I was not back until after 8, so Harry stayed with the family.

By this time, it was a shocking night – intense cold and frost – impossible to walk, so we stayed en famille for the night. I have developed a lovely cold, so went to bed early. Harry left just before 11 and I went straight to bed. It is now 1 p.m. and I have been hard at it all the morning – so the papers are beginning to take shape. I dread going out, it is so slippy, although I have the bike. I have still got to get some things.

Oh Wally, my dear, I miss you terribly – I spent hours looking into the fire last night thinking of you and us – I am sure they all wonder why I am getting so quiet. But my dear, it is you – what more can I say?

I love you,

Your very lonely,

Peggy

From this time on, my mother's letters are less restrained in her expression of her feelings for my father. She seems to have written quite a few letters during that Christmas period:

The Connacht Tribune.
Monday, December 23rd 1935

Good morning, darling, it is only 9.30 and I am here since 9.05, working hard, but am going to try to get this off before Jack and Daddy etc. come rushing in. I kept thinking of you and I – somehow I cannot separate us at all now. Saturday I spent the afternoon walloping hard [*working in the newspaper office*], and after tea went to the Savoy with Harry – it was freezing hard, and I brought him home to supper and dispatched him early – at 11.15 to be precise. Yesterday he came to dinner and afterwards we went to the Savoy matinee – and by the way the picture was disappointing – came home to tea and sat en famille all night – in other words he had only about an hour alone with me in all.

He was to leave this morning at 9 en route for Cork [*Harry was a primary school teacher and may have been teaching in a Galway school during this period*] – I hope he gets on all right – the roads are awful. And now, you have my weekend, my dear, and I am terrified I shall slip and break my neck – it is a pity that you are not here to hold me up. Wally, it seems ages since Friday – will it ever be next Friday?

11 a.m. – being a continuation of same.

My dear, I was so disappointed – I thought I would get a letter from you for sure, and the Connemara post has come in – at least I have McHugh's stuff but nothing from you. Are you as frost-bound and frozen as we are? I suppose so, but please, please, Wally, come back for sure on Friday, no matter how you work it – won't you?

Wally, it must be the grand passion – really and truly. I'll have lots to tell you when you come back. How grand it sounds – but I wish Friday had dawned, and I would feel happier. If only we got a break somehow, I would make a dash for it anytime.

I must really stop, darling, unless I get time to write more, but it's doubtful, as we have a bit of a rush today – I do hope I get a letter from you my dearest.

Your distracted,

Peggy

The letter she was waiting for from my father finally arrived on the same day, so she immediately wrote yet another letter in response:

The Connacht Tribune.
23rd December 1935

This is Monday, my dear, and I have just got the mid-day post and TG your letter, so I am going to begin mine for tomorrow – as I have the chance. I am sorry I bothered you on Friday with that tale of my tears – everything in that direction has panned out all right so far TG and I have heard nothing more since. My life is a blank – old stuff but true nevertheless – and I was awfully glad to get your letter. I shall be there on Friday night at 7.30 on the dot – let's hope that the frost will be gone by that time darling.

Darling, I so want to talk to you again, and waive all my troubles away, and Wally, don't swear so much – your letter was full of it – I'm only joking, my dear, they brought you closer than ever. I wonder what are you doing now? And I wish I was there no matter what it is. This going away business really drives me crazy – honestly it is no exaggeration – it gets me down – probably that is why I wept so much on Friday – they were very bitter tears too and my eyes were a treat for the rest of the day. Harry thought it was my cold, and I did not disillusion him.

At this moment, Desmond is sitting beside me frantically sending off Christmas cards – and from indications to hand, his postbag would seem to rival at least President Roosevelt's.

Wally, it is ages since we had a decent walk – don't you wish it was spring and we could fare forth – and how lovely early summer will be. Think of all the millions of things we could be doing Darling, darling, you are in my mind all the time – think lots of me. I must stop now until tomorrow, the 'Sentinel' is just ready – au revoir, my own dear.

This next letter is a short note from my father; although it is written on Taibhdhearc headed-paper, I think it might have been written from Ballinasloe where he had been sent to do some drama work in the local schools:

Wednesday 2.30

Liam Ó Briain has gone away for the Whit [*weekend*] and left us two Joe Soaps sitting on our hindies [*hind-legs*] holding the bag. The dear professor will not return until Tuesday evening which means that we will not have to go until Wednesday which means that this chicken will be waiting for you when you come on Wednesday night – whatever time you come. So if you get this in time try and let me know how I will be able to see you on Wednesday because I will have to see you. So wire or write but please figure it out darling, and let me know.

Next is a letter written by my father from Rosmuc, where he had again gone to improve his Irish:

c/o Post Office, Rosmuc.
12.20 p.m.

My very darling Peggy,

I might as well, love, break the bad news early. There is no bus on Sunday but there is one on Sunday week. I can, however, manage to get in on some other day. The bus leaves at 9.30 from here. I'm telling you all this love so that you won't say again that I am trying to be diplomatic and writing the bad news at the bottom of the letter. I am writing this at the window-sill and the moon is peeping in. This Rosmuc is the most beautiful place I ever saw in my life. It would make an ideal setting for our love. But since my love is absent it has the gloomy appearance of a graveyard.

The house I'm in is not too bad. It has slates on it anyway and that's something. I haven't had time to explore the countryside but please God I will start early in the morning. Mind you darling, my Irish is not so bad as I thought it was. All it needs is a good brushing up. Criostóir [*Mac Aonghusa, a local teacher and radical writer*] and his wife are terribly nice really. Not what I imagined he would be. He is very literary, has French and all the latest books and plays on the very tips of his fingers. Painting too, he seems to know all about it, so at least, I won't be without somebody to talk too.

I miss you terribly my love. The bed doesn't look too bad and the place appears to be clean. It is now 12.30 and we were talking in Criostóir's house for ages, all about the Taibhdhearc and all in Irish so that it is a relief to get back to the mother tongue.

I love you indubitably and irrevocably, so please darling don't miss me too much (and don't miss me too little) so the best thing you can do is become a living paradox in order to satisfy the cravings of the young man who is mad, potty, lunatic, crazy about you and who will not rest until he slips a little band of gold upon your finger. This place will give me the inspiration of how to marry you. I will make it my problem and solve it somehow somewhere. After all it is only a problem, the same as any other and I will try putting it down on paper and working to a solution and ending at the jolly old altar rails. I will finish this in the morning if I have time before the bus goes. And I will go to bed now and dream about you and cry because I miss you so much. God bless you and me. I love you – until death, my own darling.

Your Wally until Hell freezes over

In this letter from my mother, it refers to my father being away, presumably still in Rosmuc:

Thursday 1 p.m.

Wally – I am simply raging with you – I have just got your missive saying you are not coming, but I suppose you cannot help it – but you are missing the best opportunity we are ever likely to have – Daddy and Lou [*her stepmother*], BOTH OF THEM mind, went to Dublin this morning until Saturday night, by car, and I had fond hopes of you and I having that long awaited peaceful evening by the fire tonight and we could have repeated it tomorrow night – however, it cannot be helped.

Here is another letter from my father, written from Rosmuc:

Rosmuc.
Tuesday 6.30 p.m.

My darling Peggy,

You may have composed a lot and you may have written and

published a lot but you never wrote as nice a letter. It was charming, my love and rose the old spirits accordingly and God knows they would want some raising because right now the rain is lashing and the wind howling. I will be in on Saturday and if your family are away on Sunday we will have a beautiful long Sunday, thank the Gods. The bus leaves at 9.30 and gets to Galway at around 11.30. Well then I can stay until Monday when the bus leaves as usual at 7 in the evening. Then I will be home for good on Friday morning at 11.30 and Friday being your half-day we will have a big long time and so on ad infinitum.

Weds 10.30 p.m.

You will note my own darling that I didn't continue after tea yesterday evening and I hope you will forgive my lapse but the cursed rain was so damn depressing that I felt that if I didn't get anybody to talk to I would go nuts. So I journeyed to Criostóir's and we talked everything and taking it in turns we read Omar Kayan [*Khayyam*], and believe me love his philosophy was balm to my troubled soul. I got wet then and went to my lonely couch.

The sun is shining a little today and it looks as if it is going to be fine. I think I will take bathing togs and will climb a mountain, strip and get burned. If you wanted a dip here you would probably have to walk about forty miles.

Your letter yesterday was really beautiful. It gave me strength to bear the Rosmuc yoke. You can't honestly believe how lonely it is here without you and it could be such a different place if only you were here. There are so many places where we could lose ourselves and talk and look at one another. This love business is really terrible. I can't go anywhere without you love, you are with me everywhere. There is only one solution and that is to get married as soon as God is good and issues the permit …

I have been reading here as well. Criostóir has a most comprehensive library. I have read Goethe's *Faust*, plays by Lady Gregory, a beautifully sordid book by Liam O'Flaherty and a short story collection with stories by all the leading writers including James Joyce, Seán Ó Faoláin, Liam O'Flaherty, Mary Arden, Bates,

Houseman and a million others. It is a great primer for technique.

I think the time for your letter will never come, I want it so much. You see I love you and I become impatient if I am not with you and the only way to satiate my impatience is to feed it something, your letters feed mine but is only like nibbling in comparison to how I want you. And all that is written in the cold light of the morning I pause after every little while and start thinking about you, and how much I love you and where our future lies and what are God's intentions towards us. It is in places like this that you come into contact with God but you are very likely to rebel and that is the terrible thing.

You know I love you Peggy darling and it feels like Saturday will never come. Two days seem so long before I see you again but thank God it is better than a week hence. I love you and always will and please don't ever question it because its roots are too deep to be uprooted.

Goodbye darling, I miss you an awful lot,

I've terrible feelings that I'll die if I don't see you soon,

Your old Wally

Here is a letter from my mother, writing about what she sees as good and bad love letters:

Wednesday night. In my office – ahem and so forth

It is now 7.25 p.m. exactly and there is a slight slackening of the rope – I mean metaphorically of course – I am seizing my jolly old typewriter and shall seek to reply in some small measure to your MSS. Wally. I must say I enjoyed very much your description of those love letters – but may I be permitted to voice my opinion? From the viewpoint of a mere female I speak – and an alleged blonde at that …

Anyhow, to be mundane and matter-of-fact once more I cherish or rather relish, distinct memories of a nasty schoolboy calling me Carrots long ago – mind that long ago – when I used wield a

camán for my first Alma Mater – Taylor's Hill. I knew not that I
have reached Page 2 [*of her letter*] – I'll best you to it yet – I'm sure
that Daddy, who is next door doing the leaders, thinks I'm doing
something great – if he only knew.

But I seem to have strayed from my original theme which was
to talk about love letters. I'm rather mixed about them. Definitely
like all the rest of my sex I am wont to admire the beautifully long-
winded epistles of the early days, scented and accompanied by
bewigged and be-flowered footmen – I leave you to find the period
– I am a bit foggy.

But we will never get those now – so that's that. I think I can
always find the sincerity in the ones I do get – and I have had some
nice letters. I am rather sorry in a way that we have got so self-con-
scious as to drop all the nice little customs such as sending flowers
– how silly it would seem now.

But did you know that I love flowers – particularly, smelly ones
– that is the simplest way to express it, I think. My favourites are
violets – but I'm sure I told you that already. In fact, here is rather
a pretty story – or not exactly a story, but a custom which brings
the scent of violets back to me every spring. Balla, where I was
at school – or to give it its more fairy-taleish name, Athavallie
Demesne, is a marvellous place for flowers. When I was at school
there, the gardens were in pretty good condition. But anyhow
there was a dear old nun who was in charge of the refectory and
the flowers, and she discovered my particular weakness for violets
– so every spring, I would be presented with a bunch, on the quiet,
of course and every single year since I left school, she manages to
send them to me somehow – with my little sisters or else through
the post.

Honestly they put me in good humour for days – fancy that. I
think they are beautiful, so simple and sweet and with such a fra-
grant scent bringing pictures of lovely gardens in which they only
hold a low place.

I would really love to possess a big garden – but I don't suppose I
would be much use at keeping it as it should be kept. But, oh Wally,
haven't I drifted far away from the love-letter topic.

I fear that now I must get back to work – I still have lots to do and what a rush tomorrow is going to be – I shall need my Angel by my side to get through it successfully. I hear the editor walking around and so must really stop – goodnight, my dear, although I shall be seeing you at rehearsal later. Hope this is not too devastatingly long-winded, sounds like May O'Flaherty at her best.

Peggy

Incidentally, my mother became a wonderful gardener and built a garden in every house she lived in.

Another letter came from my father in Rosmuc:

Rosmuc.
Sat. 10.30

Although the sentiments of yesterday are like last year's snow, I feel as if there has not been any thaw. I had intended to surprise you and go in on the 9.30 bus this morning. It was 10 when I woke. I told the lady of the house to call me, she failed. That sounds very bald on paper and just like my customary goings-on but please believe me.

It's true and I feel sore at myself and I can hear my darling Peggy saying nothing but thinking in her heart – yes, he failed again. He really isn't worth it and a few other things. I will be in next Saturday morning and if you still love me we can have tea in the scullery and I will not come back to this joint until Monday on the 7 bus.

Do you mind, darling if I tell you a little about this place, Rosmuc. It's terrible – beautiful if you like but still terrible. The house I am in is nice. I have a big clean room, all to myself and I also eat here. It is awfully lonely. When I had posted your letter yesterday morning, I hitched up my breeches and went mountaineering. I climbed a mountain and looked out over the world.

I could have nearly touched the heavens with my head. It was a pretty stiff climb. Then looming away in the distance, I saw another mountain, separated from me by miles, by the valley between – the lake strewn valley – the small lakes nestling in its bosom like jewels set in a diadem. It was dotted here and there with cattle and two horses. So apart from them I was alone.

A hare sprang up and like a flash disappeared from my ken. With a dull whirring of wings, a grouse rose and fumbled away. I could have killed him, had I a stone or the inclination. I felt away from all the world. The sun was making a shy effort to break its cloudy bonds and now and again succeeding, it poured its rays into the drenched valleys It was beautiful but terrible in its loneliness. I descended into the valley, up the other mountain and down into Rosmuc. I liked being in the mountains because they are so impressive and austere that they forbid you to have any thoughts of your own. They rob your soul of its own fretfulness and infuse into your being with their own power and fill you with their own bigness.

Once you are back in the valley of Rosmuc and looking backwards at the monarchs you have left behind, your soul closes and the wounds and pangs of love and loneliness open up again and the pain oozes forth. I called for May Kilmartin and we went for a walk until 2. Then I had dinner and called for her at 3.30 whence we repaired to the schoolteachers and talked with them until 7. Then we had the tea. It started to rain and May K. stayed at home. I walked until nine and then returned to my lonely room to work and think.

That's the tale love and I'm sure you can see the poignancy of it all …

Goodbye, my darling,
I love you always,
Your lonely,
Old Wally

Here is another letter from my mother where again she is lonely and worried, and Harry Casey is still clearly on the scene.

5 The Crescent, Galway.
15th April 1936

My own darling,

I don't know how to tell you or even to begin to explain, how miserable I am. It is just 2.30 and I have had a long and busy day up to this; indeed, you could have come in to see me, because Harry Casey arrived just before I and is now gone to golf with Des. And I want to see you, dearest. He is going to the Taibhdhearc tonight, and I will collect him when I am finished here. I am all mixed up every way – sounds complicated, but perhaps you can follow my reasoning as usual.

Emotionally I seem to be exhausted – I only know that I want you, my dear, I always will. I get all teary and sad today when I think of us. Honestly everything seems to be against us, but that is all the more reason why we must do something.

You got a very nice critique from Fitzie [*Billy Fitzgerald, a 'Connacht Tribune' reporter*] – I imagine you will like it. I notice that the dailies, except for the 'Irish Press', gave nothing about it at all today – I shall have to talk to you when I see you. Remember I love you, sweetheart.

Always,
Peggy

Here is another of my father's letters from Rosmuc:

Rosmuc.
11.30 p.m.

My dearest darling Peggy,

I'm writing this letter to you now because tomorrow being a holiday, I will have to rise early and undertake the expedition go dtí an tAifreann [*going to mass*] and it is over 3 miles away. And now how are you my very own love. I have been thinking and dreaming about you today and I am sorry if the letter I posted you today was gloomy or morose but that was just the way it felt.

Although the day was fine, it was breezy and going up a mountain, I stripped to the pelt, as they say and let the rays of sun trickle over my body. My colour, bodily, is a cross between a red Indian and the skin of a Spanish onion …

The old Irish is improving anyhow but the whole expedition is a fallacy for the simple reason, that none of us – and that includes Dermody and all the directors – save Liam Ó Briain can talk Irish. Our knowledge of the language is only superficial and you would want to spend about 5 years at least in the Gaeltacht before you could acquire even the semblance of a blas. And I find out here that I am like a German talking bad French to Alexander Dumas. They don't know what the devil I'm talking about and they have nothing on me because I don't either.

I note that I haven't yet given you an account of my day. Having posted your letter (and thanks muchly, darling, for the stamps) I procured the book of stamps and wended my way up the mountains. I also brought along my togs. This was midday. Reaching a secluded nook I pondered whether or not I would divest myself of my apparel, it was breezy, ye ken.

Ah to hell with it, I say and in a few moments, I was as God had made me. Then stretching myself to the full height of my young naked manhood, I inhaled the fresh mountain air. I pulled the togs over my loins, made a note to start a nudist colony in Galway and stretched myself on the grassy sward, ticklish withal but wholesome. For awhile I pondered on the joys of an open air life and then my thoughts turned to you. I spent from 12 to 3 – three solid hours – thinking about you continuously.

It was beautiful up there, you can't realise how beautiful – and to feel the mountain grass against your bare flesh and the warm wind gently massaging your naked body. It was pagan, I admit, but oh so beautiful. I haven't suffered any ill-effects so far and my upper legs are the only things which are stinging a little. I journeyed to the school to Criostóir. We read a bit of Kavanagh until 4 whence I journeyed to dinner, got your delightful letter, read the 'Irish Press' avidly and shaved.

I saw May Kilmartin on the road. She had just come back from some forsaken spot where she had been staying a day and a night with a female – tá sé (probably a teacher). She told me she had a telegram from Liam Ó Briain and he wanted to know if she could find a room for Eibhlin (he would then send her out) [*Eibhlin Ó Briain, another Taibhdhearc actress*]. She found a room for her and cabled Liam about it. She went home and I went to Críostóir's house. We read James Clarence Mangan, Byron, Dr Anderson, some Irish pieces and had a delightful time – we talked women, sex and appeal and other things which I can't mention to you or you'd think I was horribly vulgar.

Then we went to the local football pitch. Boy! It was great fun while it lasted and I now know that, though slim (or is it skinny) I can yet succeed in bowling over many rustics of robust build and savage inclinations.

We left the battlefield at 11 p.m. I came home, grabbed a delicious cup of milk – fresh from the cow's udder – and locked myself up to write to you and be with my own darling sweetheart. I will go to bed now – it is 12.40 – and thank God for his munificence in giving me you to love and hold and hide and mind for ever and ever to infinity.

I love you, love you, love you and I say it to myself about, at least a million times a day. I'm sure you must hear me! Saturday love – don't forget, lock it into your mind. I will be in Galway at 11.30. If you could leave a note in the house, it would help. I'm simply crazy about you Peggy, darling – nuts – foolish. Love me and miss me until Saturday.

Your own lonely,
Wally A.

My mother writes about her worries for their future, particularly their plan to elope:

Good morning, my darling,

I did not see you so far today, and I was sure you would be there this morning [*she expected to see him at early morning mass*] but, however,

I prayed for us as I always do and always will. Somehow, during my prayers at the Novena last night, and they were more in the form of a meditation than a prayer, I felt they would be heard. I have started praying to my darling Esso – and if anyone can do anything at all for us, I am sure she will. I only know that my happiness lies with you – my life is irrevocably bound up with yours.

Pa is coming in and there are some things to be cleared up. I believe our female friend [*a reference to her stepmother*] is in bad humour this morning – alas Darling, I won't be able to stand much more of this, won't you hurry and try and do something? As I said before we will be so careful that nobody is going to suspect until we are quite ready [*a reference to their plan to elope*] – you know what I mean, dear heart. My heart is full again today, I find it hard to write all the lovely things God has engraved in my heart – my beloved how I long for peace and you – you mean peace of mind and soul to me.

I have been kept busy since I came back, my own darling, but I love, love you, sweetheart, that is all I can say. Darling, my heart is stretching out to yours, it always will – I'm so horribly lonely when I'm away from you sweetheart.

I'll have to stop, now darling,

I love you, love you,

Peggy

Another letter from my mother gives a true idea of the difficulties the young couple were facing:

Thursday, 3.00 p.m.

My heart and indeed my mind are both so full, darling, that I don't know what to write to you – however, by this time, I think you know how much I love you – I'd like to emblazon it to the world at large. I feel like Isolde must have felt without Tristan, for so far away do you seem to be from me now.

Although I don't feel in the least optimistic today, yet I say again we have got to do something – desperate circumstances need those desperate actions we are so fond of talking about. But now we must go beyond dreams – vain dreams – I seem to have spent my life looking forward to a fulfilment which ever eludes me – this time with God's help, I shall somehow find my happiness and yours.

You cannot imagine how terribly hurt I felt when you were spoken of as you were today and yesterday [*probably by her stepmother*]. My soul wept with the angels – of course, let us be sensible and remember it is all meant. Put yourself in their places – oh, those well-meaning friends who never consider the finer feelings which make everything worthwhile – and you will see that it seems on the surface justified.

I am sorry for everyone now when I begin to see things in their true perspective and realise that come what may – and I see plenty of trouble ahead – it is inevitable that you and I will be together always. It matters not where, or how, you know that. I am still seething though I did not let you know that today, so you see I can hide some things even from you, my best beloved. If only, Wally, you got a break – this financial question unfortunately has to be considered in circumstances like ours, or if only I was not Peggy Kenny – but it is no use saying if, ad infinitum.

My head swims when I try and think of anything feasible. I forgot whether I told you or not, that I wrote a desperate letter to Mr Delacey yesterday, asking him if he could suggest anything at all. You know I look upon him as one of my best friends and I would value his advice accordingly. Of course he is a delightfully inconsequential person, so he may not write back anything in return at all. But, it is no harm, and anyway it relieved my harassed feelings yesterday immensely to write him, even a guarded letter.

Is there nobody you could write to and act to help us out? I would do almost anything, but we must devise a very careful plan of campaign – go slowly to a certain extent, and see what we can do. Yesterday and again today, I felt an awful loneliness. This is what made me so weepy, I wanted my poor darling, Esso so much – she would be such a help now – if only she was left for another few years.

Fitzie says that Wilmot [*Seamus Wilmot, a director of the Taibhdhearc*] said today that May Kilmartin was excellent in the play and that Mr Macken was very, very good on the second night. You were the only two he mentioned. May [*Peggy's sister*] has just been giving out – she heard the reverberations of what I got yesterday – and she says that everyone should mind their own business. How I wish they would, dearest. Wally why didn't we meet some years ago – and we could have had everything settled up long ago. Please don't say you would die without me, darling – you will always have me in spirit – for I find my mind wandering off answering yours in the weirdest way at times.

There is a definite communion of spirit between us and we must keep it beautiful and like that – like it was on Monday – you remember? Heart of mine, I love you, that is the only thing in life for me – we shall have to be brave, and that especially applies to me – and now I have to earn my four guineas too – so God bless you, my darling Wally, and keep you for me, and bring us to our goal soon.

Always,

Peggy Edel

Here is another letter to my mother from my father, who spent around a month in Rosmuc, although he tried to get to Galway at least once a week to see her:

Rosmuc.
Tuesday morning 10.45

As you doubtless notice I over-slept myself this morning. I didn't waken until 10.30 and it's a horrible day. The sky is just one black mass of clouds and it is raining like hell. What a spot and what a climate and I have to wait until nearly 3 before I get your letter. My Irish is terribly poor. I didn't really know how poor and weak it was until I came out here. I'm barely able to put a sentence together and as a matter of fact I don't know whether it is broken Irish or broken English, I am speaking …

My adventures yesterday were null and void. At twelve I went to the Post Office and just managed to catch the post and give them the letter I wrote to you. Then I returned and called to pick up May Kilmartin. The plan was to go to Críostoir Mac Aonghusa's school and that he would put the boys talking and we listen to the blas. When we got to the end of the road, May K. said that she was damned if she would go to any old school and listen to a crowd of kids so she whipped two cigarettes off me and went in to spend the time with Mrs Mac Aonghusa. She would wait there until I came out of the school.

Having arrived at the school, Críostóir and myself did all the talking and it was only later that he thought about the kids. He has a most original way with them. He puts four of them, one on each side of the room and lets them hammer away at each other. They do everything but beat each other. Epithets like 'gander,' 'lark', 'bushy' and so on fly through the air and they can tell you what Michaleen Thomas' mother's grandfather had for breakfast. Talk about washing dirty linen in public.

And the essays those babies can write! Each and every one of their essays is 50% better than the one I did for my Leaving Cert, and that's a fact. They sure can use their imagination. When we got tired of playing with the kids, he sent them out to play and then he started in on me.

I'd read a bit and then he would correct my pronunciation. He's certainly well up in Irish. There are millions of different words that I was pronouncing incorrectly and he pointed out each and every one to me.

After school I trotted back to the house for my dinner and then procured your two letters. When I saw them my heart nearly stopped because I thought that something might have happened. But all was well. After dinner, I went back to Críostóir and we went walking until 7 when I had tea and Críostoir and myself talked until 10.30. I mentioned about going to Galway on Saturday and was trying to think up a real good 'one' when he said, I probably wanted to get in to see my girl. I see the post car coming and I must be away. I love you, love you, love you. Please keep thinking that always and know I miss you like hell. Goodbye love and keep missing me until Saturday, a red letter day in the lives of men.

> Goodbye love, God bless you,
> Your lonely,
> Wally

In the following letter, my father refers to their need to do something about their situation:

Rosmuc.
Thursday morning 10.40

My own darling Peggy,

Thanks for your nice long letter of yesterday. It shook up the old heartstrings. I note that all the bad weather is not converging on Rosmuc alone. I think I wrote you a fairly gloomy letter yesterday. I think it all depends on how you dream during the night and what you are waking up to.

I admit the necessity of doing something and the futility of 30/– a week and we'll have to step out and go places. We will too. I hate trying to write about things like that because I kind of imagine that what I say may sound insincere. And it isn't you know, darling. It's driving me nuts and that's a fact. Thank God for tomorrow because it means a salvation of sorts. I'm not surprised to hear about Liam Ó Briain's knowledge of my visit to Galway for as I told you he saw me on the bus.

My day off yesterday was completely lacking in interest and barren of adventure. Posting your letter, I returned to the house and read a bit of mythology – which incidentally is extremely obscene in parts – and then went down to the school at 1.30. I started to talk English to the kids and as true as the Bible, there is only one of them who can talk it at all ... most of them don't understand a word of what they read. English is a foreign language to them.

It's no wonder that the country places are overflowing with pisreogs [*superstitions*]. Last night was very calm and as I walked home to my digs, I stopped now and again and the sounds that greeted my ears were uncanny to an extreme.

I love you darling until the cows come home and when they do, we'll have palaces and silks, jewels and laces. We are bound to reach our goal because there is no power on earth to prevent us.

One o'clock today darling,

Your Wally

There are so many letters from Rosmuc it shows how much my father hated being away from my mother. Here's another one:

Rosmuc.

Monday 10.15 pm

My dear darling Peggy,

Your letter was like a spring well to a man straying in the desert. I hope you won't be mad with me darling when I wasn't in on Sunday, but really I couldn't do it. There was no car to be found and no bus. I can see that you are lonely too and I realise perfectly that choked up feeling.

Yesterday was terrible. It was Sunday and we had to go to mass. The Church is three miles away over hill and dale and believe me it is some walk. You have to leave at 10 a.m. and you just get there at 11 by the skin of your teeth. May K. went to mass with the daughter of the house-hold. I saw her there and we walked back to the digs. She met a teacher friend of hers and she spent the day with her.

I did the lonely exile act and I went down to the sea and played the mandolin and charmed the rocks until dinner-time. After dinner, I climbed a mountain and there was a bitter wind blowing, so I crouched down behind a huge rock and gave myself completely to you. I closed my eyes and went back to the very beginning of you and me. I traversed step by step our happy-unhappy love and I enjoyed all once again its moments of beauty and felt again its pangs of pain. I think I must have gone into a kind of trance because when an hour – maybe two hours – had passed, I woke suddenly and found that it was bitterly cold and that a slight drizzle was beginning to fall. So I kissed you goodbye and scampered back down the mountain. I seem to be able to find you best when I go there. So now you know where to let your spirit wander …

I will have to go and post this and I want to drop a line to mother also. Please don't forget me darling and love me and write to me because you can't possibly realise how marvellous it is to get a letter from you. I love you, love you, my God, if we could only find a more expressive language than this.

I'm afraid that there is not one word in the whole world sufficiently large to cope with my feeling for you, love, crazy, nuts are all right as expletives but this emotion is so much deeper than that – immeasurable, indefinable and all the rest of it. I suppose, however, that we have to be content with what we have. So I will say that I love you, my God so much that there is no power on Heaven or Earth powerful enough to make me stop.

Au revoir love,

I love you always will and I am lonely for you,

Wally

Here is a letter from my mother:

The Connacht Tribune.
Tuesday June 9, 12 noon

My own darling,

It's only now I have a minute to write you a letter, and I like to get it in the first post here so that you will be sure to get it the following day. We are very busy really. Jack and Daddy have gone off to Castlebar for the flying. So Fitzie and I are alone at the moment

– wouldn't you like to be here with me? Do you get my letters early in the day or late? I am sending you some stamps, you must have run out of them long ago.

My dear, I'm still missing you terribly. We have Saturday to look forward to. I do hope the family go away on Sunday, else I don't know how I'm going to slither out of the procession – I always march with the College every year and Pa will probably expect me to go out again with them.

Of course if Pa and Ma go to Balla for the day, that will make things much simpler. Anyway we will have all the rest of the time, TG.

Don't forget to tell me what time your bus arrives at, etc. I hope you are doing plenty of Irish and improving by leaps and bounds. Honestly darling I live for your letters these mornings, and I am so sorry when I have them read, because then I have nothing to look forward to for the rest of the day ...

I wish we could make some plan. I have such a lot to say to you my darling and yet I cannot write coherently even now. Keep writing me long letters, they are my salvation and do tell me how long more you have to stay in that awful place – I would like to know the worst at once.

My own beloved sweetheart, I must stop and get down to my beastly work. Sweetheart I hate to stop writing but I must. I love you and I am terrible lonely.

Peggy

My mother wrote to my father again on Wednesday:

The Connacht Tribune.
10th June 1936

Darling, darling, it is lovely to even get time to write to you. Your letter was grand and long this morning – what on earth would I do without you? You don't know how I'm looking forward to Saturday, my heart lifts when I think of it. I hope my old cold gets better quick and that my arm improves. Imagine it is 12 mid-day and this is the first minute I have had to take a break, even now I should be working as there is a pile of work waiting for me, but as I have until 10 tonight uninterrupted to get at it – it should be taken care of all right.

Darling, I'll see you at the Augustinians at 1 on Saturday – I expect that is the best and I'll be able to manage it DV. Last evening I went to the pictures with Molly Keegan, after a choir practice.

The picture was good – 'Sanders of the River' – although very peculiar, it was clever giving a great idea of the native tribes and the work of the British administration out there. Paul Robeson [*one of the stars of the film*] has a wonderful voice, but he only sang twice, which was rather disappointing.

Darling, I have lots and lots to say to you – I wish it was Saturday, everyday when I get up, I say to myself, thankfully only three more days and tomorrow it will be only two. My own Wally, how I love you, it is beyond human comprehension, I love you with all my heart, my own sweetheart, I always will.

Your own lonely,
Peggy

In another letter from my mother she talks quite openly about her love and her worries:

The Connacht Tribune.

Wally, darling sweetheart,

It is in the cold grey light of an extremely frosty morning and I am filled with love. Dearest, you will never know how I love you. It is sweeping me away, making me queer, moody and cranky for nothing. I think most people go through this phase though – and I will honestly try to forget it from this on.

I find myself getting into ridiculous rages for nothing these days – the fact that you are going to be away from me for so long probably has a lot to do with it.

Please, darling, try to understand. It is extraordinary but I have not quite got over the Diarmuid and Gráinne thing yet and I was quite sure I had. [*Reference to my father playing the part of Diarmuid and May Kilmartin playing the part of Gráinne. May was younger than my mother and very pretty; my mother probably felt insecure watching Walter acting as her lover in the Taibhdhearc production of Michael Mac Liammóir's famous play. Peggy played the part of the queen – the older woman and Gráinne's mother. This production was staged between 8–11 October 1936. I sometimes get an impression from the letters that at times my mother felt May Kilmartin could be a threat to her.*]

And, oh Wally, I love you so, and I know you love me. If only we could do something – soon. Let's get married soon, darling, if only we could both go off next week and do that – wouldn't it be grand? You know, Wally love, people in love – meaning me – are very selfish. I am jealous of your work now – ridiculously jealous of the Taibhdhearc – and all that sort of thing. But DV it will all pass, I know it will. I was so happy yesterday, so secure in the feeling that I had you, you had me, and everything was all right with the world, and then suddenly last night for no accountable reason, that old pall of gloom descended on me again.

College too, last night, made me feel lonely – for the time when I was a carefree little jib [*a first year university student*] – ahem – and full of hope for life, a great career – I used to think that I was going to do marvellous things, like writing books and seeing the world – Darling, if we could only get out of this – if we were married really, we'd get on so much better.

I don't know whether I'll give you this letter or not – it is rather incoherent, I'm afraid, but I just had to get in touch with you some way. If I do give it to you, dearest, please burn it when you have read it. I promised then I wouldn't be cross anymore – to God I mean – and I won't either, wait until you see, but I can't help being cynical about the old Taibhdhearc – it is a petty and small-minded place.

My own darling, I love you, every bit of your dear self,

I always will,

Peggy

So for those two years, 1935 and 1936, they saw each other as often as possible. By the end of 1936, my father was growing restless. He was still earning 30/– a week and he realised that he could not continue like this if he ever hoped to get married. At that time, his two sisters, Eileen and Birdie, were working in London and they advised him to come to London where, they told him, he would have no trouble getting a job. He made up his mind to go and arrangements were made whereby his sisters obtained a job for him as a door-to-door life insurance salesman. It is possible that one of his sisters also worked for the company.

One night when Walter and Peggy were down at his house having tea, Walter's mother asked him what he was going to do about Peggy. So he told her his plan was to go to London himself first and then, having found a place to live and earned some money, to invite her to come over and join him. His mother had a very clear idea of what they should do: 'Why don't you get married first?' she suggested.

They looked at her and my father made the decision there and then. He was always a very decisive man and in this case, once his mind was made up, they just had to organise it. Of course, my mother then had to make all the plans and see that everything worked out.

6

MARRIAGE AND LIFE
IN LONDON

It was the right decision, as my father would not have been able to survive in London without Peggy and she would have been equally bereft without him. My mother knew that her father would never give her permission to marry so she had to plan the elopement. They contacted Larry Delacey, their friend at the *Irish Times*, and he knew of a priest, Fr Leo McCann, who acted as an unofficial chaplain to people in the theatre business. They made contact with Fr McCann and he agreed to officiate at their wedding. My mother had to get a letter of freedom from her parish priest, Canon Davis. She went to see the canon, told him of her plan, and asked him to provide her with the letter of freedom. His response was immediate: 'What's your father going to say to me when I tell him?'

The canon was a close friend of her father's, but he knew Walter and his mother, and believed that Peggy's future husband would look after her well, so he gave her the letter of freedom and wished her well.

The last production they appeared in together at the Taibh-dhearc, before they eloped, was between the 8–10 January 1937.

My father and May Kilmartin were in the first play, *An Feilm*, a new play written by Seán Ó hÓgáin, and my father also played the man of the house in T.C. Murray's play, *Sovereign Love*, with my mother playing one of his daughters.

When my father resigned his position in the Taibhdhearc, Frank Dermody gave him a great reference. It is dated 8 February 1937, the day before they married in Dublin:

To all whom it may concern

Walter A. Macken has been employed as leading man and business manager (at 30/– a week!) in the Gaelic National Theatre (subsidised by the Free State Department of Education) since July 1932, entering the theatre while still attending the Patrician School, Secondary Education Branch, Galway. Since then he has taken leading parts in thirty full-length and thirty-six one act plays – including well-known plays of George Bernard Shaw: 'Arms and the Man' etc.; Molière: – 'Le Bourgeois Gentilhomme' etc.; Sheriff: – 'Journey's End'; Gogol: – 'Marriage' etc.; W.B. Yeats: – 'Caitlín Ní hUallacháin' etc.; J.M. Synge: – 'Riders to the Sea' etc.; William Shakespeare: – 'Macbeth' etc.; Henry Gheon: – 'The Marvellous Life of Bernard de Menthon' etc.; Sierra: – 'Two Shepherds'; Eugene O'Neill: – 'Where the Cross is Made'; Lennox Robinson: – 'The White-Headed Boy' etc.; Lady Gregory: – 'Jail Gates' etc.; Dunsany: – 'Night at the Inn' etc.; Douvernois: – 'Le Professeur'; Chekhov: – 'Three Sisters'; Tolstoy: – 'Michael'; as well as several original plays by Irish writers.

Mr Macken is in my opinion the most outstanding character actor (comedy and tragedy) in Ireland today not excluding the Abbey Theatre. My contention may be substantiated by a perusal of many press notices which he has received. As regards his personal character I have always found him to be honest, upright and trustworthy in every respect. Although his departure will be an irreparable loss to this theatre, nevertheless he carries with him into what we are sure will be a brilliant theatrical future the best wishes and recommendations of myself and my co-directors, knowing as we do that his success will also reflect credit on this theatre which he in no small way helped to bring to its present influential position in Irish Theatre.

They made their plans for their elopement and made all the arrangements during the Christmas holidays of 1936. They set the date – Tuesday 9 February, 1937. My father would travel to Dublin by train a few days beforehand and my mother would leave at the weekend. She packed one small suitcase with her essential clothes and looking around her bedroom regretted that she could not take her violin and many of her books. Then she sat down at her desk and wrote a letter to her father. In it she explained to him how she loved him, but that she also loved Walter Macken and now they had decided to get married. It was a long letter and written lovingly, but sadly I do not have a copy. However, my mother told me about it in later years.

The cover story she gave to her family was that she was going to Dublin for a weekend break, although I am almost certain her sisters, and maybe even her brothers, knew what was happening. She then left her home and went to the railway station. She took the train from Galway to Dublin and arrived at Westland Row, now called Pearse Street. My father met her there; I think it was probably Monday 8 February and he brought her to a hotel right beside the railway station. They probably had tea in a local restaurant and then they retired to their separate guest bedrooms. This was 1937, and there was no question of an unmarried couple sleeping together.

I think my mother would have been missing her friends and her family, but would eventually have slept. She was woken up at about 2 a.m. by Walter knocking on her bedroom door. She opened the door and he came in. My mother described to me what happened:

> He had got one of his feverish things, he was pouring sweat. [*This was a type of nervous flu that my father got as a direct result of stress.*]
>
> I had to sit him down and calm him down. I asked him what was wrong with him. He looked at me and said: 'This is an awful serious business you know, what we are doing tomorrow. It is marriage and it's for life, that's what frightens me.'

When she had calmed him down, he went back to his own room. The following morning they went out to the church in Fairview, and there waiting for them was Fr Leo McCann, the best man, Gearóid McKeown, and best woman, Josephine Delaney. It was the first time that Gearóid and Josephine had met and they later married, although their marriage eventually ended in divorce. After my parents' marriage and mass, they all went to a local hotel and had a wedding breakfast, including the priest. Whenever Fr McCann met my mother or father down through the years, he would say to them, 'When I tied that knot, I tied it well!' After breakfast they made their way back to the railway station where they caught the boat train to Dún Laoghaire and then took the boat across to Holyhead. From there, they boarded the train to London and my father's sisters met them there. They brought them to their flat in Ealing and helped them settle them in. They had a week to celebrate their wedding before my father started his job at the insurance company. My mother had taken one hundred pounds from her bank account at home and they had a great time, going to the cinema and eating in restaurants.

The following week they faced the reality of life in a London suburban flat. When my father went to work at his insurance company's office, my mother was left in the flat trying to come to terms with being a housewife. Among the challenges facing her was that she had to learn how to cook. As the eldest daughter and a working woman in Ireland, she had never learned how to cook. The Crescent house always had maids and none of the children ever had the experience of working in the kitchen with their mother. She spoke to me about those first days in her flat in Ealing:

> It was quite a cultural shock in all kinds of ways. Having come from a very Catholic town where everyone was married and living together with husbands and wives in stable family relationships, in these flats you were confronted with many different family arrangements, men and women were living together and there were women living on their own. There was an acceptance of unmarried people living together and this I found shocking as a young newly wed woman. However, I must say that they were all very nice to me. When I told them I couldn't cook, they advised me to buy some cook books and to learn. But they also showed me and they were really helpful, giving me little tips that they had learned themselves.

My father gives a vivid description of the kind of job he was doing in his second novel, *I am Alone*. Essentially, it was his job to sell life insurance door-to-door. He cycled everywhere and got on very well with the housewives he called on. Many of them had already bought life insurance policies from the company where he worked and it was his job to collect the one shilling a week they were required to pay to keep the policy going. My father had great personal charm and this was very useful in the job he was doing. It was exhausting work and he did not enjoy it. A typewriter was sent to their flat in Ealing by the family at home to try to encourage my mother to keep up her writing, but she never used it in London. It became my father's first typewriter and he began to work on it by writing articles for the Irish Independent.

I find it hard to understand how, once she married my father, my mother completely gave up all ideas of working outside the home. With her experience and background, why couldn't she continue to work as a freelance journalist? When I asked her, she told me my father was very insistent that it was his job to earn wages and to look after her and any children they would have, and that her place was in the home (although in one of the letters she wrote to my father when they were back living in Galway, which I quote below, she refers to writing two articles for the *Irish Independent*). She provided him with a safe and secure home where he never had to worry about his meals, the fires, the beds – everything in the home was in her care.

They never had anyone in to help with the housework. I believe my father's privacy was important to him and that he felt if they had a housekeeper or maid their private world would be invaded. He also did not want to have to live like his mother, always having lodgers in their home.

Almost a year after they arrived in London, they were expecting their first child. My mother's sister, Auntie May, told me that my mother being able to give birth to two children was a miracle, as she had a blood disorder when she was younger which could have resulted in her never having children. But my mother produced her first son on 10 April 1938. They named him Walter and he became known in the family as Wally Óg.

While my mother was in hospital, my father wrote to her:

Britannic Assurance Co. Ltd.

My own darling,

I am writing this under fire for time. I did not arise until half nine and then had to finish accounts. I have left all the washing up for the 'Bird' [*Auntie Birdie, who was probably taking care of my father while my mother was in hospital*] so she will probably curse me. I do not know what the wages are going to be – they are likely to be bad – that is no better than usual.

You can't imagine how I miss you, Pegs, darling. It's even about the bloody money, I know it will fly out of my fist as if it never existed. I hate the responsibility of it. I always said you were a wonderful manager and now I am sure of it. How you can make the few shillings go the places they do go has me beat.

So please hurry up and come home to me sweetheart because nothing is the same without you – honest to God. This whole kip-shop has a lousy look to me at the moment and no more than myself, it is crying out for you.

We will have to go back to Ireland and once you and W2 [*Wally Óg*] are on your feet again, we will get moving. I hate going into the office. I hate the gang in the office and my only consolation is that I will be seeing you in the morning. I can never tell you how much I love you Peg. I never could anyway but just now it is very much worse than usual.

Keep the old chin up because Thursday is not too far away and then I will be with you again. I hope you slept well last night and that you dreamed about me and mind yourself well because you are the only thing in this crazy world that I love and appreciate. The trouble is I am never articulate enough to tell you how much. I must go now and catch the bus darling, so until tomorrow farewell for just a little while until I can kiss you again and have another look at our beautiful son.

Your lonely,
Wally

Life went on and the young couple were constantly hoping and praying that they would find a way to get home. The year 1939 was a turning point. War clouds were gathering and my mother was shocked when civil defence officials called to their door and measured both my mother and the baby for a gas mask. When my father came home from work that evening, my mother told him what had happened and said they had to get home before the war broke out.

7

RETURN TO THE TAIBHDHEARC

Fortunately for my father, in 1939 Frank Dermody was offered a job with a film company in Dublin and he decided to leave his job in the Taibhdhearc. I don't know whether my father contacted the Taibhdhearc or whether they got in touch with him, but he was offered the vacant position of producer and the family returned to Galway. The exact date of their return is unclear, but the programme for a play called *Clann na Gealaighe* (*Family of the Moon*), staged at the Taibhdhearc between 20–23 April 1939 in which my father played a leading role, suggests that they must have returned to Galway before that point. May Kilmartin was also acting in that production.

They stayed with my father's mother in Henry Street for a short period and then my mother started looking for a house to rent. She found it in Shantalla and they lived there for a few months. During the 1940s as well as working in the Taibhdhearc and writing, my father occasionally travelled to various drama festivals to adjudicate at them. From what I heard of these experiences, he was a very severe critic. He was such a professional actor, producer and director, that he demanded perfection from these drama groups. What annoyed him was if he gave an adjudication on a particular group and advised them how they could improve, when they came back in front of him the following year in another play, they would make the same mistakes. He found that very frustrating.

While working as an adjudicator, he wrote letters back to his wife and child. Here are some extracts from one of the letters written in Roscommon, where I think he and May Kilmartin were acting as adjudicators for a drama festival:

Greally's Hotel,
Roscommon.
18/05/39

My dear Pegg,

It is a beautiful morning in Roscommon. I missed you an awful lot last night. I hope you are missing me too. I have no idea at all of the time and am busy writing this before breakfast and as usual I'm starving. May Kilmartin has come down now so it looks as if we can go and have the breakfast and then I can go to 10 mass. You know it's awful funny to be writing to you like this. It seems years you dote since I have done it before and I find that I have a sluggish pen. The dramas don't start until 1 p.m. so it looks as if we will not be home until 11 p.m.

The hotel is damn nice except that they have no hot water in the room. They leave it in a little business outside the door. So when I was shaved and dressed etc., I came out the door, didn't see it and knocked it all over the joint. I bet the cleaners are saying what nasty man was occupying room 16.

How did you get on without me last night? I hoped you missed me a terrible lot and Wally Óg too. Breakfast has arrived and I will say goodbye and I will post this on my way to mass and we will have great fun reading it tomorrow. I love you Peggy at an early hour of

the morning and it's killing me until I get back to you and little
Wally again.

Love Wally

My father's work with the Taibhdhearc took him away often. I
have a few letters from my mother to my father in late June/early
July 1939 from Shantalla, while he was in Furbo studying Irish
once again. They give a flavour of the kind of life my parents were
living:

Naomh Antoine,
Upper Shantalla,
Galway.
Sunday night

My own darling,

Mick Lohan and May have just left, they have been here since six
and I am expecting Mother and Mrs Spellman now, Mother is
going to have a bath [*my grandmother must not have had a bathroom
in her own house in Henry Street*]. Oh darling, I was very lonely after
you last night but it's good to think that I shall see you on Saturday
night. It was nice to have Joan [*one of Peggy's sisters*] sleeping here
last night. She came down and lit the fire at 7.30 and went to 8 mass
in St Joseph's. I got the breakfast and after doing the baby went to
10 a.m. mass in St Joseph's too. Captain Seán and Mr O'Connor
and all the kiddies were there too, all at Holy Communion [*they
later became close family friends*].

It's a nice wee cool church to go to – is never crowded like the
Jesuits. When you are home again I must try and go to 7.15 every
morning. I miss the daily mass. Joan stayed until 1 p.m. and after the
baby had his dinner, we went down to Mother and stayed there until
5. I walked home with him around Taylor's Hill. It turned out a lovely
evening here. I hope you get out a bit today, darling, don't forget you
need some air.

Monday 11 a.m.

Darling, I'll have to finish this as I can't do a thing with the child and I have to go down and order coal, etc. Anyway, tired as I am the only thing is to take him out, I can't do anything with him in the house alone. I love you sweetheart and wish you were home – hope I have a letter soon – I'm very lonely. God bless you darling.

All my love always,

Your Peggy

I have a second letter from my mother from the same address:

Sunday night

My own darling,

You will forgive me if this letter is short tonight but I'm really dead tired. Mona and Enda [*friends of the family*] brought Wally Óg and myself to Ashford, Cong this afternoon, we had tea there and were not home until nearly 7 – they had to take some friends of Mrs Emerson out there to see it and they decided not to go to Furbo. Anyway it was a lovely drive but Wally Óg was dead tired when we came home. He gets on great with Mona and he had his tea with her, demolishing yards of bread and butter.

So I could not get down to Mother at all today but will bring her the money in the morning [*my father gave his mother something every week*]. I was at 8 o'clock mass this morning, Joan at 10. Joan was really early last night fortunately.

Well, what has me so tired is that I have just finished off two articles, one historic that I started the night long ago in St Jude's and the other, old stuff about the races, I will post them tomorrow and I am addressing them to the Literary Editor of the 'Irish Independent' ... When I read them over, I thought they were tripe so I have not much hope for them – still one never knows, and God is good, one might get in and the money would be very useful. I must honestly try to write during the winter when you are home. I am very rusty and much slower with ideas than I used to be.

Now I have a ferocious headache so will stop, dearest. I will post this in the morning. I love you with all my heart and we miss you terribly. God bless you sweetheart and I am looking forward to Saturday.

I am very tired,
Goodnight love,
Your Peggy

And another written the following Tuesday:

Tuesday 2.30

My own darling,

It was grand getting your letter today. On Sunday unfortunately, Enda had to take a friend of his Mother's as I told you, to Ashford, Cong and took us along too and we had a grand afternoon, but I told you all that in yesterday's letter, darling.

Joan was in bed with a cold yesterday and I therefore could not arrange to get her to stay in for me last night. They called for me at 9 to bring me out to see you but of course, I had to send them off without me. However, they came back about 10 and had a cup of tea and stayed gossiping until 11. [*My father was staying in a guesthouse in Furbo about ten miles from Galway city.*] They are really an awfully nice pair.

Anyway the latest sensation is that Billy Emerson is getting married tomorrow in Gort to a Miss Clune from Craughwell, Billy's mother does not approve but she had to give her consent on account of stopping the affair with Phyllis Browne before, so they are all of a doodah.

We went out shopping in the morning yesterday and I called in to Agnes and gave her the 10/–, Eileen was there and Harry [*his sister Eileen's future husband*] came out to talk to us, but whatever it is the baby roars every time he sees Harry.

Downtown we met Des [*her brother*], he posted the articles and your letter for me and asked could he come to lunch with us today – so I said yes and proceeded to buy two pork chops accordingly. He duly arrived and enjoyed his dinner very much – he says I feed you well …

Des tells me that Daddy sent off his article on Race Week so that washed out mine, however, perhaps they will use the other one. Let's hope so, so that I can get a costume. Wally Óg is sneezing a lot, I hope he has not got a cold. I was talking to Liam Ó Briain yesterday too [*Liam Ó Briain was now chairman of the Taibhdhearc and sent my father out to Furbo*], and he said to ask you to write him a letter in Irish, till he sees just how you are getting on and that he will send it back to you with remarks; he also said that he might go out to see you sometime, he is delighted that you are out there and said you should stay as long as possible.

Wally Óg is getting restive so I must stop, my darling, I love you with all my heart, God bless you, and I am longing for Saturday night.

Your Peggy

The fourth letter of this group again from Naomh Antoine in Shantalla:

Weds night

My own darling,

I have been working hard since tea – made two cakes, a sweet cake and a soda cake and then set to and spring-cleaned the kitchen.

It was not so nice here today, lovely in the morning but quite cold in the afternoon. We went down to see Agnes after I had written your letter and stayed talking to her for a good while. The visitors had gone to Spiddal since 3 so maybe you saw them. They did not go to Cong yesterday only as far as Oughterard and were back at six, so afterwards they all went to the pictures, including

Agnes. She enjoyed it very much. She is thrilled at the thought of going off next Friday week, and I think she feels the time flying while they are here. [*Agnes spent some time living with her daughters in England each year.*]

I cannot go to see them in the morning because the baby gets very tired about 11 and I have to put him off for an hour's sleep. I'll have to try and mange the money better when you come home darling.

I laid it all out this week, yet it seemed to fly away. I don't know how we are going to manage to get curtains and things but I suppose it will all come in God's good time. I must try and buy the lace curtains for the baby's room out of this week's money.

So we went all around Salthill in by Threadneedle Road and back to Shantalla, what a walk – I am fagged. However, it should be good for both of us. Met May Fogarty [*a close friend of Peggy's*] this afternoon, she was asking for you, and she said we must go down to her again after the Races, she is delighted we have a house of our own at last.

If only you were home, my darling, I could start to appreciate our own house. Wally Óg is coming on great and I really think he misses you a lot, he shouts for you at intervals and looks expectantly at the door to see if by any chance you are hiding outside. He is an awful handful of course, but that is not his fault.

I forgot to tell you in the letter today that I was in the Crescent last night. I went down Shantalla to meet May and Ivor was waiting for me on New Line to bring me way over to the house (Daddy is away); and when I got into the house, he insisted on showing me his college blazer, etc. May showed me all her things she has collected and they are lovely. It was awfully strange being at home again, and I felt awfully lonely and queer while I was there. I was not in the house very long and the maids were delighted to see me. Wally darling, I love you, you know that and I miss you. I'll die with excitement when you come home again.

From,

Peggy

It was during this time that my father wrote my mother a letter in Irish, and I have taken the liberty of translating it. Here are some extracts:

c/o Bean Uí Chualáin,
Coismeag Mór,
Na Forbacha.
Wednesday

Peggy darling,

It's one o'clock as I'm writing this letter. Today was a beautiful day here, very hot. I will be going swimming after the dinner and going sunbathing also. It was a lovely night last night and myself and a young lad called Murray who is camping nearby, we almost walked to Spiddal. There is great heat today, it's a bit like the weather we had in June. It's the old story about my love for you which is as new as it was last year, and even stronger. There are only two days left until I am back to you. It's a pity that you are not here and we could go swimming together. I am too old now to be mitching from school. I would love to see young Wally again, and especially to see him walking the way he does. I suppose my mother is surprised to be going to England. I don't know whether Eileen and Harry are coming to visit me out here. I find it hard to talk to them. God bless now and I will see you on Saturday and there will only be a few days left until I am home for good. I love you, Pegs, Saturday will never come quickly enough.
    Your own,
    Wally

Having lived in Shantalla for a few months, my mother went looking to find a more suitable house to rent and eventually she found a house just off White Strand Road looking down on Grattan Road Strand and they lived there from 1940 to 1948. My mother's time in Galway in the 1940s was stressful. When she came home in the

summer of 1939, Wally Óg was only eighteen months old. Her
father did not attempt to contact her as he had written her out of
his life. One day, she remembers, she was walking in Galway with
Wally Óg in the pram and she saw her father walking toward her.
As she walked past him, he just said a gruff hello. Shortly afterwards,
in 1940 at the age of fifty-three, he died suddenly of a heart attack.
My mother was summoned to the Crescent and had to take control
of everything. She made all the funeral arrangements. When they
prepared the body for the funeral, they found that Tom Kenny had
put the letter Peggy wrote to him about eloping beside his heart.
My mother then went into the newspaper to write articles about her
father and write the editorials. After those few days, she returned to
her normal life in Grattan Road and the Taibhdhearc, where she still
acted and helped out my father.

In the course of his work at the Taibhdhearc, my father would
do many different things, and occasionally he was invited to work
as an actor for different companies; in April 1943, he was invited
by the famous theatre director, Carl Clopet, to play the part of
Captain Jack Boyle in a Belfast production of O'Casey's play, *Juno
and the Paycock*. While rehearsing in Dublin, he wrote a few letters
to my mother, now pregnant for a second time, and the extract
below comes from one of these:

Milano.
Easter Monday 9 a.m.

My dear Peggy,

Here I am again, and thank God the Dublin episode is drawing to a
close. I haven't got the Permit yet [*a travel permit to work in Northern
Ireland was probably compulsory, as the UK was at war*]. I have to go

in tomorrow morning and try for it and hope that it can be procured before Thursday morning when we are going to Belfast.

On Good Friday, we had no rehearsal. That was the day I rang you up. I stayed here all day and desperately learned the part and I think, Thank God, that I know it at last. I went to bed at 11 last night. Saturday we had a rehearsal at 11 in the morning, one in the afternoon and one at night at 7 p.m. I got back to Dalkey at 11 and hopped straight into bed. I haven't seen a picture since I came here or a show or anything and have very little intention of doing so.

Yesterday we had a rehearsal at 11.30. I went to mass with D. [*probably Deirdre Halligan the actress*] at 10, then on to the rehearsal, came back here at 3 p.m., talked with D. and Sonny and their aunt until tea-time. Then we all went for a walk and I was in bed at 10.30.

Michael Clarke [*owner of house where he was staying*] is acting this week in a show in the Theatre Royal and the poor devil is half dead, doing 3 shows a day. I'm asleep when he gets home (he's sleeping in the same room as me in order not to disturb the baby when he comes home late) and when I get up he's asleep so we haven't had much time for a chat.

Sonny [*Michael's wife*] is very kind and they are feeding me like a turkey cock. She is feeding the baby herself and keeps asking me questions, what you did with Wally Óg, etc. She thinks Wally Óg is the most marvellous child she ever saw and who am I to deny it? I told her when I ring you up on Wednesday night she can talk to you and ask you all the questions she likes because I can't remember half of the things you have to do with a baby, so I proudly say about all you know and how you have it all written down and everything. And the doctor she has doesn't seem to have told her anything. You were really lucky to have had Dr O'Rourke.

You will be glad to hear that nobody in the company drinks much. When they heard that I didn't drink at all they didn't seem to mind very much. As far as I know Carl Clopet himself only takes a bottle of stout now and again after rehearsal. Noel Purcell (who is 42 by the way) still drinks sherry and never drinks whiskey or stout. I gather he has been that way all his life although they all tell him he is a sissy drinker. I still don't know the names of the people in the Company, apart from the odd Joe and Nicky, without knowing their last names.

Poor D., I feel so sorry for her sometimes. She is crazy about Des [*Deirdre Halligan's husband*], and there's no doubt now Peggy, I'm afraid, that he was all wrong for her. It's pathetic really. Every day she seems to expect that he will write to her and say that he has seen the light at last and that he is coming flying back home to her.

Ah well! It's a cruel thing to say but it makes me thank God that we are so happy with our whole lives before us to be together whatever sun falls out of the skies ... I'm afraid the time has come for me to be rushing off to catch a train for the rehearsal, so I'll be going. I don't feel quite so lonely when I'm writing to you. I can see you reading this and knowing that you love me and that's all that matters really. I love you Pegsi. I kind of knew it the first time I saw you rehearsing for St Bernard de Menthon. I remember you had a brown costume on and Paddy Walsh [*a friend*] saying to me: 'God, Wally, Peggy Kenny has a damn nice leg.' I wish I was a bit nearer to that damn nice leg now. Goodbye for awhile Peggy darling and tell the little embryo that I love her (or him) [*that embryo was me!*].

Your adoring husband,
Wally

My father added a brief note to my brother with the letter:

My darling Wally Óg,

Hello, here is your old Daddy to say hello to you and to tell you that he loves you right up to China and beyond. You will be going to school next Monday. I will be thinking of you all day even tho' it will be my first night and my birthday. Have some buns on that day for your tea. Let your Mammy and yourself have a good feed and pretend Daddy is there with you. Mind your Mammy well. She is very precious.

Your loving,
Daddy

This is another letter written to my mother from the Dublin house:

Wednesday 28th April 1943

My darling Peggy,

I got your two letters yesterday morning, and was so glad to read them and read that you still love me. Reading letters from you reminds me of the time we used to be hurling massive missives at each other and loving every minute and word of them. Them were the days.

It's nice to look back on them but it is much nicer to know that we are married and that we are the proud possessors of one and a half children. Imagine what life would be like without our lovely Wally Óg. I'm dying to get a look at him again and get a squeeze from him and several squeezes from his mother.

The longer I'm away from you, Peggy darling, the more I love you. That's not so strange either. The Dublin episode is drawing to a close. It would have been a miserable period if I hadn't been staying here in Dalkey with the Clarkes and their little baby who seems to be getting bigger every day and makes me long for the time when we can be having fun with our own little morsel.

I will continue this journal of unexciting events where I left off last. It was Monday morning, I think. Well I went into a rehearsal which started at 11 and finished around 2. By the way the play is in great shape now, I think. I imagine it will be good. There is really nobody bad in it, and it sometimes has very excellent moments. Still we must wait to see what the audience think about it, after all they are the principal people.

After the rehearsal I came back to Dalkey, had lunch, and went for a walk with Sonny and four dogs. I don't feel as excited about

acting in English and Belfast as I ought to. I don't know but somehow it doesn't seem to mean such a lot after all. I seem to be more
interested in all the small things about it, like getting travel permits,
getting in and out to Dalkey. I seem to have a very clear vision of it
somehow. You'd imagine I wouldn't feel like this going back to the
Taibhdhearc. That I would feel stymied in the Taibhdhearc and look
forward to acting in English in Belfast. But somehow I want to get
back to Galway. I want to go back to the Taibhdhearc. Maybe I'd
feel differently if you were here, I don't know.

Whether it is ambition dying out in me or God giving me a
clear perspective of the smallness of these things we imagine big
from the distance, I don't know but I feel happy in our mode of life.
I see our house and love it, I love my garden even though I hated
doing it. I like to imagine myself sitting out on the seat and just
letting my mind idle away – to put out my hand and touch you, to
hear Wally Óg talking away to Wally Gung [*Wally Óg's imaginary
friend*], to feel the sun on my face and that I'll soon be going into the
house to eat a beautifully satisfactory tea cooked by my lovely Peggy.
Now I see darling that all these things mean a terrible lot to me and
I would rather remain unknown and have them, rather than to gain
what passes as fame and be without them.

I'm terrible for rambling amn't I, but I love writing all these
things to you because I know that you know what I mean. I better
continue with my 'adventures'.

It was around 3 when I had finished everything and had lunch
in town with D (by the way the grub in Dublin restaurants is lousy).
Then I decided that instead of going home, I'd go to meet the train
to see Johnny and Eileen and Billy Naughton (who was supposed
to come but didn't). Only Eileen was there so I saw to her cases and
walked to the digs with her and arranged to meet her after tea and
take her to a picture. Poor Eileen was thrilled at the idea as she said
of 'a night of sin' out at the pictures with a married man. [*Johnny,
Eileen and Billy were all family friends.*]

It was a relief to talk to her after the other people whose minds
are buried in the clouds or in themselves. We saw 'Bambi' the Walt
Disney picture. You'll love it and Wally Óg will be charmed with it.

Joined a train queue at 11.30 and met Michael Clarke and Harry Webster [*another actor*]. We missed the last Dalkey train and had to get the Dún Laoghaire train instead and had to walk home. We got home at 2 a.m. Michael told me all about how they all loathe Frank Dermody, he also told me the entire Des story with clarity. We will be going to Belfast at 1 o'clock on Friday but I will write a letter to you in the morning, before I catch the train. You know I love you and being away from you has only made me love you more.

Your adoring husband, Wally

Here is another letter of this batch. It was written the day before going to Belfast:

Thursday 9 a.m., 29th April 1943

My darling Pegsi,

It was very nice hearing your voice last night. When they couldn't get through to the Taibhdhearc, I was imagining all sorts of horrible possibilities. What did you think of the Des business?

I meant to tell you about the financial situation. Clopet will give me £15 and the train fare. I suppose then that he will pay me £16-9-8 as the train fare from Galway was £1-9-8. I have spent the £2 I brought with me (it's amazing how it goes and you don't know where the hell – just lunches, fares and cigarettes). I borrowed £1 from D. and I will have to repay her when I get paid. Taking poor Eileen Ó Briain out [*to the cinema – see previous letter*], knocked a hole in that. It's amazing the way it goes.

I reckon it will cost £3 or £4 for digs in Belfast so I am reckoning that I should at least be able to bring £9 or £10 home with me. I think I will go off the cigarettes altogether in Belfast.

It would break my heart to be handing out 2/6 for 20 lousy cigarettes. I won't forget your stockings and of course Wally Óg's present. I will also have to get something for Sonny's baby and something for the maid Nellie who is very good to me. I think I told you, Michael

Clarke is in the Theatre Royal in Bernard Shaw's Signal Fires. I will have to go along and see it today. He is getting £15 a week so he was jumping for delight this morning to hear that its run was being extended for another week.

I am going into Gings [*a company that supplied theatre costumes*] today to get the costume for Captain Boyle. I will ask about the costumes for the Taibhdhearc while I'm there.

Has Patsy [*wardrobe mistress of the Taibhdhearc*] sent on the measurements? If not would you ever get after her and tell her to hurry up with them. If there is a letter for me from the Dublin Gaelic League, use your judgement about sending it on to me in case it would never catch up with me in transit.

I'm afraid, darling that this letter will have to be short as I have to catch the train. I will make it up to you again. Once we are in Belfast, I would feel that I am so much nearer the time to go home. I love you and God bless you and mind my little embryo. By the way, Sonny says that her baby hardly kicked at all before it was born and she says you must be going to have a girl if the stirrings are faint. I don't mind really darling if it is not a girl. Another fellow like Wally Óg would be all right by me.

Your doting old man,
Wally

Later he wrote from Belfast:

c/o Carl Clopet Co.,
The Royal Hippodrome,
Belfast.
Saturday, May 1st 1943

My darling Pegsi,

It was a grand surprise today to get your letter when we went to rehearse in the Hippodrome. The letter arrived all right – like ourselves. It was grand hearing from you again. You and Wally Óg don't miss me half as much as I miss you and that's a fact. We duly left Dublin yesterday morning. I wrote the note to you and then departed for the big city. I went to Gings and got a costume. I told the girl in Gings about the other costumes (which reminds me will you get after Patsy again and get her to get off the measurements). I had a cup of tea and went to the station where we joined up with the rest of the people. The train was terribly packed and we only got a seat by the skin of our teeth.

There were custom examinations on the train to be gone through and we finally got to Belfast at 6.30. We went first to have a meal and then went to look for digs. What a job that was. The whole city seemed to be packed with people, workers and things and all the lodging houses were packed. We walked and walked and searched and searched, meeting with refusals everywhere. We couldn't even get into hotels. Finally at 11.30, I managed to get a room in a small hotel here called 'The Station', for £3–5–0 a week. But it is nice and clean and the food is very good. Having chatted with the landlord for a long time, went to bed at 1.30 and went to sleep immediately. I got up at nine this morning and went to the Hippodrome for a rehearsal at 10.

The Hippodrome is an enormous place. It was built especially for stage shows and was eventually changed into a cinema. It is bigger than the Gaiety in Dublin with an absolutely enormous stage and terrific acoustic properties. We are having a dress rehearsal in the morning at 12.00. Don't forget to say a prayer that I will be okay and that the show will go well. The rehearsal was over at 12.30. I went to the hotel and had lunch and then went back to meet Clopet and went to see the Noel Coward movie 'In Which We Serve'. It was a grand film, very realistic.

The trouble about Belfast is that you can't get away from the war, even for a minute. The greatest proportion of the population seems to be in uniform – there are uniforms everywhere.

After the picture, I came back here and had tea which brings us right up to date. None of the other chaps are staying here with me and I am rather inclined to be grateful for that, than the reverse, because I find it fairly hard to talk to them.

Anyhow I love you Peggy darling and I'm so glad to hear that the little embryo is doing well. Tell 'it' I love 'it' already. I love you Peggy darling. Write to me soon again, it will help to cheer up your despondent husband. I wish that Juno was a memory I had to look back on instead of forward to it.

Your loving husband,

Wally

The production of *Juno and the Paycock* was part of Pla-Vaude-Band, a three-hour show presented at the Royal Hippodrome from 3 May for six days only. The show opened with the play and then it was followed by a variety show featuring Peggy Dell and her band and a range of other acts. The shows were presented twice daily at 2.30 p.m. and at 7.00 p.m. My father was one of the stars, in the billing for the play he was named above the titles in the following manner:

CARL CLOPET PRODUCTIONS
Present
Diane Romney, Ann Clery, Roland Ibbs
Noel Purcell and Walter Macken
in
SEÁN O'CASEY'S
JUNO AND THE PAYCOCK
in three acts

The next letter was posted on Tuesday 4 May from Belfast:

My dear Pegsi,

It's Tuesday morning and I can give you all the news, reactions, etc., after the first night. I couldn't get a moment to write yesterday or Sunday and anyhow, I felt all googly as you know. On Sunday morning,

I went to ten mass in St Malachi's church. It's a very peculiar church, balcony all around on top, not a very big crowd at mass but I gather that 11 and 12 are the most popular masses – as they are in Galway.

After mass we had a rehearsal at 12 which lasted until 4.30. I thought they would never have the stage ready for the show at all. After tea, I spent the rest of the night with Clopet looking at the Variety acts. (There are Variety acts on with the play.) I got to bed early. Got up next morning and spent it wandering around the theatre until lunch, then back to make-up. The play started at 2.30. It was a peculiar audience but the play went down well. I thought I was forcing it a bit and decided to improve in the night show. Back for the tea and who walked into the Hotel but Joe Mullen, a Galway boy, I don't know if you know him. He is in the Fire Service here and he tells me that Sonny Hynes (Molly's brother [*a Galway friend*]) is up here with him too, so I am looking forward to seeing both of them – they will be a hell of a relief from the Carl Clopet Company.

They remind me very forcefully of the bad old days in the Taibhdhearc na Gaillimhe when Dermody and intrigues were rampant. They do nothing but back-bite one another and talk about one another and be jealous of one another until you'd wonder how the hell they can stand it at all. As far as I can see the fair Diana Romney is really the moving force behind it all. She tells people (for their own good) what the other fellow is saying. I will enlarge on this when I see you but now it is for the private ear. They have tried to pull me in to it. Some of them, tuppenny halfpenny actors, got annoyed at the show because the audience was laughing at me during their dialogue. Can you beat it! When I see the last of them, I will breathe a long sigh of relief.

It will be a pleasure to be home in Galway – because I am dying to see you darling – and my beautiful Wally Óg. What I would give for a sit in my garden now is nobody's business. Playing the big-time in Belfast has done one thing for me – it has killed my ambition to be a star. Oh I long for the peaceful worry of my little Taibhdhearc with the tiny audience. There were about 2,300 of an audience in the Hippodrome last night and I would have given the whole of them for just six Taibhdhearcites. From all of which you may think that the play is a flop. Actually it isn't, it's an enormous success but I'm fed-up. Funny isn't it, often when playing to an empty house in Galway, you'd say, 'If only I was acting in a decent theatre with a big audience, how different it would be.'

Funny isn't it that I don't feel anyway different in the Hippo-drome. No matter how I try, I don't seem to be able to get a kick out of it that I thought would. That's life all over, isn't it? Thank God, I see the grand life we have in Galway – a wife, a child, a house and a job, what the hell more could the heart desire, all that and to win £100 for my play in Irish! [*There is no record of what this prize was for.*] There you are!

We got one thing, we long for one another. It makes you laugh. I feel in good humour this morning all the same darling because I love you and although the week is crawling to its end, I will soon be home to you. I will regale you at length with the experience of a bumpkin in the specious metropolis of Ireland. I wouldn't take them on a plate. They are as foreign to my nature as goat's milk is to a cow.

God bless yourself darling and mind yourself until I come home to you. I love you more than anything this life could ever give to us. I think of you often and I know I am never far from your thoughts. Don't miss me too much but miss me just enough so that you will be hopping with delight when I come back to you. I got your letter yesterday (my birthday), a better present than a £1,000 or even £100 from an Irish play. Mind yourself and keep loving me.

Your adoring husband,
Wally

The next letter also comes from Belfast:

Thursday 5 p.m.
6th May 1943

My own darling Peggi,

We're on the last lap at last thanks be to God – just 5 more shows and then I will be on the way home. It's bloody awful, having to do two shows a day of a big long play. My voice is beginning to fail, I'm afraid. I'm dosing it with TCP and hoping that it will last it out. I won't tell you all about the show, etc., until I get home, when I will have gathered my impressions together, etc. In a way I'm sorry that I ever came at all but that's nearly done now, Thank God and I'll soon be home with my beautiful wife and son. I will be home Tuesday definitely and may yet be able to make it on Monday. It all depends on what trains are leaving on Sunday if any, etc.

I was over with Paddy Hynes [*a friend from Galway*] this morning at the place where he is working, there are a terrible lot of southern Irish here. A chap called Higgins, a Corkonian said he met you one time. Poor old Wally and school, I had to laugh today when I got your letter. Imagine him and his being a school boy. I'm absolutely dying to see him and yourself darling. It won't be long now, Thank God. If I can't get home on Monday, I will ring Tommie in the morning in the Taibhdhearc. Tell him not to leave the place between 11 a.m. and one. I will tell him what time I want you to ring up Dublin. If I do manage to get down on Monday I will either send a telegram or get Sonny to ring the Taibhdhearc and let you know.

Your lonely husband,
Wally

He also wrote a short note to Wally Óg:

Dear Wally Óg,

I am very glad to hear that you like school and that you have a grand schoolbag. I will soon be home now to see you and the bag and then you can tell me all about it. I love you over to Mexico and I am dying for a hug and a kiss.

Xxx your loving Daddy

Walter and Peggy Macken were expecting their second child in the summer of 1943. My mother was hoping I would be born on 15 August, the Feast of the Assumption, but I didn't oblige. Then she thought I would arrive on Our Lady's Birthday, 8 September, but I still didn't arrive. I was finally born at St Bride's Nursing Home in Galway on Friday 10 September, weighing in at 11 lbs; a brother for Wally Óg who was then just five years and five months old. My father wrote a play to celebrate my arrival called *Bhí Mac Agam Tráth* (I Once Had A Son) – the play ran for one week in the Taibhdhearc in the autumn of 1943.

Later, while working as an adjudicator in Sligo, my father wrote to my mother:

Grand Hotel,
Sligo.
Monday

My dear Pegsi,

Here's just a few lines to you to tell you what's what. I am duly established in Sligo. So far it hasn't been too bad. We got to Sligo about 8 o'clock on Saturday night. Talk about a bloody train journey. The train stopped at seventeen stations between Athenry and Sligo. Actually the Murphys [*Professor Murphy, one of the directors of the Taibhdhearc was probably travelling with him*] weren't so boring at all.

They are quite nice at close range. I went to the hotel then. It's quite good, old fashioned (no h & c [*hot and cold running water*]) but the grub appears to be good – I hope. I left at nine and went to the pictures. Murphy forgot the play [*presumably the play he was going to make an adjudication on*], so I had nothing to do, no books. I saw a proper stinker at the cinema. Then I went into a café and had a cup of coffee …

Sunday I went to mass at 9 and then went fishing on Lough Gill. Say fishing! Saving your presence it was pissing rain until three o'clock. I got wet right into the pelt and no fish. It is mostly a salmon lake but it is very beautiful. The rain stopped at about three o'clock and it was all right after that.

If only I didn't have to work today. There is a fishing competition on the lake today. The sun is shining and there is a great breeze blowing, but duty calls. I went walking this morning with Charlie Hughes. He is the producer of the Sligo drama group. I'm going down to lunch now and then have to go off to my purgatory.

He added a brief note for the sons also:

Dear Wally Óg,

I miss you very much and Ultan, I'm crazy about you,
    Your Dad

As well as these jobs outside Galway, my father threw himself into the job at the Taibhdhearc from the moment he arrived, working like a Trojan. He organised the translations of various classical theatre works into Irish and gathered a group of young men and women to form the casts of these classic plays. Over the course of eight years, between 1940–48, he produced about seventy individual plays, many of which he translated himself. Although his Irish was reasonably fluent by this time, my father himself said that he didn't believe that anyone could learn Irish completely unless they spent many years in the Gaeltacht. When translating the plays he nearly always called on the help of a native speaker, such as Tomás Ó Maille, Professor of Irish at University College, Galway, and a director of the Taibhdhearc. One of his first productions was a translation of *Charley's Aunt* by the English writer Brandon Thomas.

As well as writing the basic texts, he also starred in many of them, playing the lead roles, and in many cases my mother played the female lead. Although it was difficult to build audiences, my father and the Taibhdhearc began to build a strong reputation, particularly among the Dublin media.

In 1940, when Seán O'Casey blocked the Abbey Theatre from performing any of his plays because of his dispute with W.B. Yeats, my father wrote to him looking for permission to stage *The Shadow of a Gunman* in Irish at the Taibhdhearc.

O'Casey gave him permission and after the production, when my father wrote again, the playwright answered with the following:

Tingrith,
Station Road,
Totnes,
Devon.
November 26th 1940

Dear Mr Macken,

French control only the Amateur rights of the plays, sold alas to them when I was on the rocks. The delay you mention doesn't matter much. The fee for the performances of 'The Gunman' and for all subsequent performances, will be the ones paid by the Abbey Theatre, namely: 5% on the gross nightly receipts up to £40, over £40 up to £60, 7.5%, over £60 it would be 10%. So the fee for you will be 5% on your receipts of £10–18–00.

I hope that may be suitable.
With all good wishes,
Seán O'Casey

My father's production of *The Shadow of a Gunman* was so well received that the Taibhdhearc Company was invited to bring its production to the Gate Theatre in Dublin for a number of special performances. They put together three performances: the Irish language version of *The Shadow of a Gunman*, a performance of Dúbhglais de hÍde's play *Ag Casadh an tSúgán*, and a presentation of poems presented by about ten actors. Dúbhglais de hÍde, the newly appointed president of Ireland, attended the performances. Also in attendance was Gabriel Fallon, a leading expert on O'Casey plays, and in his review he said it was the most authentic production of the play ever staged and really true to the spirit of its author. My mother told me she would never forget the way my father staged the poetry readings: 'The actors were choreographed just like a choir, they were superb and he brought out the best in both the actors in the poetry they were reading.'

Two years later, my father again sought O'Casey's permission to do an Irish language version of his famous play, *The Plough and the Stars*. The playwright replied as follows:

Tingrith,
Station Road,
Totnes, South Devon, Eng.
November 4th 1942

Dear Walter Macken,

It was interesting to hear that you are going to do 'The Plough and the Stars in Irish'. I hope it may be a success with you. I haven't the slightest idea what royalty was asked for, or given, on the performance of the 'Gunman'. I daresay it was 5% on the gross receipts. I don't see how I could ask for more from the slender audiences the plays in Irish bring together. Say 7% then, if you think the first is too small.

Anyway, in these days (and before them, I'm never likely to make even a tiny fortune out of what I write), with three chiselurs, and things as they are, everything helps my lad; so however wee the cheque may be, it will be welcomed with thanks. I'm sure you're up against a big thing trying to get drama in Irish over to the people. Indeed the work of Gaelicising Éire is as we say in Dublin, a job and a half. They didn't go about it the right way from the start.

They kept it too much of a respectable middle-class movement. All the tony [*snobbish*] persons swept into the Ard Craobh and the Keating Branch of Dublin, and let the poorer branches go to hell. I remember proposing to the Dublin Coiste Ceantar – Seán T. O'Kelly – in the chair – that all Gaelic Leaguers should be required to become members, and regularly attend, and help in every way, the branch that worked in the district where they lived. That didn't go down well.

In the branch that I was attached to then – Drumcondra – the boys and girls of Hollybank Road, St Alphonsus Road, Home Farm Road, and the like, went to these branches, and we hadn't one member from these tony localities in our branch, save a President, F.J. Thunder, an old man of ninety-nine, who came once a year to say – a cáirde go léir – I wrote an article in the 'Irish Peasant' then edited by Liam P. Ó Riain, about the whole question, a rambling article, but to the point; so much so that I was rebuked by no less a person than Mrs de Valera – then of course Sinéad Ní Flannagáin.

These two tony branches were top-heavy, and the rest dwindled away. That must be at least 30 years ago. Between ourselves Hyde wasn't much of a leader, O'Hickey [*a well-known member of the Gaelic League*] would have made a much better one.

Reading the 'Irish Press' Irish articles daily, one hears all the old things said over and over again as they were being said thirty years ago. Only the other day, a speaker, the Gaelic League Tánaiste, I think, told his hearers that the Gaeilge was the one shield between Christianity and Paganism. As a Catholic, that fellow is very close to the sin of despair. And me just after reading in a Catholic journal that each Sacrament has an Archangel to take care of it! I'd love to have a chat with you sometime.

Ever yours,
Seán O'Casey

Although he was writing in Irish both for the Taibhdhearc and with a view to publishing, eventually my father came to realise that there was no future in writing in Irish in terms of earning a living from it. He hoped his Irish language writing could help him establish himself as a writer, but on the other hand, he realised quite soon that publishing plays in Irish would earn him very little money. So, according to my mother, he made a plan: 'I'm going to write a play at first and then a novel and then I will submit them to a major English publisher.'

Although he had submitted one or two plays to the Abbey Theatre before this, using the pseudonym Nicholas Retlaw, none had been accepted. Here is a letter of rejection for one from the Abbey Theatre:

Nicholas Retlaw Esq.,
2 Whitestrand House, Galway.
7th February 1942

Dear Sir,
I return herewith your play 'Rude Forefathers'. For your information I append below criticisms of it which have been furnished to the Directors.

Yours faithfully,
Ernest Blythe/Manager

1. I considered the first play by this author a very successful attempt at a farce – with the conception of a play realised as something apart

from a comedy. What I meant was the kind of thing that Edward McNulty could occasionally write so well. This play, although it is in the same manner does not seem to me to improve on the first one. It has a good deal of the same crude laughter-making quality, but has not quite the same richness of comic invention. One realises the same machinery [*is*] in motion once more, but the movement of it is not so deft or successful this time. One finds in it just a variation of the comic crook play of other lands, although the characters are to a large extent the author's own.

2. It would seem a pity to discourage him, but at the same time it seems a pity that he seems unable to conceive of a larger framework for his wit. He may of course be only a one-play man, and that this is the only way he can do it. This notion would be supported by the fact that this second play is, in its essentials the first one all over again, only less good.

3. Vulgar and ridiculous – Curtain according to the author goes down on 'gales of laughter'. It hardly raised a smile for me.

This is the kind of criticism which my father, like all writers, had to endure.

8

FIRST PLAYS AND
NOVELS PUBLISHED

My father had stated a plan and he stuck rigidly to it – to write a play in English and then tackle a novel. He based the play on the lives of people he knew very well and had lived among as a child, the dockers. These men lived in the tenement buildings in the centre of Galway city and some of them lived opposite the Taibhdhearc. One family, the Murrays, were I think the inspiration for some of the characters of this first play, *Mungo's Mansion* (originally called Mungo and the Mowleogs). There were eleven children and this was a normal-sized family among the working class of Galway at that time. He drew on other characters he knew in Galway as well. Many people who saw the play remember there was a real character called Mowleogs and also thought they recognised some of the other characters when the play was performed. But my father always said: 'I never use real people, each character in my plays, novels or short stories is an amalgam of a range of characters.'

The characters he created in *Mungo's Mansion* come to life even on the page. Mungo, the principal character, is a docker who has broken his leg at the beginning of Act I. He's confined to his bedroom and all the action in the play takes place in this one room. Downstairs there is constant chaos as Mungo's wife tries to control the children. Mungo is sitting on a chair, with his broken leg in plaster and the characters come in and out of Mungo's room, talking to him. My father drew on all his experience as an actor and theatre director in writing his plays, and for the dialogue in this play and in *Vacant Possession*, my father emphasised in his notes that the characters must speak with a 'ferocious' Galway accent.

It's clear from listening to the conversations between Mungo and his son and daughter that there is conflict between them. The two young people want to get out of the tenement and get a house in the country, in Shantalla or Rahoon, while Mungo is determined to stay in the tenement where generations of his family have lived. The doctor is called for one of the children, who probably has contracted TB from the unhealthy surroundings, and the doctor warns Mungo to move. Mungo's wife never appears on stage, she just calls on him occasionally from downstairs. Another character is Winnie the Wild Duck and upstairs there are other tenants in the house, like Jack Manders and his wife.

Mungo's best friend is Mowleogs – someone who looks like a tramp, but is a fixer. He feeds Mungo's gambling habit by telling him he has information on a horse that is a cert to win a race that afternoon. Mungo reluctantly gives him the money and Mowleogs heads out. Mowleogs does not put the money on the horse and instead he buys Mungo a Hospital Sweepstake ticket (this was a bit like the Lotto – people bought a ticket and if their ticket drew a horse that subsequently won a race, they could win up to IR£250,000). Mungo's ticket draws a horse in the Sweepstake draw. Then they have to borrow a radio and have it set up in Mungo's room, so that they can hear the race. Mungo's horse wins and the household rush out to tell the neighbours. During all this excitement, no one noticed Jack Manders and his wife slip out of the room and go up to their bedroom. Manders murders his wife and soon afterwards walks into Mungo's room to talk about the murder.

While reading through contemporary copies of the *Connacht Tribune* in the 1930s, I came across a court case where a young man, a former member of the British army who had fought in the First World War was brought to court and convicted of murdering his wife in their home. That report would have been read by my father and could be the origin of his Jack Manders character, as the murder occurred in an area of Galway quite close to where my father lived.

My father finished the play in 1944 and submitted it to the Abbey Theatre. They accepted it and then my father wrote to the publisher Macmillan asking them would they consider it for publication:

2 Whitestrand House,
Grattan Road,
Salthill,
Galway.
12–10–'45

Dear Sir,

The Abbey Theatre Company, Dublin, are shortly to produce a play of mine, entitled 'Mungo and the Mowleogs'. Would you be interested in reading a copy, with a view to publication?
Yours sincerely,
Bhaitear Ó Mhaicín

Macmillan wrote back straight away:

Bhaitear Ó Mhaicín Esq.
2 Whitestrand House.
16th October 1945

Dear Sir,

We write to thank you for your letter of October 12th and to say
that if you will kindly forward to us the MS of your play, 'Mungo
and the Mowleogs' we shall be pleased to give it our careful consideration.
    We are,
    Yours faithfully,
    Macmillan & Co. Ltd.

My father sent them his manuscript on 18 October. Ernest Blythe
in the Abbey Theatre asked him to change the title of the play
so he called it *Mungo's Mansion*. Six weeks after submitting the
play to Macmillan, he had completed his first novel, which he had
begun in November 1944, and he wrote to them again:

2 Whitestrand House.*
3–12–'45

Dear Sirs,

Some six weeks or so ago, I sent you a copy of a play, 'Mungo and
the Mowleogs' for your consideration. This play will be receiving its
premiere in the Abbey Theatre on January 7th next. In connection
with this, I have altered the ending of the play and I am sending
you a copy of the alteration. If you reject this play it won't matter; if

---

* Where addresses are repeated they are not set out in full each time.

you accept it, it probably will. The name of the play has been altered to 'Mungo's Mansion'. Rather belatedly, I enclose a postal order to cover the cost of returning the manuscript, if found unsuitable. That's that.

I would like to say also, that I have just completed a book, en-titled 'With Men of Blood, O God' and wonder would you be will-ing to read a copy of it?

Thanking you,

Bhaitear Ó Mhaicín

Having received a positive response from Macmillan he submitted the manuscript of his first novel to them on 13 December 1945. By this stage they had written to him to tell him that they had accepted his play for publication (they also arranged for its publication in America):

Whitestrand House.
13–12–'45

Dear Sir,

Naturally enough, I am very glad indeed that you find the play, 'Mungo and the Mowleogs' good enough to publish.

About the name of the play, it is altered by the Abbey Theatre to 'Mungo's Mansion', they were of the same opinion as yourselves that the original name was too obscure and likely to injure the play with the public, so since both of you are agreed about that, 'Mungo's Mansion' it will have to be.

About my own name, I have no objection at all to it being anglicised because I was born Walter Macken anyhow, but since I am a producer of Irish plays, I have to use the Irish version constantly, and I had an idea about my name being more appealing in its un-understandability, in the same way as the original name of the play.

Should we compromise and call me Walter Ó Maicín? I leave it to yourselves to choose either that or plain, Walter Macken, whichever is best from your point of view (and from my own eventually). Under separate cover, I have sent you a copy of 'With Men of Blood O God', and hope it's of some use.

Thanking you again for your courtesy,

Walter Macken

My father and mother had an anxious few months waiting for the postman to arrive with the response to his first novel. Less than two months later, the publisher sent him the following letter:

Macmillan & Co. Ltd.,
St Martin's Street,
London WC2.
7th February 1946

Dear Sir,

We have now spent some time considering the manuscript of your novel, 'With Men of Blood, O God'. It is an original piece of work, and you are to be congratulated on the possession of a talent which can produce almost, it seems, simultaneously two works so dissimilar in treatment and form as the novel and your play. We have made an agreement with you for the publication of your play. We hope that it may be possible to arrange for the publication of the novel, but before proceeding to an agreement there are several points which we should like to discuss with you.

The good things in the book by far outweigh those which we might venture to criticise. There is a vigour to the story, quite remarkable characterisation, and fine passages of descriptive writing; all of which should commend it to the public. We feel, however, that the first chapter or two are not in key with the general tone of the book. A quieter beginning would be infinitely more effective.

The details about Stephen's birth, and the early adventures of his mother in service, seem unnecessary, and might, we suggest, put the reviewer against the book, not to speak of the general public who are inclined to glance at the preliminary chapter or two of a novel when they take it down from the library shelf. There are so many good chapters coming after; it seems a pity that their effect may be lost by these first chapters which are so different in tone from the rest.

We must speak with more hesitancy about the end. The reader of your novel is led to expect a 'happy ending'; instead he is given a ruthlessly tragic one. It may well be that this is the way you saw the end while you were writing the book. If you have a strong conviction about it, we should not like to persuade you to change it; and an ending is undoubtedly more difficult to revise than the first chapters. We feel, however, that it is only fair to point out that the ending will come as a blow to many readers, who after so fine, so lively and realistic story, with many humorous elements in it, will feel themselves let down by a melodramatic conclusion. Perhaps you would consider this point and let us know what you think.

The book will make 432 pages of print. That is long for a novel, and in these days of drastic paper shortage, length is sometimes detrimental to a book's chances. If you could make some cuts when you are rewriting the first two chapters, and if any seem possible elsewhere when you re-read the MS, it would be helpful.

We hope you will realise how genuine is our interest in your work. We have a high regard for what you have attempted here. It is a good book as it stands, and the criticisms we have set out in this letter are meant only to improve its chances of publication. We are sending back the MS under separate cover, and we shall look forward to hearing from you when you have had a chance to consider the suggestions we make. Revision is never easy or pleasant to do, but we hope that in this case you may agree that it has been well worthwhile, and that the artistic integrity of the book has been in no way impaired.

We are,

Yours faithfully,

Macmillan & Co. Ltd.

Four days later, my father replied to their letter:

2 Whitestrand House.
11–2–'46

Dear Sir,

I thank you very much for your letter of the 7th, and as is only reasonable, I am glad that you think, 'With Men of Blood, O God' is not without merit and I hope sincerely that it may be possible for you to publish it. About your criticisms, I am grateful for them, because, you have forgotten more about books and the public than I would ever learn if I lived a lifetime.

I will take the first things first. Looking back over the first chapter, it seems to be more of a synopsis of another book than an introductory chapter, but my idea was to build up the character of the mother since she has such an effect on the life of her son. I note that the first two chapters comprise 32 pages. I will start into my story straight and compress these two chapters into one of about 10 or 12 pages, without, I hope, losing anything that has a bearing on what follows after. In the succeeding chapters I will cut lines here and there and eliminate in all about 20 more pages. Will that meet with your approval?

About the ending, I will have to make a speech at this point in order to try and explain what I have in mind.

Up to this time, the people of Connemara have been represented by writers (no names, no pack drill) as blue-eyed, misty colleens in red-petticoats and natural complexions, blushing charmingly at the approach of strangers, while the men were big and strong and silent, looking out over the Atlantic with large lumps of Celtic twilight aura-ating them like plaster saints. These people were set up like puppets with no feelings, in fact, emotional eunuchs. This of course is entirely false. I have tried to set them down as I know them. They are a very turbulent people. If I sent you a copy of the local papers for the past week you will see reports of fighting where they use knives and stones.

I myself saw two Connemara men fighting in a public square in Galway. The fight finished with one opponent taking the thumb of the other and biting clean through it. This of course is only one side of them and their break-outs are not as frequent as you may gather from all this. Apart from their emotional moments they are a nice kindly gentle people and as good company as you would wish to meet.

You would want to understand all this to know what I am saying in the end of the book is not melodrama but stark facts. A few years ago a soldier was attacked by three men. He received nearly sixty pen-knife wounds in the face and was left for dead. He recovered.

This is my point. Stephen in the book virtually murders Malachi. After that there can be no happy ending, from a moral sense, what I did was to make him suffer, but not to die, a fact which I don't seem to have brought out very clearly in the end.

He is lying in the road with the doctor's car approaching, and I want to leave an impression in the mind of the reader that the Doctor got to him in time, and that he is the author of the book, so that the reader will get a picture of a large man with many scars, hunched over a writing pad.

Also the readers will say to themselves, 'Well after all, if he hadn't suffered that way, he might have been hanged, and they can see the Judge saying, 'You have suffered sufficiently for what you did in a moment of great stress, Stephen O'Riordan, I hereby sentence you to imprisonment dating from your arrest. Therefore you are free to go.' That was my idea and I think it could be brought out more clearly which I will do.

So please, if you can, leave me with my ending and I am almost certain that the reader will get satisfaction out of it.

I want to thank you again for your helpful and courteous letter. It is very encouraging to think that publishers can be so helpful. That is why I hope we can come to an agreement on this novel, because I feel that as I gradually become more practised that some day I may be able to turn out work that is worthwhile.

Thanking you again and hoping to hear from you soon.

Yours sincerely,

Walter Macken

Macmillan replied to his letter on 19 February 1946:

Dear Sir,

Thank you for your letter of February 2nd. You have taken our suggestions very well, and we are sure that the alterations now agreed will greatly improve the book. As our earlier letter indicated we attach much more importance to compressing the first two chapters than to altering the end. Your defence of your own ending is spirited and persuasive, and we would not venture to press upon you any suggestion for altering it.

The MS will no doubt have reached you by now. When you have made the necessary alterations and excisions will you return it to us and we hope and expect then that it will be possible to come to an agreement for the publication of the book.

Within two weeks, my father had completed the re-writing and revisions and he sent the new MS back to Macmillan:

Whitestrand House.
3–3–'46

Dear Sir,

Keeping my fingers crossed, I enclose under separate cover the re-vised MS of the book 'With Men of Blood, O God' which I hope you will find acceptable.

The first two chapters of 33 pages have been telescoped into one chapter of 13 pages and going through the book I have cut out over 600 lines of typescript, which would be almost 18 pages as well as the 20 saved in the cutting of the early chapters. I think this has improved the book a lot, because it tightened it considerably, and it has given me the opportunity of eliminating unnecessary or uncom-fortable passages, but of course you have the last word …

> Hoping that this thing is now satisfactory.
> I remain,
> Yours sincerely,
> Walter Macken

They acknowledged receipt of the revised manuscript on 8 March and by 9 April they wrote to him to tell him that they had accepted his revised edition of the novel. He replied with new suggestions for the title:

> 2 Whitestrand House.
> 15–4–'46
>
> Dear Sir,
>
> I thank you for your letter of the 9th, and needless to say am duly delighted that you find the book worth publishing. I find the terms satisfactory, and since these times are hard times will be glad of the advance with the signature of the Agreement.
>
> With regard to the name, I have given it a lot of thought and have come up with quite a few. My favourite at the moment is 'Here Comes the West Wind' but in case you don't like that I am enclosing herewith another list of names that you might like or other of them. 'The Tide Flows Past', 'The Years are Empty', 'My House is Violent', 'The Man and the Mountain', 'I will wash My Hands' and 'The Earth is Brown'. If none of these suit, I will keep thinking and turning up something better on hearing from you again.
>
> Thanking you,
> Yours sincerely,
> Walter Macken

Macmillan replied to my father's letter within a few days. This time, for the first time in the correspondence I have from them, the letter was written and signed by Daniel Macmillan, one of the founders of the company:

Macmillan & Co. Ltd.
18th April 1946

Dear Mr Macken,

Thank you for your letter. I am glad that you find the proposed terms satisfactory, and I enclose a formal agreement. If you will kindly sign this and return it to me I will send you a duplicate signed by ourselves and the £50 advance.

In the agreement I have called the book 'Here Comes the West Wind', but we will consider the other titles which you suggest. Anyhow there is no particular hurry, as the actual title need not be settled until the book is all set up and ready to put into pages.

Yours sincerely,
Daniel Macmillan

The publishers wrote again looking for some biographical information which they could include in the dust jacket of his novel. They asked him for about 600 words as a profile, which he duly sent to them:

2 Whitestrand House.
10–5–'46

Dear Sir,

In answer to your letter of the 2nd, I enclose herewith the story of my life, with photographs. I'm sorry to say that I couldn't stretch it to anything like 600 words and am dully appalled at the dull life I must have led up to this. About the copyright on the photograph, I am enclosing a letter from the photographer and if you find the photographs suitable maybe you could get in touch with him.

Here is the biographical note he wrote with the letter:

Walter Macken

He was born in the City of Galway on May 3rd 1915, making him 31 years age in this 1946. His father also a Walter Macken was killed in World War I as a private soldier. His mother and two sisters are living in London. At present he is actor-manager-producer of Taibhdhearc na Gaillimhe (Galway Gaelic Theatre), a small theatre subsidised by the Irish Government for the production of original and translated plays performed in the Irish language. The theatre was founded in 1928.

At the age of 17 he became an actor, at least he commenced the business of becoming an actor in the theatre where he remained until the age of 21 when he married and went to live in London for two years, returning then to take up the position as producer etc., in the theatre, a position he still holds. He has two young sons.

He wrote his first play at the age of seventeen, and fortunately it was never produced anywhere or he would have had a hard time living it down.

After that he wrote three 3 act plays in Irish, 'Oighreacht na Mara' (Heritage of the Sea) which was published by the bookshop in Galway and two others, 'An Cailín Aimsire Abú' (Salute the Servant) and 'An Fear ón Spidéil' (The Man from Spiddal) both published by the Government Publishing Company – An Gúm.

In February 1946, his first play in English, 'Mungo's Mansion' was produced at the Abbey Theatre, Dublin. He has also written other plays, long and short which have been produced at the Taibhdhearc.

Daniel Macmillan wrote to him in June 1946, suggesting the

revised title 'Wild West Wind' for his first novel. My father replied on 13 June 1946:

Dear Mr Macmillan,

Thanks a lot for your letter about the title. I like very much the asso-nance of the three Ws. The only objection I can see to it is that some people looking at it might think it was a cowboy yarn, you know, the wild west. Have you thought of this side of it? I know it's almost an insult to the house of Macmillan to say it but apart from that I think it is grand and will look well.

I had meant to write to you before this with the suggestion of a title which came to me while I was reading a poem in Irish. The title was 'Quench the Moon'. The verse which I took it from goes as follows, roughly translated:

You took the south from me, you took the west from me,
You took the bright heart within my breast from me,
You quenched the moon and took the sun from me,
My fear is great that you took God from me.

What do you think of that? It is more or less a summary of the plain-tive bits of the story. The poem itself is beautiful and is the cry of a girl about a departed lover. Excuse this tangentising into Irish poetry but since this thing was in my head, I thought it best to tell you of it.

However it is, I give my full blessing to 'Wild West Wind', if you think that 'Quench the Moon' is not so good. After all you know more about titles than I do and of what is likely to be the most suit-able, and whatever you decide I thoroughly and heartily agree too.

Yours sincerely,
Walter Macken

My father was modest about his ability to choose the correct titles for his novels – *Quench the Moon* was the perfect title. Macmillan accepted it.

He had chosen Macmillan as they were the English publishers who had published Yeats, Frank O'Connor and Seán O'Casey – it was a good choice and he was to stay with them all his writing life. That they agreed to publish his first novel was a major breakthrough for my father and he began to concentrate on writing as much as possible. As with *Mungo*, Macmillan arranged for the novel to be published in America.

The principal character in *Quench the Moon*, Stephen O'Riordan is a young schoolboy in Cleggan when the story starts. The story clearly draws on my father's own experiences. Stephen's mother Martha is a strong character who loved to tell her only son stories. Quite early on in the story, she becomes ill with breast cancer and before going to hospital in Galway, she writes him what is essentially her last letter. She tells him how she had discovered a suitcase full of manuscripts under his bed and she compliments him on his writing saying that although it has faults, it is good and he should keep it up.

Stephen meets Michilín when he is just a child. Michilín, Stephen learns, is the best poacher in Connemara and when Stephen gets older, Michilín brings him along and trains him in the fine art of poaching. When he grows up, he falls in love with Maeve, who happens to be the sister of the family of bailiffs. Having had a bad fight with Malachi, one of the bailiffs, who he kills, and nearly killing his own father, Stephen decides to leave and find work in Galway. As he travels to Galway, there are wonderfully vivid pictures of the beauty of the road from Clifden to Galway. The book has a number of tragic incidents, the final one is where Stephen is knifed by the bailiff's brothers and left for dead.

When the book was published in January 1948, the *Connacht*

Tribune wrote a critical review, making the point that the author was living in the past and that incidents like the stabbing did not happen anymore. Right beside the book review was a brief news item which said that a man was admitted to the Galway Hospital from Connemara with thirty-eight knife wounds! Two months after the book was published, the Irish Censorship Board banned it – possibly because Stephen and Maeve make love and she becomes an unmarried mother. This deeply hurt my father. He considered appealing the ban, but as can be seen from a later letter from Lovat Dickson at Macmillan, he received no encouragement from the publishers to do so, and gave up on the idea.

There was great excitement towards the latter half of 1946, when an English producer, Irene Hentschel was interested in setting up an English production of *Mungo's Mansion*. After various false starts with manuscripts of the play being lost in the post, the production received the green light in September 1946. The following letter spells out what was to happen:

Tennant Plays Ltd.,
Globe Theatre,
Shaftesbury Avenue,
London W1.
30th September 1946

Dear Mr Macken,

We are hoping to do 'Mungo's Mansion', beginning rehearsals some time in December and opening on the road in January, coming into the Lyric, Hammersmith at the beginning of February. I enclose a copy of your usual agreement for the Lyric, Hammersmith. Will you read it through and let me know if you find it satisfactory, in which case I will draw it up for 'Mungo's Mansion'.

I am not very happy with the title as it is only good if one has seen the play. What one wants is a title that is attractive and will arouse people's curiosity and make them want to see it. Will you try and find some other suggestions and I will see what I can think up. I am coming over to Ireland at the end of October, perhaps you could meet me in Dublin and we could discuss further details.

I have approached F.J. McCormick, but I am afraid we can't get him. I have now sent the play to Arthur Sinclair. What do you feel about him for 'Mungo'? He is a beautiful actor and if we can discipline him, I think he should be very good but he is a bit slow. For 'Mowleogs', I suggest Max Adrian. He is an Irish actor who has been playing for some time in London and I think he might be excellent. I am sure we can't do better than Eileen Crowe for 'Winnie', but I don't know yet whether she is available. I have written to her. Can you possibly get me a half a dozen copies of the play in book form and send them to me? I will of course pay for them if you let me know the cost.

Kindest regards,
Yours sincerely,
John Perry

P.S. The suggestion is that Irene Hentschel shall produce the play. She is one of the foremost producers over here and in addition I feel we are all under an obligation to her as she brought the play to our notice.

My father replied to John Perry almost immediately:

2 Whitestrand House.
3/10/46

Dear Mr Perry,

Thank you for your letter I am glad that you are going to produce 'Mungo', and hope that the venture will prove to be successful.

About the specimen agreement you left out American rights or production or something but it will be all right anyway you can incorporate it into the agreement you make for 'Mungo'. It's a pity that you are not happy about the name. The reason I say that it has been produced in the Abbey under that title and is being published under that title and it seems a pity that you can't stick to it. So I would be obliged if you could pin your faith on that name.

If you find such a thing impossible, however, I will spend the next few weeks browsing over it. All I can think of to throw up at the moment is 'Mungo the Monarch'. If the title has to be changed, can't it wait until you come to Dublin, where I will be delighted to meet you and have a chat and you can trot out your suggestions and I mine and maybe we can triumph in that manner.

It's a pity about McCormick, I have never seen Sinclair acting but he has the reputation of being slow on the words. However, that is your baby. I know that you will get the best cast you can. The only person I would like to suggest (if available) is Denis O'Dea for the part of 'Manders'. He was magnificent in the Abbey and if the play is produced a thousand times that part will never be done as well. He was completely satisfactory. His wife, Siobhán McKenna did the part of the daughter exceedingly well. She is a young Abbey star now and learned her craft here with myself in this little theatre of ours. However, since I am out of touch with the acting talent in Dublin and London, you do what you think best yourself about the casting.

I am delighted that Irene Hentschel will be producing. I have read about her frequently and anyhow her championing of 'Mungo' from the beginning makes her a natural as far as I am concerned. I haven't a single book copy of the play myself. If I write to the publishers maybe they'd arrange for half a dozen page proofs to be supplied to you. Would it be worth your while to drift into their offices – Macmillans of St Martin's Street – I am sure they would facilitate you, because the production of the play will probably have a favourable action on the sales of the book. Let me know.

Hoping I have forgotten nothing and looking forward to meeting you.

Yours sincerely,

Walter Macken

9

DISAPPOINTMENT
AND SETBACKS

It is in this correspondence about the English production of *Mungo's Mansion* that we are introduced to Lovat Dickson of Macmillan, for the first time. My father dealt with him right through the 1940s, 1950s and even into the 1960s and had great confidence in him. This is his first letter to Dickson:

2 Whitestrand House,
Grattan Road,
Salthill,
Galway.
19/10/46

Dear Mr Dickson,

Thank you very much for your most clarifying letter of the 17th and I am gratified, if not a trifle smug, that you are taking all the worry of the business into your capable hands. I would be obliged if you could talk to Miss Hentschel about the arrangements as to her fee and so on.

Mr Perry in his letter said something about coming to Dublin at the end of October. I'd very much like to meet him but don't know if he had changed his mind about this. If he hasn't, I would be glad if you could inform him that I will be engaged in our own theatre with a play from the 4th to the 10th of November but any time before or after those dates would suit me. We produce a play the first week of every month.

The only claim that the Abbey have on the play is that they are entitled to 15% of the film rights if it is sold to the films. Apart from that, the play cannot be performed by any other company in Ireland, including Northern Ireland without prior consent in writing to the Society [*The National Theatre Society*] within one year from the date of the first performance at the Abbey (February 11 1946).

About changing the name of the play, I myself seem barren of ideas, but perhaps yourself or Mr Perry would hit on something that would suit, since he knows his audience and you know the public. If I think of a startling name, I will communicate it immediately.

There is something else I want to say, which has nothing to do with the matter in hand, but I thought I might as well say it and get the thing settled in the one letter. For the past year, I have been working on a second novel to succeed 'Quench the Moon', and have recently succeeded in completing it. It is entitled 'Cockle and Mustard' and I was wondering if you would read it and see if it is worth publishing. In the same period or before it really, I have beaten out another play called 'Three Days in the Gantry' and wondered if you could take both medicines together.

I don't know if all this sounds over prolific to you, but it is well over two years since I wrote my last play in English – 'Mungo's Mansion' – so I had time to brood over this second play, and it is over a year since I finished 'Quench the Moon', but nevertheless I feel that I owe you an apology for bombarding your firm with MSS in this manner. However, it could be that you may not like either of them, and then there will have been no need for an embarrassed feeling on my part. Thanking you heartfully for taking the play negotiations in hand and hoping that I have forgotten nothing else.

Yours sincerely,
Walter Macken

Lovat Dickson worked very hard on the negotiations with John Perry and also with Irene Hentschel's agent, the end result was that 1% of gross profits would be assigned to Miss Hentschel, but in another letter written on 26 October, he again refers to the manuscripts of the new novel and play:

> I am grateful to you for the offer of £25 advance on the publication of 'Mungo's Mansion' and will accept it with thanks. I am grateful for all the work you have put into the play and hope someday to be able to thank you in person. I have dispatched under separate cover, the MSS of 'Cockle and Mustard', the novel and the play, 'Three Days in the Gantry'.
>
> I got the title of the novel from one of the gospels which I can't trace at the moment about a man sowing mixed seed and cockle and not knowing whether the result would be the useless cockle or the useful mustard. It will be easy enough to dig up the reference if you find the book acceptable or the title or both. Again thanking you for all you have done and hoping that our joint work will be beneficial to all of us in the future.
>
> Yours sincerely,
> Walter Macken

The reply to this letter came from the Macmillan company rather than Lovat Dickson, who was on holidays:

> Macmillan & Co. Ltd.
> 31st October 1946
>
> Dear Sir,
> In Mr Lovat Dickson's absence we thank you for your letter of October 26th and for the return of the contract with H.M. Tennant duly signed. We have sent this to Mr Perry today.
>
> Thank you for your generous view of Miss Hentschel. We have written to Miss Olive Harding [*Miss Hentschel's agent*] today

confirming that we will pay over one percent of the gross receipts from the production.

We enclose herewith a cheque representing an advance of £40 against the publication of 'Mungo's Mansion' [*it is unclear why this increased from £25 agreed earlier*]. As you are a resident of Éire, British Income Tax has to be deducted here, but you can probably reclaim it. A certificate is enclosed.

We are so glad to hear that you have sent us under separate cover the manuscripts of 'Cockle and Mustard', and of the play, 'Three Days in the Gantry'. We will read these with great interest and let you know our feelings about them as soon as we have a chance to consider them carefully.

Yours faithfully,

For Macmillan & Co. Ltd.

My father missed his chance to meet with John Perry when he was in Ireland. In a letter dated 7 November, he wrote that he still could not think of a new title for Mungo; among his suggestions was *Galway Hurdle, Galway Merry-Go-Round*. He thought he might be able to get up to see Perry during the second week in November once the play at the Taibhdhearc was over. Eileen Crowe was unavailable for the play and my father suggested May Kilmartin to John Perry. May had worked in the Taibhdhearc, at the Abbey for a while, on a tour of Ireland with Equity Players and then had returned to teaching in London. John Perry replied to his letter on 20 November:

The Company of Four,
Lyric Theatre,
Hammersmith,
London W6.

Dear Mr Macken,
This letter will confirm our conversation at Woodroof. We have

definitely decided, with your agreement to call the play, 'Galway Handicap'. I am writing to May Kilmartin today and asking her to come up and see me and Irene Hentschel with a possible view to her playing 'Winnie'. I do not have any more news for the time being, but I will let you know as soon as anything is definitely settled.

Yours sincerely,

John Perry

During the years in Whitestrand, my parents waited anxiously each day for the postman to come. If he was carrying a large parcel, they knew it was bad news, as it was probably a rejected manuscript. A few days after they received the November letter from John Perry, they received Macmillan response to his second novel and his second play. The letter was a mixture of good news and bad:

Macmillan & Co. Ltd.,
St Martin's Street.
21st November 1946

Dear Sir,

We are glad to be able to tell you that we should be pleased to publish your play, 'Three Days in the Gantry' on the same terms as for 'Mungo's Mansion' – a royalty of 10% of the published price on the first 5,000 copies and 15% thereafter; 6d on copies sold at reduced rates overseas and 10% of the English price for America and Canada. If this arrangement suits you, we will send you the usual formal agreement and pay an advance of £40 on account of royalties on signature.

You must forgive us if we once more suggest that the present title is not at all attractive, and ask you to think of something more likely to appeal to the reader or, as we may hope, the play-goer. 'House Divided', 'Vacant Possession' (if the term is used in

Ireland) or 'Rent Free' would represent the kind of thing we have in mind.

As regards the novel, 'Cockle and Mustard', we are afraid that what we have to say may be something of a disappointment to you. It has been read by the advisors who reported for us on the works we have undertaken to publish, but they are of the opinion that in this instance you have not done yourself full justice. The characters and background are well depicted and convincing, but the sense of drama and the memorable descriptions of rural Ireland which impressed them in 'Quench the Moon' are lacking in this new story. It is possible that, though you may have had the theme in mind for a long time, you may have hurried the writing, but, whatever the reason, the book has not the depth or the emotional quality of which your other work has shown you to be capable. It would not, we feel, be in your best interests if it were issued at any rate in its present form.

Though we are returning the manuscript by registered post, we should be ready to reconsider it if you decided to present it again when you have been able to revise it. In that case you might like to consider our reader's suggestion that Joseph's excursion with the cow is not particularly relevant, and that Nancy's tussle in the car would lose very little if it were described with more restraint. On the other hand you may be inclined to leave this story for a subject and a setting that will give you wider scope, and that might well prove to be the wiser course.

We hope to publish 'Mungo's Mansion' in January next (1947) and 'Quench the Moon' in the following autumn. The new play would come out at the beginning of 1948, and it would suit us very well if you had another novel of yours ready for the autumn of that year. It is still a slow business to produce even a straightforward book, so that the manuscript of a new novel should be in our hands about a year before it is intended to appear. We need scarcely say that we shall look forward to seeing anything that you may have to show us.

We are sure that you will accept our comments on 'Cockle and Mustard' in the right spirit, as they arise from our high opinion of the promise shown in your first novel and our anxiety for the rapid and permanent establishment of your reputation as a writer.

We are,

Yours faithfully,

Macmillan & Co. Ltd.

What a heart-breaking letter to receive! My father answered the letter within a few days:

2 Whitestrand House.

25–11–'46

Dear Sir,

I thank you for your letter of the 23rd and find the terms for the publication of the play completely acceptable, and I will endeavour to think up a title on the lines you have suggested. I don't seem to be very hot on titles, do I?

Naturally enough, I am disappointed about the book. Of the two books it is the one which I have had the ambition to write since I came to the age of reason. The first one I had in mind was to give an essay on life in the country of Connemara and the second one was to be my masterpiece, life in an Irish city as it has never been depicted before, and based mainly on my own memories and in the environment in which I grew up (even the cow incident was the way I learned the facts of life on a visit to the country).

I realised of course that depicting the city life, here there would be no scope for sweeping beauty or violent nature, it would be the difference between the breeze of a tall mountain and the air of a stuffy city kitchen. I knew that there would have to be an abandonment of beauty, but I thought that the vision of the new Ireland struggling up from the chaos of the 1920s would in some way compensate for what I was losing. Well there you are. Perhaps I wanted to write it too much. It has been boiling in me so long that it probably became hard, like an egg too long in water.

I am not quite clear about your letter and what it means. Do you mean that you do not think that it would be possible for me to revise it so that it would be acceptable to you, that it would be better for us all if I let the dead rest? You say, on the other hand you may be inclined to leave this story for a subject and setting that will give you wider scope, and that might well prove to be the wiser course. Do you mean by this the story of the book as a whole or a reference to the Nancy incident?

I accept all you say in the proper spirit because I realise that you know what you are advising, and indeed it is good to have somebody who is sufficiently interested to tell you when you are putting a foot wrong, so I would be glad if you would tell me what exactly you mean about the book.

I would be quite willing to sweat over a revision of it, and in one or two chapters apart from those you mention if I thought that in your honest opinion such a proceeding would be of value to make something out of the book. But if you think that nothing can be made of it at all, I would be grateful to be told that too. I am grateful to you for your letter, your acceptance of the play (this came as a bit of surprise to me), your gentle methods of criticism, your suggestions, and your unfailing courtesy, and remain.

Yours very sincerely,

Walter Macken

Macmillan answered his letter within days, an excerpt of which is below:

5th December 1946

Dear Sir,

We write to thank you for your letter of November 25th, and to enclose a formal agreement for the publication of your play, at present entitled 'Three Days in the Gantry'. If you will kindly sign it and return it to us, we will send you a duplicate signed by ourselves.

As regards your novel, 'Cockle and Mustard', we should like to consider very carefully what you say, and to consult our advisors once more, so perhaps you will allow us a little time to do this. We are very anxious to give you the best advice in our power as regards the revision or abandonment of this particular work, and we must thank you for the way in which you accepted the observations we have already made upon it.

My father answered their letter quite quickly:

2 Whitestrand House.
9/12/46

Dear Sir,

I thank you for your letter and the contract and return the latter duly signed. With regard to the title, I have been thinking about it and I have reduced it to three: 'Free for All', 'Vacant Possession' or 'Free Forever'.

I like 'Free for All' on account of its double meaning, but I don't know whether I like it better than your suggestion of 'Vacant Possession', which is a very good title, so I leave it to yourself to pick the one of the three which you think most suitable.

I am looking forward to your decision with regard to 'Cockle and Mustard'.

Yours sincerely,
Walter Macken

While worrying about his novel, he received a letter from John Perry concerning the forthcoming production:

The Company of Four.
December 11th 1946

Dear Mr Macken,

The cast of the play is as follows: Arthur Sinclair, Max Adrian,

Marjorie Rhodes for 'Winnie', E.J. Kennedy for the 'Doctor', Brian and Dennis Carey for 'Mairteen' and 'Mr Manders', Phyllis Ryan [*later to become an important theatre producer in Dublin*] as 'Nellie' Billy Kelly as 'Mr Skerrett' and Norah Lever as 'Mrs Manders'. We start rehearsals next Monday and open at Bournemouth on January 20th. We then play Cambridge and come in to the Lyric Hammersmith on February 4th.

By all means give this information to the 'Irish Press'. Let me know when you are coming over and if we can help you about arranging accommodation.

Yours sincerely,

John Perry

Macmillan wrote to my father that same week with bad news about his novel:

Macmillan & Co. Ltd.
16th December 1946

Dear Sir,

We wish to thank you for your letter of December 9th and to en-close your copy of the agreement, signed by ourselves, for your new play, together with a cheque for the advance payment of £40 less tax. Of the three titles you mention, we prefer 'Vacant Possession', and we propose to use that instead of 'Three Days in the Gantry', unless you happen to think of something that would please you better.

As we mentioned in our letter of December 5th, we asked our advisers to tell us, while the book was fresh in their minds, what they felt would be the best advice that could be given about your 'Cockle and Mustard'. Their replies, which are quite independent, as neither had seen the other's report, are in close agreement, and they recommend that in your own interests you should not attempt to re-construct the book, but should devote your time and talents to an entirely new piece of work. 'Cockle and Mustard', they feel has possibly been in your mind too long, and it has in consequence lost the freshness and savour that marked your 'Quench the Moon'. They have a keen sympathy with any author who is advised to take such a course with a book by which he himself sets store. It demands a great deal of courage to make this sacrifice, but they believe that if you could bring yourself to let this book go, you would in the long run have no reason to regret it.

Other authors have had a similar experience when their gifts have not at first displayed themselves in a wide enough field, and sometimes their personal feeling for a story they have discarded has worked itself into a later book with impressive effect. We therefore hope that you will not be unduly discouraged by this verdict upon 'Cockle and Mustard', and that you will feel able to turn confidently to another theme and perhaps a larger setting.

Material considerations cannot, of course, be ignored, and it occurs to us that possibly a little financial assistance from us would enable you to approach your new work with a freer mind. If you felt inclined to accept it, we should be pleased to arrange for you to receive £3 weekly for a year, beginning on January 1st 1947, this sum to be charged to your general account with us – by which we mean it would ultimately be charged against the total earnings of your books, reckoned together. Perhaps you will kindly let us know if you would like us to do this.

You probably know that at present we are bound by law to deduct tax at 9 shillings in the pound from any payments we make to you. If, however, you will obtain form K3 from your local Inspector of Taxes in Éire, complete it and forward it to the address on the form, we should in due course be authorised to make any payments to you in full, without deduction of tax.

Any advice we can give you in all these matters, or as regards your literary work, is always at your disposal.

We are yours faithfully,
Macmillan & Co. Ltd.

While it must have been disappointing for him to get the bad news about his novel, their offer of £3 a week was a generous offer considering at that time he was earning £3–15–0 in the Taibhdhearc. My father thought about their letter for over two weeks before finally composing the following letter in answer to it:

2 Whitestrand House.
31/12/46

Dear Sir,

I thank you for your letter of the 16th, and thank you for the copy of the agreement and your cheque, and your advice about form K3 of which I had never heard. About the title of the play, I think you should leave it at 'Vacant Possession', because it is very apt, dramatic and it would be hard to think of a better one.

And that duly brings me to the question of 'Cockle and Mustard'. I suppose by now you are very used to the vagaries and temperaments of the people who try to write things, so you will understand the many moods through which I passed before I got down to write this letter. I put it off over the Christmas until my final feelings could mature.

Well having passed through the wounded ego stage first during which the honourable firm of Macmillan & Co. suffered exceedingly, I then passed to the despondent stage during which Macken got it in the neck and from that to the present stage of reality, or quasi-reality.

And the result? Well I suppose you could easily foretell, I have more or less decided to inter the book, but the final obsequies I will postpone until I can have a chat with you in person (if such is possible). My wife and I will be going to see the London production of 'Mungo', and we will be in London from Tuesday to Friday February 3rd to the 7th, and I wonder if I could call to see you on one of those days. I would like to hear more of why you dislike the book so that I can avoid the same mistakes when I tackle the next one. I have decided to tackle the next one which will be called (by me) 'The Laughing Lady' and hope to have it completed by autumn of next year, but I would prefer to postpone its tackling until I talk to you. If C and M is such a botch, how on earth is the next one going to be any better, I know it will have to be but there's no such comfort in that.

I appreciate very much your offer of £3 a week, but at the moment I'm refusing it, but would be obliged if you would leave it until I can talk to you about it. It would mean an appreciable difference in our finances, but I feel it is better to write from necessity. It at least provides the urge, and if I take that I would feel bound to set to because I was eating my own tail.

Now that the wound to my ego has healed, and taken its place amongst the many other scars of the same article, I would like to say that I am grateful to you for your advice and appreciate that it is all for the best, and apart from that it is always a good thing, lest a man get a little above himself, that he should get a solid kick. It reduces things to their proper perspective and, we may hope, makes a better man out of him.

Thanking you again, and hoping that we may be able to fix a date.

Yours sincerely,
Walter Macken

The next letter I have came from Lovat Dickson:

Macmillan & Co. Ltd.
3rd January 1947

Dear Mr Macken,

Thank you for your letter of December 31st. I am glad that you agree about the title of the play. We shall, then, leave it at 'Vacant Possession'.

I am glad to hear that you are coming to London from Monday February 3rd to Friday February 7th and I look forward very much to the opportunity of meeting you then. Would you and your wife have lunch with me on Wednesday February 4th? If this day is convenient to you, will you call for me here at ten minutes to one and we will go to a restaurant nearby.

Can you send over to me before that the MS of 'Cockle and Mustard'? I should like to read it again before we meet, to refresh my mind about the details of the story. My fellow directors and I would be only too glad to talk over with you the problem of this book, and I am glad that you have postponed the interment until after the inquest!

Yours sincerely,
Lovat Dickson

The Company of Four theatre group wrote to him to tell him they would arrange accommodation for him and his wife in London and that the play would be opening at the Palace Court Theatre in Bournemouth.

Lovat Dickson sent him a short note on 13 January:

Macmillan & Co. Ltd.
13th January 1947

Dear Mr Macken,

Thank you for your letter of January 7th. I meant Wednesday 5th February and look forward to seeing you and Mrs Macken here at about ten minutes to one that day. I am glad you are sending the MS of 'Cockle and Mustard'. It and the short MS you are sending with it have not yet arrived, but they are no doubt held up over the unpleasant strike we are experiencing as the moment. We will look forward to reading it, and will try and give you a helpful opinion on it.

Yours sincerely,
Lovat Dickson

There was news from John Perry about the opening of *Galway Handicap* (the English title for *Mungo's Mansion*) in Bournemouth:

The Company of Four.
January 21st 1947

Dear Mr Macken,

The play went well last night and had a good reception. It wants a good deal of work done on it, and I hope we shall be able to do this during the next fortnight. We may have to cut it, as parts of it seem to drag with English audiences, though it is difficult to make certain about this for a few performances, as naturally the company was very nervous and some of the performances were rather ragged.
Looking forward to seeing you very much.
Yours sincerely,
John Perry

A few days later, a telegram arrived at Whitestrand House on 28 January:

Play going much better – please tell any Irish contingent who want seats for first night on Tuesday February 4th to apply to Lyric Hammersmith – John Perry.

My mother and father went to London in February and while they were away a letter arrived at Whitestrand House from Macmillan with good news, outlined in this excerpt:

We are publishing your play, 'Mungo's Mansion' on Friday February 7th and we are sending you the usual six author's copies.

While in London my parents attended the first night of *Galway Handicap* and when my father came home he wrote to Irene Hentschel about her production of his play:

2 Whitestrand House.
Monday, 17th February 1947

Dear Miss Hentschel,

Sufficient time has passed over our heads to dispel the glamour of the big city and to return our feelings to normality. I duly take my typewriter in hand to drop you the promised line. I'm very sorry to see that the weather has continued as sour as it can, and believe me when I say that I am principally sorry for yourself and the actors when you have hammered such a magnificent job on 'Mungo'. They will never be able to take that away from you anyway. I heard from a few Galway people who had been to see the play and they say that you'd swear that the producer had been born and bred in Galway and personally I think that is the highest tribute that could be paid to your work on the play.

I did not believe – (having suffered exceedingly at the Abbey last year) – that it could be done so well and was accordingly shocked with surprise and delight when I saw it unfolding in front of my eyes, the play which I had written and not just a bowdlerised version, gelded by half-wits. So from Walter Macken to you a thousand thanks, and appreciation which I find hard to put into words, and regret that can only find form in words, since at this stage of my life they are my most precious possessions.

It was also a pleasure to look at the lovely team-work of the actors from the eye of a producer and remarkable when you think of it, that there wasn't a line that didn't come across, remarkable because here you had an audience listening to actors selling them people and places and twists of speech that were as unfamiliar as a tortilla in Piccadilly. So would you tell them from me how much I appreciated their work and the knowledge that if the play was done a thousand times in other climes that it will never be better done.

Peggy and myself are still very grateful for the evening we spent in your home – (even though I was skilfully being put to work much against my will) – and for the opportunity of meeting your husband.

To tell the truth we were both secretly hoping before we went at all that we would have a chance to meet the great Ivor Brown since we had been so familiar with his work for years and years and we could hardly believe it when it happened – just casually like, but we are still sorry for having tucked into your rations with heavy Irish appetites. It's a bit late, now that we have demolished them of course, but the sorrow was there anyhow and sure someday if you both find your way to this town beside America we will put on an act with a few fatted calves.

It's very nice to be home again – (although some of the Galwegians stare at me when I say that) – but I feel better working among people who despise me a little for being willing to stick in a small Irish town 'playacting' and playacting in Irish to make it worse. Someday when we are all dead and buried they may understand. Of course they think that I am a millionaire now that I had a play on in London and they are all only too willing to give me credit or 'tick', and are a little surprised to see me going to work on an old bicycle instead of a Rolls Royce with a gold bonnet. It's quite a struggle to take them at their word about the credit but so far we have refrained and hope to be able to hold out indefinitely.

Well, as promised, I am sending you one play under separate cover. It's one translated from Irish called 'Salute the Servant' ('An Cailín Aimsire Abú') and when you have digested it, I will have the other one that Macmillans are publishing ready by then. This farce has never been performed in English and I never bothered to send it to a publisher even. I don't know why unless it is that I may be a little ashamed of it since it is not drama with a capital D. I wrote it with the idea of taking the Irish Play out of the kitchen, where it seems to be getting bogged down. It was successful in Irish and I can assure you that this is a recommendation, people came to see it.

It is a mixture of an English farce, broad Irish comedy and a sprin-
kling of satire and is of course pure box-office.

Anyway let me know what you think of it and you needn't be
afraid of hurting my feeling because owing to the many difficulties
I have been up against for many years, I have I hope acquired the
glimmering of a philosophy about these things, so when you are
giving a verdict on it would you tell me at the same time whether in
your opinion it would be worth my while sending it to a publisher
apart from its producibility. It's my only copy so would you try and
preserve it for me.

I have been long-winded enough now I think, so I will take
myself away from your sight, and hope I have said all the things
I meant to say, which is a ridiculous assertion since it's a thing no
Irishman has ever succeeded in doing. Once again thanks for all you
have done about 'Mungo' from the cradle to the grave so to speak,
and I hope we may meet again in the future and that as a writer of
the play you had to produce that I have not been too obnoxious.

Yours sincerely,

Walter Macken

Mungo did not have a successful run in London and my father
was so depressed about it that he wrote to Macmillan saying that
he probably owed them money instead of them owing him any
money. They had asked him also to write a 200-word description
for *Quench the Moon* which he did. The following letter was sent
to him toward the end of March 1947:

Macmillan & Co. Ltd.
25th March 1947

Dear Mr Macken,

Thank you for your letter of March 19th. I am sorry that you feel
a little disheartened about the fortunes of 'Galway Handicap' in

London, but I hope that it is only a temporary mood. After all, it was an achievement, and I feel sure that people would have gone to see the play if conditions had not practically confined them to their homes. [*There was snow, frost and ice throughout the run of the play.*]

I am told that the 'Company of Four' do not intend to take up either of their options, and as they have both lapsed, you are free to make any other arrangements. It seems to me that it would be certainly worthwhile to let your friend in New York see what he can do there for the play. If you will let us have the name of the producer you have in mind, we will see what can be done through our New York house.

The broadcasting and television rights are your own. We will certainly send Mr Fred Donovan of the BBC Television Department a copy of 'Mungo's Mansion'.

As regards the financial position, you are about £10 in our debt, but we can, of course deduct this from your book royalties next autumn.

Thank you for the photograph and for the note about 'Quench the Moon'. I think they will both be useful to our Publicity Department.

With all good wishes.

Yours sincerely,

Thomas Mark [*a director of the firm*]

During this period, my father did carbon copies of all the letters he wrote, typing them all. Unfortunately in the 1950s, he changed and instead wrote all of his letters to his publishers in long-hand, keeping no copies. When I tried to get them back, I only managed to obtain a few from Terese Sacco, the editor who succeeded Lovat Dickson. Mr Dickson had returned to his native Canada, taking all the letters he had from my father with him and I failed in my attempts to contact him before he died, so was unable to retrieve them.

By this time my father knew of the failure of *Mungo*'s London run and wrote a follow-up letter to Irene Hentschel in March:

2 Whitestrand House.
27–3–'47

Dear Miss Hentschel,

I have just heard today from Macmillans the summation of the catastrophe and it sounds like nothing else but the laconic communiqué issued after a last battle. So I thought I would write to you and I don't know whether I should apologise or sympathise. If it is any help I would like you to know again that I know how much infinite trouble you took with the play and all the work you put into it, and after that it deserved to be a success. The fact that it wasn't is a severer blow to you than it is to me and I think with dismay of the mountains of energy and talent that was expended on the thing when all the time the jinx was on it.

If it hadn't been for you the play would not have gone on and it seems all the worse that you didn't make enough out of it financially to buy a pound of tea and it is unusual for you to be mixed up with anything that smacks of failure.

I am sorry about the whole thing and I think with horror of the second play which I sent you to read [*a script of 'Salute the Servant'*], knowing the way my name and fame must by this time be stinking in the nostrils of theatrical men, so if you would return the thing to me, we will forget that you ever had the misfortune to be mixed up with me and that I have ever had any aspirations to being a playwright and will concentrate on the art of novel writing, an art which the human equation nor the elements of nature ever enter. Once again thanks for your kindnesses and accept my condolences over the corpse of poor oul Mungo.
Yours sincerely,
Walter Macken

His second play, *Vacant Possession*, is set in the same milieu as *Mungo's Mansion*, in a condemned house called the Gantry. One Saturday night four people break in to sleep there for the night. They are Fixit Maloney, Gunner Delaney, his wife, Maggie and their son, Chicken. In the course of the weekend other characters come in: Mister Kilcullen (nicknamed Dummy), the representative of the Corporation; Jamesy Horgan (Revenge), the bailiff; Wee Wee Brady, a smart aleck type of crook; Gabbler Blake, a gentle old man; and Sergeant Matterson, a member of the gardaí. The setting and language of the play was so similar to *Mungo's Mansion* that Ernest Blythe and the Abbey rejected it for a production, but Macmillan accepted it and published it in 1948. It was never produced professionally until the 1990s, when Sheila Meehan produced and directed it on stage in Galway (with myself playing the part of 'Revenge'). It ran very successfully to full houses both in the Taibhdhearc for a week and later in as part of the Galway Arts Festival, for another week.

In April another letter came from Macmillan. My father was in Dundalk where he was adjudicating at a festival, giving his judgement on the plays.

Macmillan.
18th April 1947
Walter Macken, Imperial Hotel, Dundalk.

Dear Mr Macken,

Thank you for your letter of April 14th. We will attend to everything as regards sending 'Quench the Moon' for the MGM awards, but we thought it would be interesting for you to see the announcement. Thousands of MSS will be submitted, of course, but one can never tell. Can you let us have the lines from which the title of 'Quench the Moon' was taken, and we will then use them as a motto in place of the passage from the Bible that went with the old title?

It must be a grim business adjudicating on something like forty plays at a Drama Festival. I hope they give you time to escape before your verdicts go in.

Yours sincerely,
Thomas Mark

Two weeks later, Thomas Mark wrote another letter to him, addressed to his house in Galway:

1st May 1947

Dear Mr Macken,

Thank you for your letters of April 24th and April 25th with the motto and dedication for 'Quench the Moon'.

As regards, 'Vacant Possession', the title need not be settled until quite late in the day. We don't care for 'Gaels in the Gantry', which seems to have only alliteration to commend it, and promptly suggests Bats in the Belfry. The pun on 'Gaels' would not be very obvious here, and in England 'gantry' has only the meaning of the structure that supports a crane or a set of signals. If you go on thinking about the matter, I hope that you will concentrate on something short and crisp. Think of what a saving it means in ink, paper, signs and electric lights! Something like 'Hamlet' is the ideal, though that has been used already.

Yours sincerely,
Thomas Mark

Lovat Dickson wrote my father a letter in July 1947:

18th July 1947

Dear Mr Macken,

As you know, we submitted 'Quench the Moon' for the MGM
Novel Contest. We have had an announcement of the winning
competition this morning. Two novels have been given the award,
but both are by American authors. I am so sorry that 'Quench the
Moon' was not successful. I hope the news will not disappoint you
too much. There were, of course thousands of MSS entered, and
it is not at all certain that quality always wins in competitions the
aim of which is to find good material for the films rather than
good literature.

I meant to have written to you before about 'Cockle and
Mustard'. I had an illness this spring, and I have been rather pressed
with work during the last month or two, but I am looking forward
to reading 'Cockle and Mustard' in the next few weeks, and I will
write to you about it then. I hear from Mr Mark that we are to see
a new MS of yours ['And Then No More']. I think that much energy
does deserve success.

Yours sincerely,

Lovat Dickson

He received another letter the same day from Thomas Mark about
the spelling of the name of one of the characters in *Quench the
Moon*:

18th July 1947

Dear Mr Macken,

Thank you for your letter of July 14th. I am glad that you think
'Malachi' can stand for all the very good reasons you give. I am glad
to hear that we may expect to receive your new novel – 'And Then

No More' (I hope there is no dire significance in the title) – in a few days' time. I am slowly recovering from my own holiday, but the weather is not helping one to be particularly cheerful.

Yours sincerely,

Thomas Mark

There followed some very good news for my father about *Quench the Moon* from Lovat Dickson:

11th August 1947

Dear Mr Macken,

I hope to be able to give you good news soon about the American rights in your work. Mr Huebsch, the Vice-President of the Viking Press, a distinguished New York firm, has just been visiting London. I gave him a proof copy of 'Quench the Moon' to read while he was here and I had a telegram from him just before he sailed on the 'Queen Elizabeth' last Saturday to say that he was interested in the book and that he thought he would like to make an offer for the American rights. I hope to hear from him as soon as he arrives on the other side.

These negotiations sometime fall through before they are completed, so do not let your hopes rise too high; but if you are taken up by the Viking Press you will be with an excellent American publisher and your work will have every chance in the United States. I shall try to persuade them to import copies of 'Mungo's Mansion' so that they have the complete canon, so to speak. I will let you know more about this as soon as I have anything definite to tell you.

In October 1947, he received a disappointing letter from Lovat Dickson:

Macmillan & Co. Ltd.
2nd October 1947

Dear Mr Macken,

I have a mixture of good and bad news to send you with this letter,
for I was just about to write to you with our views – unfavourable,
I fear – of 'And Then No More', when a letter arrived from Mr
Huebsch of the Viking Press enclosing a contract for the American
publication of 'Quench the Moon'. I am very relieved that we have
been able to fix up American publication for you, and with so good a
firm as Viking Press. The contract is being checked in our Accounts
Department to make sure that no advantage for you is overlooked,
and when it is ready, we will send you a copy.

I have been at fault for holding on to the MS of 'Cockle and
Mustard' for so long. I read it some time ago, but I thought it would
be best to let the impression it had formed in my mind rest for a little,
as a test of the permanency. Just at that time you sent in the new MS
of 'And Then No More', and that has been under examination by our
readers since.

I am afraid that our advisers do not think well of 'And Then
No More'. From what I know of you through correspondence I am
sure it is better to be entirely frank with you than to beat about
the bush. A genuine artist can accept criticism of his work, even
if he doesn't agree with it. We have already advised you to discard
one book, 'Cockle and Mustard' and turn to something fresh; and
now we must tell you that in our opinion 'And Then No More' does
not succeed, and we cannot believe that it could be improved by
revision. Our frank advice is to put aside both these books.

After declining them both we could hardly venture to suggest
what theme you should embark on next, but speaking in a purely
personal capacity, and having just read 'Cockle and Mustard', I would
suggest to you that you are on firmest ground in using a background
you know well. The attraction of 'Cockle and Mustard' is in the
pictures, each of them quite separate, of Joe Hellegan's boyhood;
the book seemed to me to fail to hold the interest when Joseph fell

in love with Gráinne and with Socialism. There is especially in that latter part, a good deal of over-writing in the book. What there is of this in the beginning is attractive because it somehow conveys the sense of boyish urgency and enthusiasm. It becomes less attractive as Joseph grows older, and I think you should look upon the tendency to over-elaborate a scene as deleterious to the effect you want to produce. There is no doubt that you are at your best when you are economical of words, as is in describing the drowning of Daisy. Indeed as a general principle, you would be well advised to work on a smaller scale.

A long novel can only hold the reader by means of a much greater variety of characters and incidents than your theme and setting allow you to provide. The trouble with 'And Then No More' is one of construction. The interest is centred on Mabbina for the first half of the book; in the second half she ceases to be the central figure, and the interest shifts to her daughter. It comes as somewhat of a surprise that Ina's father should be Maelisa Ross. It is clear why you have introduced this character; it is to make your Ina wholly Irish. But our readers feel that your handling of Maelisa's love for Mabbina, and his subsequent life as an Art Student in Paris, a poliu [sic] in the 1914–1918 war and later a successful author, is too stereotyped. Is it possible that you wrote this part quite separately from the rest of the book? I don't know whether that is a fair guess or not, but it would explain why the story seems made up of two quite separate parts.

The background, when you stick to Ireland, is good, though it lacks the magical quality that you gave it in 'Quench the Moon'. But the trouble is not in the background, it is in the characters and the story. These are not worth the length and the treatment you have given them, and I think that you would waste your time if you tried to revise or prune this work.

'Quench the Moon' is an admirable novel, and you want to make sure that you follow that up with something equally as good. It will be some little time yet before 'Quench the Moon' is published, either here or in America, so you need not feel pressed to turn out another MS quickly. You are entirely your own master in this matter, but I do hope you will consider our advice, which is to forget these two MSS and to work on something entirely fresh. I know that it is much easier to give that sort of advice than to follow it, and I am sure that it will be a disappointment to you that the two MSS you have written since 'Quench the Moon' have both been declined by us. I am sending you a copy of 'The House of Macmillan' in which you will find recorded similar experiences by authors who subsequently became famous.

You will at least have the consolation of knowing that it is not a unique experience for a good writer to have his first books severely judged by the publisher who stands between him and his public. When you write another MS for I am sure you will do that, I hope you will send it to us. We are genuinely interested in you and your future, and I am sure that the Viking Press will feel the same way, especially as they have just taken 'Quench the Moon' and are most enthusiastic about it.

I am returning the two MSS under separate cover.

With kind regards,

Yours sincerely,

Lovat Dickson

My father accepted the criticism of his two books and put them aside. He wrote to Macmillan in November 1947:

Whitestrand House.
4/11/47

Dear Mr Dickson,

Thanks a lot for your letter of 31st October with the Viking Press agreement, both copies of which I return duly signed and witnessed. It was a cause of jubilation in Macken's Mansions and provided necessary water for the wilting ego, assisting it to pigeonhole reverses and cling to a concrete success.

'Mungo' as you know was on in Belfast with the Group Theatre.

An interesting thing occurred there. They were just beginning the seventh week of the play, and in the mad scene where Mowleogs tackles Manders, there was a bit of a scrum. Manders fell back on Mowleogs and Mowleogs broke his leg! Really broke it. It was just like the story. I said to them that in order to have it rounded off as a story, Mungo should have bought a Sweep ticket for Mowleogs and he should have drawn Fairy Fulmer in that big race. That was the end of the play, since they had no stand-in (couldn't afford one I think) but it was apparently a great success there, since Belfast is a hard-headed northern town that despises any accent that is not Ulster in origin. Hope to see you in December.

Yours sincerely,

Walter Macken

Our lives were to change dramatically in December 1947. My father was incredibly frustrated working with the directors of the Taibhdhearc, with whom he didn't always agree. Apart from two years in London, he had now worked at the theatre from 1935 to 1947 and he saw little hope of being able to survive on the small money they were paying him. At one board meeting in December, when the directors began to attack his policy of presenting a wide range of plays from all over the world instead of concentrating purely on native Irish drama, he told them what he thought of them. After that stormy meeting, he went back to his office, phoned Ernest Blythe in the Abbey Theatre, and told him what had happened. Blythe offered him a job immediately, as an actor with the Abbey Company. The following is the report of what happened at his last Taibhdhearc directors' meeting on 17 December 1947:

Maidir leis an litir ó Bhaitéar Ó Maicín a rá go raibh sé ag éirigh as a phost mar bhainisteoir-léiritheoir, do ghlac na stiurthóirí leis. Dúirt Bhaitéar Ó Maicín faoi seo go raibh brón air gur foillsíodh an scéal in sna bpáipéiri roimh an chruinniú ach nach air a bhí an locht.

(As regards the letter from Walter Macken stating that he was resigning from his job as manager-producer, the directors accepted his resignation. Walter Macken said he was sorry that the news was published in the newspapers before this meeting and he regretted it, although he said it wasn't his fault.)

10

THE ABBEY THEATRE –
I AM ALONE

So my father was to begin a new life as an Abbey actor. Meanwhile he received a very encouraging letter from Mr Huebsch, his American publisher, in December 1947:

Viking Press,
18 East 48th Street,
New York.

Dear Mr Macken,

I have been wanting to tell you how much I like, 'Quench the Moon' since last summer when we acquired the rights through Mr Dickson but for no good reason except pressure of work (which is not a good reason) kept putting it off. We have scheduled the book for publication early in 1948 and I hope that the public response may be such as to afford you and us pleasure and satisfaction. I look forward with a great deal of interest to the further manuscripts from you to which Mr Dickson alluded and also to the possibility of a meeting with you when I next go abroad, unless you should happen to be coming here before then.

With all the good wishes of the season.
Sincerely yours,
B. Huebsch

In January Mr Huebsch wrote again:

The Viking Press.
January 13th 1948

Dear Mr Macken,

I thought it would please you to read the enclosed copy of a letter
which our sales manager is sending to some of his personal friends
in the books trade. It will be apparent to you that this is not a per-
functory expression. We are planning to publish 'Quench the Moon'
on St Patrick's Day and I expect before then to send you specimens
of our advance promotion calculated to arouse interest in the book.
    Sincerely yours,
    B. Huebsch

The following is the promotion letter written by Viking Press:

A novel of present-day Ireland, this is in some ways, I think, the best
first novel published by Viking Press in years. As a newcomer, Macken
has shown himself to be a past master at character de-lineation. The
novel of the tragedy that was the life of Stephen O'Riordan portrays as
well the lives of the poor, proud and primitive people of Connemara.
    You can also see the poachers, the pubs, the weddings and wakes;
you hear the terrible silences of the old as they sit in the dark corners
of their kitchens; you chuckle at the gaiety of the young men who
are ever ready for a fight or a frolic, and whose wit shines out like
a flash of stone against stone in the roadside walls – which sometimes are taken apart for the pugnacious purposes of the lads. Sad
though the book is in spots, it also has warmth – like the warmth of
a summer breeze that barely moves the flowers of the Irish hillsides.
Never lacking in excitement – be it grave or gay – the story goes on
to a dramatic ending, and when you have finished it, your spirit may
need a poultice, but your heart has had a holiday.

Letters to my father from his publishers were being sent at this point to the Abbey, where he had started in January 1947. This is the first example from that period which survives and also the first in which Lovat addresses him simply as 'Macken', indicating a progression in their relationship to friends.

Macmillan & Co. Ltd.
14th January 1948

Walter Macken Esq.,
c/o The Abbey Theatre, Dublin.

Dear Macken,

I am glad to hear you made the break. I can imagine how you feel, but I am sure that it will all work out well in the end. Courageous moves always justify themselves eventually, and I shall look for a great book to come from this.
  With best wishes, yours sincerely,
  Lovat Dickson

The following is a list of what my father was writing during the 1940s – written by him, I think, in the early 1950s:

'Mungo's Mansion', a play, commenced in January 1944, published in February 1947
'Quench the Moon', a novel, commenced circa November 1944, published in April 1948
'Vacant Possession', a play, commenced August 1945, published September 1948
'I Am Alone', a novel, commenced February 1946, published December 1949
'Rain on the Wind', a novel, commenced January 1947, published September 1950

'The Bogman', a novel, commenced February 1949, published May 1952

'Home is the Hero', a play, commenced March 1950, not yet published

It is interesting that when he was compiling this list, he did not mention the three books he had written in the 1940s, all of which had been rejected by Macmillan:

Cockle and Mustard, the semi-autobiographical novel.
And Then No More, a historical novel.
Citie of the Tribes, a book of short stories.

During the 1940s, my father established a writing routine that continued throughout his life. He always wrote in the morning and he went to work at the theatre in the afternoon and evening. While my father was writing at home, my mother had her own routine. The 1940s was a difficult time for my parents, as my father aspired to earning a living as a full-time writer. However, he had suffered a string of disappointments after *Quench the Moon* was published. *Quench the Moon* was banned in Ireland. His second play, *Vacant Possession*, although accepted for publication in the UK, was not accepted for production by the Abbey Theatre. Ernest Blythe felt the play was too similar to *Mungo's Mansion*. Macmillan had rejected three manuscripts, including the autobiographical *Cockle and Mustard*. Having read it many times, it seems to me that Macmillan were right. His second novel called *And Then No More* also failed the Macmillan test and was rejected. He then submitted a collection of short stories called *Citie of the Tribes*, set in Galway. Again, Macmillan rejected this manuscript. I was delighted, when in the 1990s, Irish publisher Brandon Books agreed to publish *Citie of the Tribes*. Other stories were also published in a collection called *Grass of the People*.

The rejection of three manuscripts must have been very difficult for my father. He tried placing the book of short stories with other publishers, but none of them accepted it for publication. So he began writing a new novel.

My family moved to Dublin in the first week in February 1948. My father had secured for us the entire upper floor of the house where he had been staying and wrote to tell close family friends Simon and Lavinia Campbell:

20 Shandon Park,
Phibsboro.
Thursday

My dear Lavinia,

Only yesterday and in a most roundabout way did I hear of your magnificent achievement, the producing of a son, half Irish and half English, a combining [*of*] the best parts of the two nations which it gets from its Ma and Pa. I hope you won't think me the most despicable friend in history, and indeed I feel very poorly about it that I should have only heard about it a week afterwards and I don't see any excuse for me. I am in the pantomime, a chap had to fall out and I took his place, and I was rehearsing, and looking for a flat but that is no excuse for such low behaviour since I knew that the time was going to descend on you at any moment. However, maybe you will still forgive me, and remember me as being not as bad as you must think of me now. I am delighted that you have a son, and I can imagine the joy that must be flowing in Simon. I remember my first son, and nothing I have ever created since or in the future can compare with the feeling I got then, when I heard that I was a father.

So from me, all my best wishes, and the hope that you will be about soon and that I will have an opportunity of apologising to you and your son in person. Peggy and the kids will be coming to live with me next week at the above address. A grand landlady, she is getting rid of her four lodgers and setting [*renting*] the place to us.

Your friend Wally Macken

In a letter to my mother on Wednesday, 4 February 1948, he told her what he was doing to prepare for our arrival:

GPO 12.30

I spent the morning shifting furniture in the house. The CIE van will call on Friday. It's costing a fortune but I decided not to have stuff thrown anyway at all on a lorry. It's better that way. These CIE fellows know how to pack properly so that it will be worth it in the end. It won't be long now darling. I'm dying to see you all. I will be on the station platform panting to see the train. I envy you the fun you will have with Wally Óg and Ultan on the train. I love you and am dying to have you in my arms again.

Your adoring husband,

Wally

He wrote again on 5 February:

GPO

My darling,

Thanks for your letter. Good to see that you are so excited. I sent you £10 today by wire. That should cover you. I can't say what time CIE will call. The job will be done by van from Galway. This is the last letter I will be writing to you whilst I am away from you. I'll tell you I love you in person. My heart thumps at the thought of seeing the three of you again. Only two more days, imagine. All my love to speed the wheels.

Your adoring husband,
Wally

It was all very exciting for me. I loved travelling on the train. Of course in those days, the trains were steam trains with billowing smoke coming from the engine, fuelled by coal. At that time the Galway train came into Westland Row (now Pearse station), the rail line continued from there out to Dún Laoghaire where many of the west of Ireland people went to get the boat to England. I will never forget coming into the station and there waiting for us was my father. As soon as the train began to pull into the station, he ran down the platform towards us, pulled open the door, and hugged us all. I do not remember precisely how we got from the station to the house where we were to stay, but I think he called a taxi.

As soon as we arrived, I wandered off. About an hour later, my parents discovered I was missing. My mother was worried as the canal ran behind the house, but I was found in a neighbour's house chatting to an old man about his life and times.

My mother immediately began to walk the streets of Dublin to find a house we could rent. Eventually she found No 31 Ardpatrick Road in Cabra, a house in a new estate right beside Phoenix Park. We soon settled into a routine of life in our new home. My father would write for a few hours in the morning and have rehearsals in the afternoon. Meanwhile there were letters coming in from Macmillan about the upcoming publication of *Quench the Moon*:

16th February 1948

Walter Macken Esq.,
The Abbey Theatre,
Dublin.

Dear Macken,

Thank you for your two letters of February 11th and 13th. I have
sent a proof copy of 'Quench the Moon' to RKO today. RKO is a
whale-sized and very good film company.

I wish you were going to be here in March, but I suppose you are
kept hard at it at the Abbey.

Yours sincerely,
Lovat Dickson

Thomas Mark, who was a director of Macmillan, wrote to keep
my father updated when Lovat Dickson wasn't around:

Macmillan.
19th March 1948

Dear Mr Macken,

'The Irish Digest' has asked permission to use a condensed extract of
approximately 2,000 words from Chapter X of 'Quench the Moon'
in a forthcoming issue. A fee of one guinea per thousand words is
offered, and perhaps you [*would*] kindly let me know if you would like
us to accept this on your behalf. The fee does not err on the side of
generosity, but the Digest has always been helpful to us when we have
wanted to use extracts in any of our school books. They have been told
that no extract or review is to appear before the book is published.

I hope that you are having a good time at the Abbey Theatre.

Yours sincerely,
Thomas Mark

My father declined the offer. The following response to his letter notes this:

25th March 1948

Dear Mr Macken,

Thank you for your letter of March 23rd. In view of what you say, we will not authorise the 'Irish Digest' to use an extract from 'Quench the Moon' but the onus will not be placed on you.

A few early copies of the book have arrived, and I am sending one to you under separate cover. I hope that you will think it compares favourably with the Viking production.

You do not appear to be enraptured with the Abbey as yet. The change must, of course, have meant the kind of uprooting from which one doesn't quickly recover unless the compensations are very prompt and obvious.

Conditions over here have not changed much in recent months, and we have a threatening Budget before us. However, I think it is the international situation that causes most forebodings. What a return, in both cases, for our efforts in two wars!

All good wishes,

Yours sincerely,

Thomas Mark

Two further letters about *Quench the Moon* followed:

Macmillan & Co. Ltd.
Tuesday, 31st March 1948

Dear Macken,

We are publishing 'Quench the Moon' on Friday (3rd April) and I am sending you six author's copies due to you under separate cover. I know that Mr Daniel Macmillan himself meant to write to you and send these copies himself, but he is absent from the office for a few days, and I am doing it in his place. With all good wishes for the success of the book.

Yours sincerely,
Lovat Dickson

Some of the Irish literary critics were less than kind to the book when it was published, as is made clear by this very supportive letter from Lovat Dickson:

5th April 1948

Dear Macken,

We have not yet had the reviews from the 'Irish Press' and the 'Irish Independent'. These will come in from our clipping agency some time this week. I am sorry that the 'Irish Independent' should have been savage, but I hope you will not be too much hurt by what one reviewer says. There was a fair review in 'The Observer' yesterday.

Lionel Hale is a good critic, but with only an inch and a quarter to sum up the value of so long a novel, he obviously hadn't the room to spare to be constructive in his criticism. I think you probably won't resent what he says about the end of the book; other reviewers will no doubt say the same thing. The important matter is the impression you will make with this first work; the impression of the power to create a scene and characters. Hale seizes on this in comparing your work to L.A.G. Strong's.

But there will be plenty more reviews to come yet, both from here and from America. It is a good idea not to look at them until you have a fair batch to go through, when you can set off the good ones against the bad ones and get the true measure of what they think. And what they think is seldom as important as what your readers will think. They will like the book, and that is all you need to worry about.

Yours sincerely,
Lovat Dickson

P.S. RKO have written to say that they have now sent a long synopsis of the story to the coast, they will contact us if anything develops. This, I am afraid means nothing at the present stage. However, their interest has been looked after [*Macmillan had provided RKO with everything they needed to submit the novel for adaptation to a film*].

Next came another letter from Lovat Dickson:

21st April 1948

Dear Macken,

Thank you for your letter of April 19th. I am so glad to hear that 'Mungo' is enjoying a successful revival at the Abbey Theatre [*my father played the part of Mungo in this new production*]. It came, as they say at the right time.

I am glad you have not allowed the press cuttings to depress you unduly. The Americans have more paper, and the reviews enjoy greater length, though they do not always contain good criticism in the same proportion.

However, you are lucky to have got started over there with your first novel, and I hope that both there and here you will go on to greater success with the next book. By the way the press cuttings from the 'Irish Press' were most interesting. Mr Mark reminded me of what Oscar Wilde has said on the subject of life holding the mirror up to art.

Yours sincerely,
Lovat Dickson

This was followed by a letter came from Viking Press:

Viking Press.
April 29th 1948

Dear Mr Macken,

Here are a few more reviews, the latest of them being by Thomas Sugrue, which is to appear in the 'Herald Tribune' of May 2nd. Sugrue, by the way, is an interesting personality, a writer of talent and insight who has made a name for himself in the face of hopeless crippling.

I have your note of 19th. We, too, have no choice but to be philosophical about the fact of your book. The bottom seems to have dropped out of the market and we can only hope that 'Quench the Moon' and other titles on our spring list will survive until the public again begins to buy. If there should be any good news I will send it to you.

Sincerely yours,

B. Huebsch

Sad news came from Lovat Dickson in July 1948:

Macmillan & Co. Ltd.
12th July 1948

Dear Macken,

I have heard at last from Mr William Herndon, the Los Angeles literary agent whose letter you sent on to me at the beginning of May. You will remember that I said to him that we would be interested in the proposal that he might obtain a writing assignment for you. He now writes that he had not replied to the letter before as he has been out of town, and asking for a copy of 'Quench the Moon'. I am asking the Viking Press to forward him one. As I guessed in my letter to you of May 6th, he is simply an agent fishing for his 10%.

We have just received a notice from the Censorship of Publications Board in Dublin saying that 'Quench the Moon' has been prohibited entry into Éire under an order dated 30th June as being 'indecent or obscene'. As you know this happens to a great number of novels that are published, but I thought I should tell you in case you did not see it on display in Dublin bookshops.

Yours sincerely,

Lovat Dickson

His American publisher also wrote to him about the banning:

c/o Barclay's Bank, London.

28th July 1948

Dear Mr Macken,

I leave London for Sweden tomorrow and write merely to thank you for your note which I found upon my arrival here. We will meet sometime but not this year. With the limited period at my disposal a trip to Dublin would be an impossible luxury. I would have been much disappointed if 'Quench the Moon' had not been banned in your fair country. Don't they do that to the best books? I am told that it is something of a racket and that the censors give the booksellers a chance to stock up before they clamp down on the offensive volume; thus everybody is satisfied, the censors have protected virtue without interfering with sales.

Some time or other you will be telling me about another novel, won't you?

Yours sincerely,

B. Huebsch

Books in the 1940s and 1950s were banned whenever there was any mention of sex outside of marriage, so this was presumably the basis on which *Quench the Moon* was banned, as Stephen and Maeve have a child out of wedlock.

My father had completed yet another novel, *I Am Alone*, by the end of July 1948. In this novel, the principal character, Pat Moore emigrates to London from Galway. He stays with his brother-in-law and begins work as a labourer on a building site where his brother-in-law is the foreman. He meets up with a range of characters on the building site and after a period working there, he leaves and gets a job as an insurance salesman. Meanwhile he has met and fallen in love with a local girl, but he also has an encounter with a local beauty who he lusts after. The story sets out to give a portrait of what it was like to be Irish in London in the 1930s and in the course of the story there are encounters with IRA men, but primarily it is the story of an ordinary young man who has come to England to live and work. Of course, my father drew on his own experiences of living and working in London between 1937 and 1939. Ealing, where my parents had lived, was the backdrop for the novel and he used his own experiences from selling life insurance door-to-door.

He wrote to Macmillan telling them he had completed his new novel.

Macmillan & Co. Ltd.
3rd August 1948

Dear Macken,

Thank you for your letter. I am delighted to know that you have completed a new novel. 'I Am Alone' seems an excellent title, although I haven't checked to see whether it has been used, but the title is of the least importance at this stage: we will examine the book carefully and will write to you as soon as we can about it. I am just going off on a holiday myself, so one of my fellow Directors will be writing to you.

I am glad you take the philosophic view about the banning of

'Quench the Moon'. That is the view that everyone in England takes of it.

> With all good wishes,
> Yours sincerely,
> Lovat Dickson

Up to now, both Macmillan and Viking Press had been writing to him courtesy of the Abbey Theatre. Now at last through my mother's thorough search they had found their house at 31 Ardpatrick Road, Cabra, and this then is the first reference to the house from which *I Am Alone* and *Rain on the Wind* were to come. This letter came from Macmillan:

5th August 1948

Dear Macken,

Thank you for your letter of August 3rd. I am so glad that you have found a new house. Even though the rent seems exorbitant, the privacy will be worth it. The BBC have paid for the television [*rights*].

There are a number of other sums due to you, and we can safely advance you £100 on account of your general earnings. I enclose a cheque for that amount herewith. 'I Am Alone' has safely arrived this morning, and we will be dealing with it as quickly as possible. All good wishes to you in your new home.

> Yours sincerely,
> Lovat Dickson

It must have been a difficult few weeks at Ardpatrick Road waiting for the verdict, as his other work had been so recently rejected outright by Macmillan. It must have been a great relief to my parents when the following letter arrived:

30th September 1948

Dear Macken,

You have waited patiently for a decision on 'I Am Alone', but the MS arrived, as I warned you, during a period when several of us were away, and we have only now had a chance to read it and to give it all the consideration the work deserves. I am glad to tell you that we are ready to publish it, but I think you must yourself know that it is not as good a book as 'Quench the Moon'. The subject has not the same interest, and the Galway background was more attractive than the rather drab Ealing mise en scene in the new book.

I tell you these things quite frankly, for the choice of theme and background is important to a novelist, who means to secure a wide and permanent public. There is one other feature of this new book which was not apparent in 'Quench the Moon'. There you wrote with an intensity which gave attraction to your style, and you identified yourself with your characters in a way that held the reader's interest. In 'I Am Alone', you seem to write more superficially.

You are outside of all your characters; you record everything they do and think as might a friendly observer, but you are not inside them as you were in 'Quench the Moon', and although the new story runs along easily enough, it does not run as deeply or seems to come from the heart as did the other.

It is perhaps unfair to draw the comparison too closely, but I think it is important at this stage of your progress as a writer to examine what you have done and ask yourself whether you are developing characteristics of style which are not the ones you really want to possess.

Thousands of books appear every year which have the form of novels and sell their few thousand copies, but everyone knows that the world would be just as well without them. But there are books and 'Quench the Moon' was one, which show an unusual promise and talent in the writer, which the reader remembers with pleasure afterwards, and which have a special place on many bookshelves. One can tell at once they were written with intense sincerity and with enormous pain. We know that you are capable of writing books like that, but we do not feel that 'I Am Alone' comes into that category.

Nevertheless, 'I Am Alone' is a decided improvement on 'And Then No More'. It will probably be treated quite well by the reviewers and will have a sufficient sale to justify the risk in publishing it, but I doubt if it will really help your reputation, and I hope you will think very carefully about the theme of your next book, and make sure that your whole heart is in it before you tackle it.

Am I right in thinking that you didn't exactly approach this book in that spirit: that you simply thought it would make a good story and therefore turned it out with that energy which one can't help always admiring in you?

If we had known it was to be about an Irishman starting as a labourer in Ealing, going on to become an insurance agent, finding himself on the edge of IRA activities, marrying a nice girl and in the end keeping clear of disaster, we might have said then, what I have briefly said in this letter, that the subject did not promise a book of very wide appeal. But you have done it, and since we have your future at heart and want to give you every encouragement, we will offer to publish it, and if we join in the offer a little sermon on your future, you will know that we only do so because we have a firm faith in your capabilities. The terms we suggest are the same as for 'Quench the Moon', namely 10% to 2,000, 15% up to 5,000 and 20% after, 10% on overseas sales and an advance of £50.

Don't think from what I have written that we will publish the book with any lack of enthusiasm. We have every expectation of making a modest success of it, but your future as a writer is of more concern to us at the moment, and that has brought forth this letter. I hope you will realise that it is written in an attempt to help you ultimately to the success you have it in your power to attain.

With kind regards, as always,

Yours sincerely,

Lovat Dickson

My father wrote a wonderful letter defending his novel. It gives an idea of how frustrated he had been with all the rejections he had received up to this point:

31 Ardpatrick Road,
Cabra, Dublin.
October 2nd 1948

Dear Dickson,

Thanks a lot for your letter of the 30th, received yesterday with the information that you will publish 'I Am Alone', and the terms which I find acceptable.

It wouldn't have been you or Macmillans if you hadn't been frank. That is what I value most in our association, and if the day ever dawns that you cast me off completely as being barren fruit, I will always be honest and know that from the beginning any criticism of my work has always come from you for my own good and believe me when I say that I have never resented it. I have tried all my life to face up to facts as much as limited human intelligence and failings will allow, and I think I have taught myself to be very suspicious and critical of the things that come from my brain.

And that is why now I would like to justify the writing of 'I Am Alone'. If I agree with you that it lacks the heart that was in 'Quench the Moon', will you agree that if there isn't a lot of heart in it there are large lumps of brain and mind? That it is tight and con-trolled good writing, that it is disciplined after the wavering canvas of 'And Then No More'.

Before I decided to sit down and write it, I was wavering between two themes. One, a Galway one which I have been thinking of for years which I will call 'Rain on the Wind', and this. To write the Galway one it would have been essential for me to have gone back there again (which I will have to do) to get into the files of the local newspapers and go into the pubs down by the docks and learn to drink pints with the Claddagh fishermen.

'Quench the Moon' came as a germ [*of an idea*] from a three-act play I had written at the age of seventeen, and over which I had been dreaming for many years. In the same way this 'Rain on the Wind', will be coming from a three-act play I wrote in Irish called 'Oighreacht na Mhara', or 'Inherit the Sea', but it is essential that I should also soak myself in the atmosphere so that the heart would be beating in it like 'Quench the Moon'. When I do come to write, 'Rain on the Wind', the heart will be throbbing in it so loudly, that it will be heard in China.

So here I was now, I couldn't go back to Galway having to earn a living here. I was in despair after the failure of my last two MSS, I was beginning to think that I was only a tinkerer, that there was nothing in store for me except to be an accomplished actor, living a life of stupidity which only actors can lead, so I had to turn and prove to myself that I could still write. The emigrating from Galway to Dublin has reminded me forcibly of the last time eleven years ago when we emigrated too, the same heart burnings and strangeness and deep loneliness, and I had been thinking of the theme of 'I Am Alone' for a long time.

So I set out to write it under difficult conditions. I spent four hours per day at it, in a small tiddly suburban flat, with scarce enough room to breathe, smuts from factory chimneys floating in the window, and the echoes of obscene language as well from the young Dublin chisellers, bathing naked on the banks of the canal, just outside the window. So honestly I felt the theme of 'I Am Alone' very much from Pat Moore's side and also from the side of Jo Jo. I set out to present two years in the life of a very ordinary young man, and the ordinary everyday things that happen to him away from home when he is on his own and somehow I believe that it will have an appeal to any man who has left his own country and gone to another, in that he can associate himself with the thoughts of Pat Moore. It is a theme that has never been touched upon properly by Irish writers with the exception of Peadar O'Donnell, who some years ago wrote a novel about the life of potato-pickers from Donegal. Funnily enough I had been thinking about it very hard and was at a dinner in Bray, near Dublin, where I was talking to the Earl of Wicklow, who told me how much he enjoyed Mungo at the Abbey, and about a few chaps from England he had brought to see it, and he was asking me why someone didn't write a book about the ordinary young people who go to England and about whom nothing is ever heard again. I said, coincidentally, I have been thinking about that for some time, for eleven years in fact, ever since I was working in London myself. That's only by the way. I also felt this business about the IRA chaps. I knew quite a few of them. Friends of my own from Galway who were interned for seven years in the Curragh Camp here, during the war, and some of the chaps who have been released from English prisons where they have been since 1937.

They were young men then. They are not young any longer, and I think it is sad to see them come to realise that what they did was foolish, and worse, in vain because they fought foolishly for an ideal, their leaders have become legitimate [*politicians and businessmen*]. So no martyrs crown for them. No honour in their own land. They were eejits who should have stayed at home and gone to College and done their exams and gone into the Civil Service, instead of thinking that they could alter history by doing ten years in jail for burning letters in pillar boxes.

Do you understand that, what I'm after? To place the very ordinary against a background of implacable and hopeless idealism. Now I disapproved intensely of what they were doing then. (If they had to bomb why the hell didn't they go and bomb up in the Six Counties which was the seat of all the trouble. What did the poor Englishman do to them, the chap who couldn't tell you the name of a principal city in Ireland.)

All that but I felt sorry for them for being such eejits, if you know what I mean, so here you had what the Irish call – A Tadhg an dhá thaobh, a Tadhg of two sides – and I made an approach to it, as coldly and logically as possible, lest it might have dipped either way into hopeless sentimentality or partisanship on one side or the other. I wanted to get them as people and pin them as people, and I wanted to get my style of writing, concentrated and controlled so that 'And Then No More' would become a memory. And I felt it was good writing, and that the people in it were well drawn, because they were types I knew and had met, even the fair Lelia.

I don't know if despite all this splurge I have made myself clear. The fact that you will publish it, has done at least one thing. It has given me back a little confidence, because I cannot feel that you would honestly publish it at all, if it hadn't some good in it. Also I wanted to get away from 'Quench the Moon'. Can you understand that?

I wanted to get away, even once, in print from Galway and Connemara, so that having done so, I might return, to show that I could leave if I wanted to, and now I will settle dutifully back to my familiar mise en scene (like Thomas Hardy) and put all the heart back into it.

I had already tentatively returned. I had been planning a book of short stories called 'Tales of a Citie' (remembering your criticism of 'Cockle and Mustard', that each chapter seemed to be a separate incident). I have written very few short stories but the few I have seemed to be good, so I thought of slowly embarking on them. I could only turn out one a month if that, and at the end of the time I would have levered myself home again and would have been ready for 'Rain on the Wind', full again of the sea and the sky and strong men in ships. I don't know what you think of that idea. Anyhow I am sending you a sample to show what I mean, the introductory chapter and one story. I think the heart is in both of them. What do you think?

I'm sure there are lots of other things, I meant to say to you, but I have overflowed enough now. Thanks again for your letter, and more so for the sermon, because it makes me feel like a filly at the end of a rope. As long as you hold the rope maybe I won't go over.

Yours sincerely,
Walter Macken

After his splendid defence of *I Am Alone*, he began submitting his book of short stories and was hopeful it would become his fourth book to be published. Lovat Dickson's first reaction to the short story idea wasn't very encouraging:

Walter Macken stands in front of his library of books, Menlo, Easter 1967.
(Photo Credit: Jimmy Walshe)

One of the letters sent by Walter Stephen Macken to his wife Agnes when he was fighting for the British army in the First World War.
(Photo Credit: Ultan Macken)

Ultan (left), Walter and Wally Óg sitting in the back garden, 1947.
(Photo Credit: Bill Naughton)

Walter Macken relaxing on Inchagoill, Lough Corrib, 1950s.
(Photo Credit: Windsor Lewis)

Walter Macken playing the role of Saint Patrick in the Taibhdhearc in the 1940s.
(Photo Credit: Taibhdhearc Archive)

Gort na Ganiv, the house where we lived from 1951–1966.
(Photo Credit: Ultan Macken)

Peggy and Walter Macken happy at Gort na Ganiv in the 1960s.
(Photo Credit: Ultan Macken)

Wally Óg, Peggy and Walter Macken in Gort na Ganiv, 1962.
(Photo Credit: Ultan Macken)

Peggy and Walter Macken in the front room of Menlo, 1967.
(Photo Credit: Jimmy Walshe)

Wally Óg brings us on a trip into the hills behind Pamplona.
(Photo Credit: Ultan Macken)

Peter and Sabina Walsh join my parents in Madrid.
(Photo Credit: Ultan Macken)

Ultan Macken at work on the RTÉ Guide in the 1980s.
(Photo Credit: Eve Holmes. Courtesy of the RTÉ Guide)

Peggy Macken in the study in Menlo in the 1970s.
(Photo Credit: Jimmy Walshe)

Walter Macken in reflective mood in Menlo, Easter 1967.
(Photo Credit: Jimmy Walshe)

Macmillan & Co. Ltd.
12th October 1948

Walter Macken Esq.,
31 Ardpatrick Road.

Dear Macken,

Thank you for your letter of Oct 2nd and Oct 7th. I have delayed writing to you until I had a chance to read your introduction and the short story. Let me say at once that the short story is quite charming, although I think it could be tightened up at the beginning. The reader does not realise what you are getting at while the descriptions of the band, delightful in itself, is going on. It is only when the boys emerge and particularly Joe, that the themes become clear. If I were you, I should try to reduce the first four pages to two pages.

I think you will find that you will heighten the effect if you do that. It is not easy to criticise the Introduction, because there you have an excellent idea, and you have something worth saying. But here again I think you write at too much length. The point you are making is that it is a fatal thing for a person to sweep through a small town without observing the life that is going on there. But that point will be made emphatically enough if you say it only once, as you do at the beginning, and if you do not turn several times to curse the unobservant. There are fine bits in this Introduction. The description of Galway is very impressive, although I don't like 'carpeted with fish: back grounded by the blue misty mountains'; and I don't like 'She was a very beautiful girl, perfect as to figure and form.' The other bits of your writing are so much better than that.

You realise, of course, that an Introduction of this length is a very solemn thing to attach to a book of short stories. All that you say is this Introduction could really be said in a short story itself, the title story perhaps, and there it would be more effective than if you present it with an introduction, which some readers will skip and others will quarrel with.

I know that the point you are making in the Introduction is a spelling out of the background to all the stories that are included in the collection. But I am sure that will be clear enough in the stories themselves, and it need only take ten or twelve lines to say why you are calling the book – 'Tales of a Citie'. I am not sure by the way about that title. I note the way you have spelt 'Citie' and the explanation you give of the origins of Galway explain it all. But before the reader begins he will think it is a book about the streets of the Metropolis.

I am sure that the best thing for your style will be to discipline it a little more. When you are writing simply and there are no straggling bits you can be very moving, but I think overwriting and over-emphasis sometimes blur the effect. Anyone with your ability does not need to write too loudly.

Of course I agree with you that there are many good qualities in 'I Am Alone', and if there is not so much of the heart, there is a good deal of the head in it. I was most interested in what you told me of the conditions under which you wrote it. I am taking advantage of this letter to enclose the agreement for 'I Am Alone', which I hope you will find in order. If you will let us have this back signed, we will send you back a copy for your retention.

As for your letter of Oct 7th, it is true that Graham Greene's publishers made a successful appeal against the banning of that book. I think the censorship board relented because this was a very distinguished and well-known book, and very liked by a great many Catholics. I must say, I dislike the idea of having to submit the book with a fiver attached to it for review by this Board, but I will refer this matter again to my fellow Directors this week, and will write to you again about it.

With all good wishes,
Yours sincerely,
Lovat Dickson

There was a brief note from Macmillan on 21 October enclosing a copy of the contract for the publication of *I Am Alone* and a cheque for £50 as an advance payment.

A further note from Lovat Dickson came on 25 October telling him that another story, 'Homecoming', had arrived and added the following: 'I am glad you agree about the uselessness of appealing for a reinstatement of "Quench the Moon".'

My father revised the first story in the proposed short story collection, *The Boy and the Brace*, and sent it back to Lovat Dickson. The result was positive:

Macmillan & Co. Ltd.
2nd November 1948

Dear Macken,

Thank you for your letter of October 30th, and for the re-written pages for 'The Boy and the Brace'. You have done an excellent job of compression here, and I think you must agree that the effect is much more impressive. You now have a good story, and I hope there will be more to come like it.

Yours sincerely,
Lovat Dickson

Then there was bad news from Viking Press:

Viking Press, New York.
November 15th 1948

Dear Mr Macken,

The delay in writing to you about 'I Am Alone' is due only in part to my having had to postpone reading it because of the accumulated tasks which awaited me on my return to the States in October. It took some time, too, to get action from the readers to whom the manuscript was submitted. You may have surmised from the delay that there were differences of opinion about the book, and that is actually the case.

All of us found much to admire in the story, the characters the treatment, but none was wholly enthusiastic ...

In the end it came down to a question of the best procedure in the circumstances; the best for you and for us. We published, 'Quench the Moon' not so much in the hope of a substantial commercial success as in the belief that the book gave promise of still better things to come. The story has a fair critical success, sufficient to confirm our own view, but the public held aloof. The practical question which we face is whether to present a novel about which we ourselves lack enthusiasm to the trade whose first reaction – intelligible enough – will be to point out the failure of the first book. To press in on them would be to work against the tide.

We feel that it is important for your future in America to offer only the best of which you are capable. Of course, 'I Am Alone' is publishable and is much better than many books that are published, but if you are looking to build up a big reputation as a novelist rather than merely to get what you write published, a long view suggests that it is desirable to withhold and to wait. It is our thought that our common interest will be best served by not putting 'I Am Alone' on the American market now. We would like to hold back until you have a book that we can present with greater good faith than this one. It is not impossible that at a later date you yourself may wish to work over, 'I Am Alone' and re-shape it into something more powerful and effective. Your second published novel, however, should not be a let-down from 'Quench the Moon'.

Another argument – a coldly practical one – against publishing 'I Am Alone' now is that the book business is in a bad state and that novels are being mowed down as quickly as they appear. Only a few of outstanding quality survive the temper of the times. Frankly, we consider that it would be a disservice to you to offer to bring the new book out merely because [of] the faith which 'Quench the Moon' engendered in us.

I judge from your letters to me that you prefer honest opinion to evasive politeness and I am writing accordingly. Please be equally open in responding.

Sincerely yours,

Huebsch

My father wrote a very eloquent response to Viking Press:

c/o Abbey Theatre.

Dear Mr Huebsch,

Thanks for the letter of 15th and your frankness about your rejection of 'I Am Alone'. I have always appreciated frankness above all. I will look at the rejection first from your point of view, and seeing the distressing (and to me inexplicable) failure of 'Quench the Moon' in America, for my part I say, 'If the Americans didn't like that book, how the hell would they ever like anything I would write.' If I were you I would do exactly what you have done. It would be ridiculous to publish a book in which you lack enthusiasm, and for my part I would be ashamed and deeply distressed to think that you would publish anything of mine as an act of charity. I find it difficult to argue with your side of the question.

Macmillans are going to publish the book. Why? They have more or less the same outlook as yourselves on it, except they say they will bring enthusiasm to bear on its publishing. They think the story is good etc., but that it lacks power and heart, and that the mise en scene is drab. That is being very frank now isn't it, and I'm sure Macmillans wouldn't object to my giving you their views on it, so if it is any comfort to you to know that you can have it for what it's worth. It sort of backs up what you think yourself.

So here you have two great publishing houses almost of one mind, and yet about the book itself I find it impossible to agree with you. It's not that I'm not a good critic of my own work. I am, and very severe one too. I have probably written and destroyed more

229

words than a lot of writers. But I'm holding out for 'I Am Alone'. I'm afraid that I have faith in it.

I know it lacks the sweep and power of 'Quench the Moon', and above all the background of that book, but I still consider that it is an achievement in the ordinary, if you know what I mean. I lived two years in the surroundings described at the time described and the things that happened. So I wrote it cautiously in order to be non-partisan, but what it lacks in caution I consider it makes up for in solid disciplined writing, and argue with me if you will, I don't think there is a spare word in it.

It is deliberately ordinary, and deliberately drab and lacking in colour, and it was a harder book to write than any I may write in the future with my powerful romantic tendencies. I know that readers of 'Quench the Moon' will get a sad let down when they start through it. What, they'll say, what's this? Where is Connemara and Galway and the violent men and the passionate women and the colour and beauty and sun glinting on lakes and the sweep of it all? But, Mr Huebsch, I wanted to write this book, badly, about very ordinary people in a very ordinary setting. I wanted to write about an ordinary young man who left his own glamorous shores for the drabness and greyness of life in a London suburb.

It was very hard and it took a lot of sweat, but I did it and I believe in it, devil the damn do I care what they say. I have done it and one publisher has cautiously accepted the publishing of it, for which I'll be ever grateful to them, and let it be cast on the water now and sent sailing. It won't bring me money and it won't bring me fame, but it brings me faith, that I could leave all the great glory of Connemara to go to it, and now I will go home after it refreshed and I will dip a pen into the lakes and the clouds again and I will colour them like I did before and I will stir the heart, but I will do it all the better because I have succeeded in doing the other. Can you understand at all what I mean? It's very misty, I know and you will probably think there is altogether too much Celtic Twilight in it for your taste, but it is true that you find it always hard to defend the things you believe in but no matter what anybody says now or in the future about it, I will remain steadfast about it, and when I die at the age of 105 and they carry out an autopsy on me, I hope they will see 'I Am Alone' engraved on my heart.

Please believe me when I say that I can see your side of it very clearly and that if I were you I would not look at me, and I appreciate the faith you had in 'Quench the Moon', and I regret terribly that your faith in it wasn't rewarded. In fact I feel a little guilty about it all, but there is nothing I can do to atone.

My next book is buried alas, in the mists of the future. It will be called 'Rain on the Wind', but I don't know when it will be written. It will be sometime. It will be essential first that I go home to Galway for a time and look up things and suffer a few things and enjoy a few more. But God knows when, because since I can't make a living as a writer, I have to persist in making a living in the Theatre and that puts a brake on movement and means one is still subservient to Bosses, so you can't do what you like.

In the meantime Macmillan are interested in a book of short stories I am compiling called 'Tales of a Citie', the 'Citie' in question being Galway which is known in Ireland as 'The Citie of the Tribes'. Dickson has been vetting them as they come from the heart, and I think he is impressed. He has got me to alter a little here and there, but the heart is in them, and he actually used the word excellent twice. So that coming from Dickson (a stern and capable taskmaster like yourself) must mean that they are good. But you probably don't publish books of short stories or do you? If you are interested let me know and I will send on the few I have completed for your inspection. Even if you don't publish them you might like to read them to see what you think.

All the best and I think I have said everything I want to say and that there is nothing else left in me.

Sincerely,
Walter Macken

11

LIFE IN DUBLIN –
RAIN ON THE WIND

When we came to live in Dublin in 1948, we established a daily routine in the Dublin suburb of Cabra. My brother was at secondary school. At first, he went to the Marist CUS (Catholic University School) in Harcourt Street, a tough school with a tough regime of discipline. My brother was forced to play rugby and there were stories of how the sports master used canes to beat the boys on the legs if they did not form a proper scrum. He left that school and went to Belvedere College where he was much happier. I began my schooling as well, attending the Phoenix Park National School about 500 yards from where we lived.

My strongest memory of those years at Ardpatrick Road was that, for the first time in my life, I was spending time with my father. I don't know how it came about, but I seemed to spend a lot of Sundays on my own with him. Ardpatrick Road was right beside Phoenix Park and on Sundays, my father would take me for walks in the park, where all kinds of sports were played every Sunday. I was aged between five and six when he taught me the rudimentary skills of hurling and how to play Gaelic Football. But we would also watch other sports: soccer, rugby and cricket.

He would also take me to mass with him at Phibsboro church, where we usually attended the 11 a.m. mass. Right opposite the church lived my father's first cousin, Dr Christy Macken. He was married to a beautiful woman called Molly and as they had no children, they treated me as if I was their own. Dr Macken acted as doctor for anyone staying in a prestigious Dublin hotel, The Gresham, so we often ate there. He was always invited to the major GAA matches in Croke Park and we were seated in what was the old Hogan Stand (probably in the VIP area). I can remember the wonderful matches we attended: I saw such legends of sport as Nicky Rackard and Christy Ring playing. In one particular match between Cork and Galway, I recall a fast-running Christy Ring making for the Galway goal and striking the ball hard. Then the Galway goalie, Seánie Duggan, leapt up and caught the sliotar in his hand, belting it outfield.

We were not really conscious that my father was working as an actor in the Abbey Theatre. I have vague memories of being taken to the theatre, and brought around backstage where I met many of the actors and actresses. Jack Cruise, who dominated Irish variety theatre circles from the 1940s right up to the 1970s, told me he often travelled into work on the same bus as my father and he used to try out his stand up jokes on him on their bus trips.

One Christmas Eve, I remember my father sitting with my brother and me in the living room in front of a roaring coal fire and he helped us both to write our letters to Santa Claus. I remember asking for a train set. My letter was folded up and placed in the heart of the fire and then as it went up the chimney – my father explained that it would go straight up to Santa Claus. The following morning I got up at about 4 a.m. and ran down to the living room and there it was in a big red box, my mechanical railway set. My father helped me to set it up and soon the little train was making its way around the circular track. The extraordinary thing about those Christmas mornings in that Dublin suburb was that as soon as you had seen the toys that Santa Claus had brought you, you ran out into the street to tell your pals. The street in front of our house was full of children just like it would be in the middle of the day even though it was about 5 a.m.

One of the street games played in our road was called kiss and chase. The boys lined up on one side of the street, with the girls on the other side. The girls would turn their back on us, count up to sixty and we would run and hide. If the girls caught you, you had to kiss them. Myself and my best friend Paddy Mervin were the smallest boys in the road. As soon as the game began, we would hide ourselves in the garden shed, right down at the bottom of our long back garden. As six-year-olds, we were of course terrified of girls and especially of them kissing us.

On one occasion when we were hiding, I saw my eleven-year-old brother smoking with his two friends at the corner of the shed. I was shocked and immediately ran into our kitchen. My mother and father were there: mother standing at the sink smoking and father sitting down smoking. I ran in and said in a rush of words: 'Daddy, Daddy, Wally Óg is out the back smoking!' There was a shocked silence in the kitchen. My father went to the kitchen door and called my brother. When he came into the kitchen, my father asked him about the smoking. Of course my brother denied it and they believed him. My father was furious and I think he gave me a slap, the only time in his life that he raised his hand to me. I was shocked more by the fact that I had been accused of lying than by my big brother lying through his teeth!

Meanwhile my father and Macmillan were still discussing the short stories and it was very hard for him to receive letters like the following, after Lovat Dickson had rejected one of his short stories about the life of a salmon:

Macmillan & Co. Ltd.
29th November 1948

Dear Macken,

Thank you for your letter of November 24th. Mine of the 22nd seems to have upset even your equable temperament. However, differences are good things on matters of this kind, because though you may think my view is obstinate, it will represent at least what a part of your readers think. I believe that we can only sentimentalise those animals whose actions we have an opportunity to observe closely and continually, and who can themselves exhibit a range of emotions like gratitude and affection. That is why I think the salmon is out of it.

I did not mean to hint that you ought to give up writing short stories: far from it. I meant only to warn you that it was a particularly difficult medium to work in. I had an impression that you felt it was as easy to do a good short story as to do a good novel, and I happen to think it is more difficult. I am glad to know that you will persevere. As long as you do not mind a quite frank expression of opinion on the stories you show me I will always be glad to read them. I will look forward this week to reading 'Battle' and 'The Passing of the Black Swan', and I will write to you about them just as fully and as frankly as ever.

With all good wishes,
Yours sincerely,
Lovat Dickson

My father sent two more stories within weeks, which drew the following response:

Macmillan & Co. Ltd.
7th December 1948

Dear Macken,

These stories I like much better: 'Battle' and 'The Black Swan'. They are good stories both and I think will be liked. In the case of each, if I may say so, you don't approach a pitfall, but successfully encircle it. I don't want to stress too much the danger of sentiment, but it is a thing which I think you should beware of: you come perilously close to it with the old man and his boat, and the understanding scene between the Sergeant and Seán at the end of 'Battle'. But in these matters a miss is even better than a mile: you have the advantage of having worked an emotion successfully without the disadvantage of having it drown you and your story in unreality.

I hope I have made my point of view clear about that. As long as you can use sentiment as an instrument as you do in these two stories and get away with it, you are doing fine: it is only when the vapours of sentiment thicken and obscure the pattern of your story that it becomes dangerous. I begin to wonder at this stage if some little link between the stories isn't necessary? So far the 'Citie', though you often refer to it, isn't clear in my mind as the little recognisable world I think you mean it to be. I should like it to be clearer so that I should know instantly its topography whenever you refer to it. I ought to know what the bay looks like, and how the town appears against the skyline, as they sail the 'Black Swan' home at night, and where the police station is, and how far of a walk, and through what streets and surroundings Seán was led on his way to the Tinker's Fair at Eyre Square. I should like the same characters now and then to wander through all the stories, as characters do in a Hitchcock film. Adding in topographical detail in each story will not be enough by itself, but I was wondering, as I read today, whether that difficult first story or introduction which you have laboured over might not be simply a sketch of the town itself. And an assembly of the characters there who are going to come into all the other tales? Like the prologue to the 'Canterbury Tales'? I don't know, but it might be worth thinking about.

Yours ever,

Lovat Dickson

Two weeks later, two further stories prompted the following letter:

Macmillan & Co. Ltd.
14th December 1948

Dear Macken,

This note is just to acknowledge the two further stories, 'First Kiss' and 'Mary Ann'. I look forward to reading these and to writing to you about them in a few days' time. I am glad you liked the idea for the Introduction. I can see the difficulty in keeping a few characters running through the stories, but I still think it might be a good idea. These characters could be unconscious commentators. Perhaps commentators, is hardly the right word, but I mean someone whose entrance to the scene will touch a chord of memory in the reader's mind. All they need to do is pass across the scene: they need not say anything or have anything to do with the story, but the view of them will serve to emphasise the fact that these stories all have a unity of place.

Yours sincerely,

Lovat Dickson

Next came a letter with Dickson's comment on 'First Kiss' and 'Mary Ann'.

Macmillan & Co. Ltd.
23rd December 1948

Dear Macken,

These are two very interesting stories, 'First Kiss' and 'Mary Ann'. I think they both deserve to go into the collection. You come dangerously near sentiment with both of them, particularly with 'Mary Ann', but with Mackenesque agility you manage to avoid it, and I must congratulate you on both stories. By 'sentiment' I hope you will understand that I mean a state approaching sentimentality, but not quite that. This word is constantly changing in meaning. Sentiment is a necessary ingredient of any narrative, but it must be an ingredient and not the whole mixture.

Yours sincerely,
Lovat Dickson

Another encouraging letter came towards the end of January:

Macmillan & Co. Ltd.
20th January 1949

Dear Macken

I have now had a chance to read 'Colm Comes to the Citie' and 'Dad'. They make interesting reading, but my criticism in the case of both these stories is that the plot is too obvious. It is plain what is to happen to Colm; and the sort of man that Dad was to turn out to be was evident from the beginning of the story, for as you no doubt know, this theme has been done many times before.

There is further criticism to offer that they are longer than they need to be. I think the effect would be heightened if you were to cut out some of the unnecessary words. But these criticisms made, the stories have, as all your writing has, light and air in them, and the descriptions of countryside and character are excellently done. No doubt they will fit well into the collection, but I must be frank and say that I do not like them as well as some of the other contributions you have made.

We have now reached the stage, I think, when you have written enough to assemble these stories into the sort of book you visualise. The new Introduction or an introductory story needs to be written, but if you could complete that and let us have what will be the MS of a volume of short stories, I should like to show them to some of our readers, whose judgement we are bound to take. Are you ready to do that, or would you rather wait until you have written some more?

Yours sincerely,
Lovat Dickson

As a result of this letter from Dickson, my father compiled a list of the stories that he felt were ready to be included in his first collection:

The Boy and the Brace
Bill
First Kiss
Black Swan
Battle
Mary Ann
Colm
Dad
Intro
Spanish Joe
Saga
Pugnug
Tale of a Kid

The only story he put a question mark over was 'Spanish Joe'.

However, there was bad news from Lovat Dickson:

Macmillan & Co. Ltd.
25th March 1949

Dear Macken,

I am sorry that we have taken rather longer than we had hoped in considering the new MS of short stories. These went to several readers, all of whom knew your earlier work, and we have had long and interesting reports from them which reflect the careful thought they had given to the publishing problems presented by these stories. The Board has now considered these reports, and I am instructed to write to you and give you our views on the MS itself, but especially the relationship it bears to the general programme of work.

I must frankly tell you that the reports were not altogether favourable. As you know, views differ widely about short stories, and hardly any two readers admire the same thing. Your effectiveness in creating character and in getting over the idiom of the Irish countryside was universally praised, but each of the readers felt that these stories did not succeed in creating the impression that you obviously meant them to have. Oddly enough – because none of them know what the other had said – each commented on the impression the stories gave of not being worked over sufficiently. I think I remember in our earlier correspondence about this that I mentioned the same thing, so this is evidently the effect your stories have on several types of reader, at least.

I do not think there is anything to be gained by your going over each of the stories now, even if you were willing to do so. But we would suggest that you put the MS aside until after 'I Am Alone' is published. (That is to come, by the way, in our six month publishing programme.) Then we would suggest that you look at this MS again, perhaps discarding some of these stories, working over some of the others to meet the criticisms of those readers.

Whether that will result in producing a MS that passes all the tests it is hard to say, but I do believe that if you put this MS on one side for about six months, you will want to discard some of the stories and will see in the others a need for a re-writing that you did not see at the moment.

I hope you will take this advice, given with all friendliness, in good part. We have now published a novel for you and two plays and have another novel in the press. We are at the most critical point of your career, and although this is the second time (actually the third time) that we have asked you not to publish something, I believe that in offering advice that must be unpleasant to receive we are acting in your best interests. Do think it over and see if you do not agree. Meanwhile I will keep the stories here and will not send them back to you until I hear from you.

Yours sincerely,

Lovat Dickson

My father was shocked by this rejection:

31 Ardpatrick Road,
Cabra.
March 26th 1949

Dear Dickson,

Your letter of 25th at hand. You don't have to be told I am sure that I was duly shocked. The truest word in your letter is about 'the most critical point in my career' such as it is.

I'll tell you the way I feel. You published 'I Am Alone' rather against your will, I imagine. I remember you saying it would not be food for your reputation, so that reading the proofs of it now I find myself almost hating it and feeling that it is no good at all. I gave a lot to the stories you have rejected. Now frankly I have come to the point where I don't think anything I could ever write again would meet with your approval. I genuinely cannot see myself sitting down to write anything anymore without saying to myself, well what's the use, Macmillans won't like it. That of course is a fatal feeling, and I don't see how it will ever be possible for me to overcome it.

So there I leave you. There's no use going into impassioned reasons for why I think you are wrong and I am right or the other way about. You will know in what category to place me as an author, I cannot help the feeling that publishers no more than doctors have often been wrong.

I will be obliged if you will let me have the MS at your convenience and my thanks again for the care with which you read them. For the moment, I find I have nothing further to say.

Sincerely yours,

Walter Macken

My father sent another letter that same day posing a number of questions to Dickson:

March 26th 1949

Dear Dickson,

Further to my letter of 26th and to assist me in coming to a decision, would you please answer the following questions if possible?

1. Did the readers dislike all the stories?
   (If the answer to this is yes, you needn't bother with all the other questions.)
2. What stories taking an average of their report, did the readers like?
3. Why did they like them?
4. What stories met with their partial disapproval?
5. What stories met with their complete disapproval?
6. Why?

If it is possible to answer some of these questions for me without

being unethical it might be a great help in straightening out the way
I feel now.
Sincerely,
Walter Macken

Lovat Dickson replied promptly to his letters:

Macmillan & Co. Ltd.
29th March 1949

Dear Macken,

Thank you for your letter of March 26th, I am more sorry than I can
say that our decision should have upset you so much. I know quite
well what your first feelings must be, and I have complete sympathy
with you in the mood that must have been on you when you wrote.
I am returning the stories under separate cover. I hope that we
may see each other soon and talk about this whole matter. That is so
much more satisfactory than trying to get one's ideas over in a letter.
With all good wishes,
Yours sincerely,
Lovat Dickson

My father was convinced that *Tales of a Citie* was ready to be
published, so he submitted the MS to Collins in the UK:

Abbey Theatre.
July 7th 1949

Peter Wyld Esq.,
Collins Publishers.

Dear Mr Wyld,

Thanks a lot for your letter of the 5th. I'm glad to hear that the mix-up over the letter was due to such very human things as marriages and illnesses and I hope that they are all duly eliminated now.

I am enclosing herewith the MS of 'Tales of a Citie'. The delay in assessing it will be expected by me. I have learned patience in a hard school. With all best wishes, and when you have come to a decision about the MS would you please direct the body or the report of the inquest to my private address below.

Sincerely yours,

Walter Macken

31 Ardpatrick Road, Cabra, Dublin.

However, nothing came of his efforts to get another publisher to publish the stories.

The turning point of my father's writing career happened in 1949 and it was his newly completed novel, *Rain On The Wind*, that was to bring about the change. He wrote to Lovat Dickson:

31 Ardpatrick Road.

November 9th 1949

Dear Dickson,

As you see, I am not dead but living. It's a long time since we heard from each other. I am writing now to say that I have completed a new book called 'Rain on the Wind', written about events and people on my own heath so to speak, and I'm wondering if Macmillans would read it and let me know what they think of it.

I don't know when you will be bringing out 'I Am Alone' but when you are sending me the author's copies would you include another six extra and put them against my account. I have so many relatives that have to have them.

I hope you are well and haven't forgotten me.

Sincerely yours,

Walter Macken

It seems that he wrote this novel in the period between spring and November 1949, when his short story collection, *Tales of a Citie* was rejected. Lovat Dickson answered by return post:

Macmillan & Co. Ltd.
11th November 1949

Dear Macken,

I am glad to hear from you again after so long, to know that you are well, and to have the good news that you have completed a new book. Certainly we should like to consider it. Do send it right away, and you may be sure that we will examine it, carefully, and sympathetically.

We are expecting to publish 'I Am Alone' on November 18th. The advance copies are already in the house, and so I am sending you your six author's copies, and the six further copies you require. I hope you will like the appearance of the book. I will write to you from time to time to let you know how it is going, and you will of course, as always, have weekly clippings of reviews from us.

Are you still acting? You do not say whether 'Rain on the Wind' is fiction or not. I can't help admiring and envying your energy.

With all good wishes,
Yours sincerely,
Lovat Dickson

It took Macmillan almost two months to give him their first response to the MS of *Rain on the Wind*. Thomas Mark wrote to him:

11th January 1950

Dear Mr Macken,

As Lovat Dickson mentioned to you in his last letter, I have been asked to write to you about your 'Rain on the Wind', no doubt because I was the last to read the MS.

I know just how an author feels about any far-reaching criticism of his book, but I am sure that you will realise that we should not be induced to make it if there did not lie behind it a genuine response to what you have attempted, and desire to see it presented to the best advantage. Some of our most experienced advisors – those who saw your earlier books – have reported on your novel, and several of us here have read it, so what follows is a summary of several opinions.

Everyone feels that your book contains passages that are as good as anything you have written, particularly in descriptions of action, such as the boats in the storm and the affair with the English poachers, but there is unanimous agreement that it is far too long for what is essentially a rather slight story. We estimate the extent at not less than 150,000 words, and the general view, though I shrink from conveying it, is that it should be cut down by a least a third. This will, I know, mean sacrificing passages that have cost you a great deal of trouble and are admirable in themselves, but we are sure that the abridgment will improve the book and its prospects of success with the public.

You are obviously tempted to put down everything as clearly and completely as it comes into your imagination and memory, but if every incident, dialogue, and piece of self-communing is given its fullest expression, the story tends to be swamped, and the book has the effect of a series of episodes with no marked organic relationship.

The political–philosophical passages are not very valuable, and the anti-English outbursts not only seem extraneous but are scarcely magnanimous in present circumstances, and cannot gratify many of your potential readers. If you would like to have a few specimen suggestions, I should recommend that the first two chapters could be telescoped into one, that the description of Pa might be shorter, and that the account of the mackerel fishing should be given a space more proportionate to its importance to the story. Chapter 11 is lengthy, and in Chapter 13 the long account of the Aran Islands and their people is not really relevant to the fact that Peter came there to meet his end. (I would rather have a fuller explanation of the Claddagh at the beginning of the story.) There is another long chapter after Peter's funeral, and possibly funerals altogether get rather too much emphasis in the book. In Chapter 19 a good deal of what Jo has to say could be dispensed with; she appears self-righteous and one loses one's liking for her.

On smaller points, I think that some of the short phrases might be made into more orthodox sentences, and that the 'And he … and he … and he' might be employed less freely, as the effect is spoiled when it is constantly recurring. Short single sentences treated as separate paragraphs take up room on the printed page, which is a consideration in a long book, and I have marked places where they scarcely appeared to earn their prominence.

I wonder if the end could be made a little clearer. Novel-readers always like to be certain whether or not the boy gets girl, and Maeve's thoughts on page 362 make this doubtful.

Each new novel has to win its public nowadays, for the seller's market has gone for books as for so much else. One sad instance of this is the fact that so far we have only succeeded in selling some 1,500 copies of 'I Am Alone'.

I hope that you will read these comments in the most charitable spirit, however strongly you may disagree. The most important matter is, of course, the abridgement of the whole MS, and I may end up saying, after so much that may have appeared discouraging, that there is no doubt as to our wishing to publish the book if you would reduce its extent to about 100,000 words. We are returning the MS for this purpose under separate cover, by registered post.

With all good wishes,

I am,

Yours sincerely,

Thomas Mark

My father went to work on his MS and in ten days he cut the original manuscript as suggested and replied to Thomas Mark:

31 Ardpatrick Road.
January 19th 1950

Dear Mr Mark,

Thank you for some parts of your letter of the 11th. For the pain you took with it and the advice you gave me about 'Rain on the Wind'.

I have spent the past week cutting 50,000 words out of it, and it is a terrible experience and contains a terrible lesson. I have no doubt that in the future I will be grateful for your advice and glad that after a struggle with myself, I accepted it, but at the time of cutting it seemed like chopping off the limbs of a new-born baby with a rusty knife. Anyhow 'tis done and cannot be undone. It is cut down to the bare bones (it seems to me) but I hope that the slight story (I would have preferred if you had used the word 'simple' which it set out to be) will gain stature from the painful operation. I left the end as it was but I deleted the doubtful words of Maeve on page 362 so that all doubt ought to be eliminated.

Whenever I come to writing a book again, I will not forget this past week. It will be a blue headline in my brain. I am enclosing the MS under separate cover and hope you will find that I have done with it as you advised.

Yours sincerely,
Walter Macken

Macmillan accepted the new shortened version of the novel for publication. My father was delighted:

31 Ardpatrick Road.
Feb. 11th 1950

Dear Dickson,

Thanks a lot for your letter of the 7th and your letter and contract of the 9th February.

I didn't know I had written such an agonised letter over the cuts of the book, but I regarded them mainly as a salutary lesson and felt, even though the pain was sharp, that it was all for the best and that it held a lesson for the future. And then whatever about my ego I knew that your advice was good. It has always been so and your acceptance of the revised version is encouraging to me: I feel now, cautiously that I am on a good road as long as I stay on it and keep out of the by-ways.

About Mr Latham, when I sent the MS of the book to you I also sent a copy to the Viking Press. I don't know why, unless I had a despairing feeling that two chances were better than one. I haven't heard from them about it, but perhaps you would like to get in touch with them?

They took such a beating over 'Quench the Moon', apparently, that they would be doubtful, and their ideas about this new one would be similar to your own. However, you might handle it and see what they think. The original contract is void, I think, because they turned down 'I Am Alone'. I am enclosing the agreement with this, duly signed and hope it will be good for both of us.

With all good wishes,

Yours sincerely,

Walter Macken

The publication of his third novel was on its way now and I suspect that neither he nor Lovat Dickson realised it would become the huge bestseller that it was.

Macmillan & Co. Ltd.
2nd March 1950

Dear Macken,

Thank you for your letter of February 27th, and for the copy of the letter you wrote to Mr Latham at Viking Press. We have arranged to send you an extra set of galleys of 'Rain on the Wind'. By the time you receive them, you will know what Viking Press mean to do. If they decline the book, you can send the additional corrected proofs to the New York Macmillan Company, and if they accept it, you will already have advised Mr Latham and in that case the extra set can be used for Viking Press.

We did receive notification that 'I Am Alone' is banned in Ireland. The reasons given for banning it are obviously not those in the minds of the censors. It is possible to appeal against such a verdict, but I am sure you will agree that it is not worthwhile in this case. They plainly do not want the book to circulate.

Yours sincerely,

Lovat Dickson

Some good news came in May of 1950:

Macmillan & Co. Ltd.
19th May 1950

Dear Mr Macken,

You'll be glad to hear that we have arranged for a Dutch edition of 'I Am Alone'. This Dutch edition will be published by the Catholic Book Club in The Hague. We have obtained a fee of £100 as a fee for this special edition. It is unlikely that it will be published before the middle of next year, but as soon as complimentary copies are received, they will be forwarded on to you.

Yours sincerely,

R.Z. Allen

12

FROM ACTOR TO
FULL-TIME WRITER

M.J. Molloy the playwright, wrote to my father telling him that an American producer had plans to stage his *The King of Friday's Men* on Broadway and that they wanted my father to play the part of Bartley, as he had played the role in the very successful Abbey production in 1948. In May, Peter White, from the production company, wrote to my father while we were on our annual holiday in Bunbeg in Donegal:

Mr Walter Macken,
c/o Breslins Hotel,
Bunbeg,
Co. Donegal.

Dear Mr Macken,

Michael Molloy has suggested we write to you regarding the American production of 'The King of Friday's Men'. We are extremely interested in having you to do the part of Bartley on the basis of Molloy's high recommendation and the notices you received in the 'Irish Press'. We plan an early Fall production, for which you would have to be available about July 1st. We understand there is a problem about your coming to America because of contract obligations at the Abbey. We feel confident that acting Bartley over here would foster great success for you in the American stage and motion picture industry.

We would greatly appreciate direct correspondence from you on this matter stating the conditions of your availability and your terms, should you get leave of absence from the Abbey and come here for our production. I am sure we can agreeably discuss terms, besides we are in a position to help you get additional contracts after the run of this play, should you desire them.

Sincerely,

Peter White

This holiday in Donegal was a very special one. We were staying in a hotel/guest-house right at the foot of Mount Errigal (Ireland's second largest mountain). I have a distinct memory of seeing wild eagles flying over the top of that mountain. There was a lovely river running right through Bunbeg and each day my father went fishing. He didn't catch anything and on our last day we went up beyond the waterfall. He was using a small short trout rod and he hooked a big salmon. The salmon, instead of staying in the pool, headed off down-stream. My father and I followed him, walking through pools, over small waterfalls and still the salmon fought on. Finally the salmon tired and my father was able to net him. The fight had lasted almost an hour and as we ran down towards the village, we saw the bus waiting for us. My mother had persuaded the bus driver to wait for us and there was a great cheer when we finally got on the bus, especially when they saw the large salmon my father had landed.

After the holiday, two more letters came from Peter White:

The King of Friday's Men Company,
Room 906,
1619 Broadway,
New York 19.
June 7th 1950

Dear Mr Macken,

I acknowledge with thanks the receipt of your pictures. Could you let us have word regarding your availability for our production. I see your best man, Gary McEoin two or three times a week. He hopes very much you are coming.
    Sincerely,
    Peter White

Obviously my father replied telling Peter he was interested and received the following response:

The King of Friday's Men Company.
June 22nd 1950

Dear Mr Macken,

In reply to your good letter of June 6, we acknowledge your attitude of cooperation and your friendly desire to further the chances of Michael Molloy getting a successful American production.

    We make you the following offer, which we believe is fair to both sides; round trip transportation for yourself and wife, and $1,500 for the four week rehearsal period and a two week playing period. If, the play becomes established after two weeks running period, we will pay you a salary of $250 a week. In the event that you are acclaimed a star and the play becomes what is known as a hit, we shall reconsider the matter mutually.

    A condition of this offer is that we become your American representatives, with the understanding that all contracts and commitments will be subject to our approval. David Garrity, the publisher, is helping promote the play through his Irish Book Club, and he mentioned an interest in publishing your novel if someone else refuses it.

Yours sincerely,
Peter White

By the time we returned from our holidays, it looked as if everything was ready for my father's first visit to Broadway. Another letter from Peter White added to the excitement. (It is clear from later correspondence that my father signed this contract and the $1,500 advance payment was made to him.)

The King of Friday's Men Company.
July 11th 1950

Dear Mr Macken,

Thanks for your good letter of June 26th. We are delighted you have decided to come with us. As for living expenses in New York, the League of New York Theatre Producers has recommended that the cast be put on $15 a day living expense account during the two week try-out period, which should settle your concern.

Arthur Shields' wife has just died, and this has somewhat held up the negotiations. We expect that he will be the director. We will give you the final confirmation and let you know when we want you as soon as we can.

Garret Johnson, now calling himself Gary McEoin, is currently managing circulation and editorial matters at a Spanish language newspaper in New York called 'La Prensa'. He took your address from me, so I expect you will be hearing from him. He is going to tell a new publisher about your book ['*Rain on the Wind*'], in case you have no luck with the old established ones.

Sincerely yours,
Peter White

There was more good news a few days later concerning an American publication of *Rain on the Wind*, which had been rejected by Viking Press. Mr Latham was now working for Macmillan.

Macmillan & Co. Ltd.
14th July 1950

My dear Macken,

Thank you for your letter of July 12th. We have now settled terms with the New York Macmillan Company for the publication of 'Rain on the Wind'. There is to be an advance of $750, against royalties of 10% to 5,000, 12.5% on the next 2,500 and 15% thereafter. These are very satisfactory, indeed quite generous, terms, and we are glad to have been able to work out so good an arrangement for you.

As you know, we have the English language rights on 'Rain on the Wind', and strictly speaking, we should be able to set off the American income against the English one. We have, as you know, published all your books (although we have had many a discussion with you along the way) with the firm faith that eventually you would establish yourself as a novelist on a big scale. Perhaps Mr Latham was influenced by our faith, although I like to think that what did attract him was the unusual vitality in your work which promises such good things for the future.

We propose, therefore, to deal with the American royalties as though they were yours, and we propose to act merely as your agents, collecting the royalties on your behalf, and dealing with the subsidiary and other rights. We do this for many of our authors, and we charge a commission of 20%, which I hope you will find satisfactory. I should add that in the past when we negotiated the Viking contract for you, we used to charge 10%, but with increased costs we have found it necessary to charge 20%. On the whole, as I think you will see, you will come out of the arrangement very well.

I am delighted to hear that you are going to New York to act, although rehearsing in August on Broadway will be an unenviable experience. However, the pay as you say is very good, and it is an excellent idea for you to see America and for America to see you. It will be very good if the play lasts for a bit, and the novel comes out in America while you are acting on Broadway.

That fishing story of yours is wonderful to read. You must have had a lovely holiday.

With all good wishes,

Yours sincerely,

Lovat Dickson

My father and mother always said that life-long friendships can be counted on the fingers of one hand. One such friend was an American journalist, John McNulty. They first met by accident when my father was touring with a company set up by Cyril Cusack, with John Millington Synge's *Playboy of the Western World*. My father always played the part of the father of the playboy. While he was performing in Cork city, we were staying in the Bunnyconnellan Hotel near the lovely coastal town of Crosshaven. While my father was rehearsing, we spent our time around the hotel and met John McNulty who was making his way around Ireland and happened to be staying at the same place. My mother told him that her husband was acting in a play and was also a writer and when my father met him they became fast friends. A few days later it was time for him to return to America and he was sailing from the port of Cobh in a huge liner. He walked down the hotel's garden that evening with me, holding my hand, and we had a conversation that he included in his article for the *New Yorker*, published in September 1950, and later included in a book he published. His friendship continued through the wonderful letters he wrote and the letters my father wrote to him. He was born in Lawrence, Massachusetts and fought in the First World War, where he was wounded as an

infantry sergeant. After the army he attended journalism school at
Columbia, he worked for the *Associated Press* and then worked on
newspapers in Columbus, Ohio, and Cleveland before returning to
New York in 1935 where he really found his niche as a columnist
with the *New Yorker* magazine. My mother told me that John
had been married when he was young. His wife had a nervous
breakdown and was committed to hospital. Although John was
Catholic, he eventually got a divorce. By the time we met him in
the 1950s he was remarried to a lady called Faith.

My father and mother were looking forward to seeing him
when they visited New York but, by coincidence, we received a
letter from him in July of 1950.

1 Post Road, Wakefield,
Rhode Island.
Thursday, July 20

Dear Walter,

It has been too long a time since we heard from the Mackens. How
are the Mackens doing? The McNultys are okay, but of course that
is only one man's point of view. There'll be three of us by the end of
August if the doctor is correct. Is there any notion of you coming
over here? It would be a pleasure indeed to see you all again. How's
the writing? I know the playacting is sailing along but I also know
it's the writing that interests you most.

We're in Rhode Island for the summer, it's near the sea, looks
like Kerry but not enough like Kerry to suit me. We often talk about
going back to Ireland but even if we had the money, we would not
go back this year.

Take a few minutes off some night and let us know all about
yourselves.

Best regards,
From Faith and John McNulty

My father must have already written to him about the proposed visit:

1 Post Road,
Wakefield,
Rhode Island.
July 21

Dear Walter,

That's a funny thing. Yesterday afternoon I said to Faith, it's a long time since we heard from the Mackens. And I wrote this letter which you may have now received. Well, sir, this morning your letter came! It had gone to New York, as properly addressed by you and then been forwarded up here. There is such a thing as mental telepathy, all right.

We are immensely pleased at the prospect of seeing you and Peggy and regret only that the youngsters aren't coming. You must, from now on, keep us informed of every detail, such as, who your producer is, if there is anything we can do, big or small, by way of preparing for your arrival, you have only to command us. Have you figured where to stay? We're having the baby the latter part of August and it now bids to be a big month, what with the Mackens and the heir to the McNulty millions, arriving at the same time.

I am beset with fears that you may be expecting too much of this 'fabulous America'. It isn't paradise on earth (I don't think you rate it as such anyway) and I do hope you are not counting on having too much of your salary left when you get through paying the idiotic cost of living in Manhattan, where hotel rooms for the two of you will surely run to $60 or more a week in a decent place, such as 'The Alonquin', an old fashioned hotel that's right in the theatre district of New York.

Please, Walter and Peggy, do not build any air-castles on what you will save here, because it is a sorrowful duty to warn you that it won't be much. Don't think me as a pessimist, I merely don't want you to be heart-broken at this fabulous America.

I'm anxious too, to see 'Rain on the Wind'. Is there a publication date set? I must write the Macmillan publicity outfit and tell them what a hell of a fine guy they have coming over here. This is a ballyhoo nation, and the more ballyhoo the better, even if some of it is bound to be distasteful. Among the tasteful items, however, I think I can arrange to have you interviewed for our 'Talk of the Town' department in the 'New Yorker' which reminds me of the perfidious McNulty promise a long, long while ago to enter a subscription for the 'New Yorker' for you, and I don't think I ever did it. By God, I'll do it next Tuesday when I go back to New York. As I said in my letter of yesterday, we are staying up here at the country home of Faith's folks, and I am working occasionally, but not to any fanatical excess. As they say, work is the curse of the drinking classes.

I'll try and give you all the help I can in making your stay interesting and possibly, if not probably, profitable. Please write us details as they develop, and do not hesitate to call on me to do any chores that you'd like to have done. I'll find a place for you to stay and things, like that, letting you know how much it will cost and all that, so that you and Peggy can have the matchless fun of jotting down figures and totting up miniature fortunes about to be gained – fortunes that seldom come to pass but which are fun on paper.

Do write us now,

John McNulty

We had planned, if you ever came, to have you in our guest room in New York, but that is to be a nursery, no less!

The McNulty's were expecting their first child and their excitement is clear.

Meanwhile the letters about *The King of Friday's Men* kept coming, such as this one concerning financial arrangements:

The King of Friday's Men Company.
July 26th 1950

Dear Mr Macken,

Thank you for your prompt wire. I am holding your check for your instructions. Do you want your New York agent to deposit it for you, or shall I send it on to you or hold it in safekeeping until you arrive and can deposit it in an American Bank yourself?

If your American agent has power of attorney and can deposit a check made out to you, perhaps that would be safest.

According to our latest plans the August 15 date will be postponed to somewhere in the neighbourhood of September 1st. Anita Loos is sailing for Ireland next week to meet M.J. Molloy and interview the different casting possibilities he has turned up. She will want to meet you too, but you are not to infer that your position as Bartley is in any jeopardy.

Sincerely,
Peter White

A couple of weeks later there was great news about *Rain on the Wind*:

Macmillan & Co. Ltd.
9th August 1950

Dear Walter Macken,

As Lovat Dickson is on holidays, I sent a telegram yesterday to let you know that 'Rain on the Wind' has been chosen by the 'Daily Graphic' on the recommendation of Edward Shanks as the Book Find For September. They want us to publish it on September 13th to synchronise with the appearance of Mr Shank's review, and we are of course making effort to keep that date.

Mr Harold Macmillan is now in Strasbourg, but he asked me to say how pleased he was that the book was chosen, as, of course, we all were. He hoped that you would help the 'Daily Graphic' as much as you could with anything they might require for publicity purposes. I imagine that some of it may go against the grain, but this is one of the penalties of your growing fame, as you have already found in the case of the questionnaire from our New York house.

We had a photograph and a biographical note, and we have sent these to the 'Daily Graphic'. We have also given them your address, but we did not do this until we felt that the telegram had reached you and given you fair warning. I know that you must be very busy, so if we can help you in any way, please let me know.

I only take this opportunity of sending my own good wishes, not only for they success of the book, but for your coming conquest of Broadway.

Yours sincerely,
Thomas Mark

John McNulty was also a regular correspondent with my father at this time:

One Post Road,
Wakefield,
Rhode Island.
Saturday, August 20th

Dear Walter,

The occasion for writing this letter is that when we got back I told Brentano's bookstore to get 'Mungo's Mansion' and it came last night and I read it again. I had read it at Bunnyconnellan and by gosh, I had even more fun reading it the second time.

How are you and Peggy and Wally Óg and Ultan getting on? We speak of you often.

My story on the Irish excursion will come out in an early September edition of 'The New Yorker'. It isn't really a story, really but a series of small anecdotes, one of which has Ultan as the central figure – I hope you don't mind. I'm in fear that you will find my little yarns the stereotypical episodes noted by most of us Yanks. Just the same I'm going to risk sending you that story when it comes out.

Any chance of you coming to the States? If you do there's always a room (small and dully furnished mostly with Racing Annuals) where you could stay at our house at 325 E 72nd Street.

Regards to all,

John and Faith McNulty

John and Faith were unaware of the postponement to the start date of the play and in consequence, what was happening with the trip to America.

I think my parents were pleased that there was going to be a story in *The New Yorker* featuring me. The story was published later in a book called *A Man Gets Around*, where John writes about his first visit to Ireland, and that his father came from Lisdoonvarna in County Clare and his mother from around Ballyhaunis in County Mayo. He planned to visit both places but only visited his mother's home place. He also paid visits to Dublin, Waterford and Galway and finally ended up in Bunnyconnellan near Crosshaven where he met up with the Mackens:

Our last days in Ireland were spent at Crosshaven, which is near Cobh (pronounced 'Cove' and still called Queenstown by the crew of the 'Britannic', on which we were to sail back to the United States). At odd times during those days I recalled the dreamy notions I had before we left East Seventy-Second Street. My head had been full of all the things I had heard about Ireland from the time I was a kid, at wakes, and in songs about white cottages with thatched roofs and the smell of burning peat (I learned within a week or so to call it turf, not peat). After landing there and riding around the little island, only a couple of hundred miles from north to south and less than that from east to west, I always had a feeling that Ireland wasn't exactly what I had dreamed it would be. Yet it was – in a sentence or a phrase dropped by a passer-by, or timidly passed to me by a man next to me in a pub. Often I felt these were my people, although they did not know me any more.

At the hotel we stayed at in Crosshaven, there was a little boy, the son of Walter Macken, the actor and writer. The father was down for a couple of weeks from the Abbey Theatre, in Dublin, to play in Cork, which is about fifteen miles from Crosshaven. The name of the little boy was Ultan. That is a name you never hear in the United States. It is pronounced 'Oolthawn' with the accent on the 'thawn'. It is an old, old name, older than Patrick or Michael in Irish use, and to hear the little boy's mother, Peggy, say it was to hear a caress.

The place where we were staying was the Bunnyconnellan Hotel, nestled on the side of a hill from which we could look out at the splendid harbour of Cork. Sitting on a bench in front of the hotel, in one of the bursts of sunshine that space out the rain in Ireland, the little boy and I were looking out at the sea. Ultan, who is only five, was born on the coast of Galway, where they say the sea in a rage can be a most terrifying thing. Before us, there was an empty sea, where tomorrow the ship would be.

'Out there will be the "Britannic",' I said to him, 'and if you look out tomorrow you will see her. There will be no way of seeing us – it's too far to see – but we will be there, heading back to America.'

Ultan walked away and plucked idly at a flower in the border of the path. Then he came back to me, the stranger he had known for only seventy hours or so. He, too, was groping [sic], as I had long been, because he put his little hand on my arm and he said, in his beautiful Galway speech, 'We'll be terribly froightened for you tomorrow whin the loiner, and you in it, starts out into the big sea.'

A stranger I was, in a country I felt was my own, and a little bit of a boy, with a single sentence, ended all my groping – 'We'll be terribly froightened for you tomorrow …'

Meanwhile the delays to the production of *The King of Friday's Men* continued. The latest letter came from Michael Grace, the producer, rather than Peter White:

The King of Friday's Men Company.
October 13th 1950

Dear Mr Macken,

I must apologize to you for not getting a letter off to you sooner but getting the production of 'The King of Friday's Men' in shape takes every second and the days just seem to fly by.

We are working hard to get the production going within the next six weeks and opening the latter part of December here in New York. The one thing that is holding us up is the final choice of the director.

Mr Guthrie McClintic, Bretaigne Windust from Hollywood, Sir Cedric Harwicke are all available choices for immediate production and we also believe that Margaret Webster is. Among those who can do it pending a short delay and also want to do it are Peter Glenville, Maurica Evans and very likely John Ford.

We expect to come to a definite solution within the next ten days and at that time, we will give you a definite date for your departure and your stay over here. The ultimate form of the producing unit may be legally different, such as a partnership etc. as this is necessary for reasons of tax governing the theatre. Naturally, your contract with this office is valid as per our agreement of June 22nd 1950 and this office is looking anxiously forward to its splendid fruits. I was just up to Boston two days ago and happy to hear that Mr McClintic considered your performance one of the best he had ever seen on the stage.

In this, he coincides with Thornton Wilder as you may possibly know. It is on just such things as these, and the tremendous interest that our project is already creating, that we hinge our concepts and anticipate success. The reason I have not written earlier is because I know that you more than anyone else would like to see a satisfactory director, so that the play may be given its utmost here in New York. As I am very pressed for time, I wish you would show this to Mr Molloy and the chances are before the fortnight is out, you will either see me personally here or in Ireland.

Sincerely,
Michael Grace

John McNulty wrote in October as well. He was beginning to think that my father would not be coming to the States at all:

1 Port Road,
Rhode Island.
October 18th 1950

Dear Walter,

Thank you for your letter about the 'New Yorker' piece. You spoke so highly of the magazine that I must arrange for you to get it regularly – but of course I'm always putting off things like that – so don't expect it too soon. The little anecdote you told me about Ultan was very nice indeed [*I don't know what this anecdote was*] – and I hope he is well and all of you are.

I had Brentano's the booksellers get me Mungo and the friends who have read it are very praiseful of it, especially a fellow named Bill Keefe who is a Broadway fellow.

Are you going back to Galway to live for a while? I often wonder and so does Faith. Is there any more talk of you coming over here some time? One day when you have nothing else to do, write and let us know of these things. Meanwhile our fondest regards to you and your brood – Mackens abú.

Sincerely,
John McNulty

A very interesting letter arrived from M.J. Molloy in October:

Milltown,
Co. Galway.

Dear Wally,

I had a cable from Mike Grace today. He says that the rehearsals are
opening about the middle of November and the cable continues: 'Ask
Macken for four weeks extension of option on June 26th with me.
Cable this office.' This suggests that he wants you to cable him the
option extension, but I don't get what the hurry is about. An air-mail
letter will reach him in three or four days. Send it to the Office Secretary, 'King of Friday's Men Company', Room 906, 1619 Broadway.

Peter White was sacked at the beginning of September, and
since then I have had little news. A month ago, Grace alone had
raised $50,000 and the most likely directors are Guthrie McClintic,
or Bretaigne Windust.

Best wishes,
Yours sincerely,
Michael Molloy

P.S. Mike was to fly to Hollywood this week end to talk with
Bretaigne Windust; that is why I don't see what the hurry is about. It
is just Mike's little way of wanting everything by telephone, or cable;
which is all right for him. There has been trouble between Mike and
Mrs Dahlberg [*one of the play's backers*], not without reason on both
sides, I think.

Also in October, my father received a letter in Irish from Ernest
Blythe, his boss at the Abbey:

26/10/1950

A Bhaitéir, a chara,

Tá sé socraithe again gan 'Juno and the Paycock' a dhéanamh roimh

Nollaig. De bhrí sin, caithfimid tosnú Dé Mairt ag cleachtadh Professor Tim. Tá páirt ann duit-se. Mar sin, is dóigh liom go bhfuil
sé riachtanach socru láithreach i dtaobh an turas go Meiricea. Do
bheadh sé mí-shásúil bheith idir-eatortha nios sia. B'fhéidir go dti-
ocfá isteach ag caint liom amhaireach.

    Mise le meas,
    Earnán de Blaghdh

Translation:

Walter my friend,

It's settled now that we won't do 'Juno and the Paycock' before
Christmas. So we need to start rehearsals for Professor Tim on
Tuesday. There's a part in it for you. Therefore I think we need to
make an arrangement as regards the trip to America. It's difficult to
be between two stools any longer. Maybe you would come in and
talk to me tomorrow.

    With regards,
    Ernest Blythe

There were deep discussions into the night between my mother
and my father, as to how he should reply to this letter, with the
result that he sent a letter of resignation:

31 Ardpatrick Road,
Cabra.
Oct. 27th 1950

A chara,

Go raibh maith agat as ucht do leitir den 26ú. Táim ag macnamh ar
an scéal le fada, agus ar an mhí-shástach sa chaoi ina bhfuilfímid i
ngeall ar an turas go Meiriceá, agus sé mo thuairim nach bhfuil ach

bealach amháin sásúil as agus sé sin go néireodh mé as mo phost mar aisteoir sa Mhainistir.

Dhá bhrí sin cuirim chugat le seo fógra faoi go bhfuil mé ar éiri as an bhfoireann. Seo é an uair is fearr mar nach bhfuilim páirteach i ndráma ar bith i láthair na huaire, is ní raibh le déanaí, agus nilim páirteach i gcleachtaithe agus ni ghortóideadh m'imeachtachta an amharchlann nó an complacht.

Mise le meas,
Walter Macken.

Translation:

Dear Sir,

Thank you for your letter of the 26th. I have been thinking about my situation for a while now and the unsatisfactory position vis-a-vis my trip to America and it's my opinion that the only answer is for me to resign my job as an actor in the company.

As a result, I'm sending you my resignation with this letter. This is the best time for me to leave, as I'm not taking part in any play at the moment as I haven't been for a while, and I'm not involved in any rehearsals either so my leaving will not damage the theatre or the company at this time.

With regards,
Walter Macken

We were told by my parents that he had no choice, that he had to retire from the Abbey, but as Blythe's reply to his letter makes clear, he would have been happy to welcome him back when he returned from the USA:

27/10/50

Toisc a mhí-chinnteach is tá data do imtheachta go Meiriceá ba dheacair tú chur i ndráma a leanfadh, bhféidir go Nollaig. De bhrí sin ceapaim gur fearr mar shocrú tú éiri as an bhfoireann go seala-dach. Glacaim le do litir díorscoir ar an dtuiscint sin. Fé mar a dúirt leat, beidh fáilte romhat nuair a bheas tú saor chun teacht ar nais go dtí an bhfoireann.

Translation:

Because of the uncertainty of your trip to America, it was hard to cast you in any play that would last until Christmas. Therefore I think the best arrangement is for you to resign from the company on a temporary basis. I accept your letter of resignation on that basis. As I told you, you are welcome to come back to the company when-ever you are free to do so.

Judging from the correspondence it seems that my parents went to New York in November and while they were away, my father's mother, Granny Macken as we called her, took care of us.

Here is a letter from Macmillan which was sent to my father at the end of November, while he was in the USA. It was sent to his agent, Ruth May, who had been appointed on Macmillan's recommendation. They felt that now that *Rain On The Wind* was successful, he needed to have a literary agent, so they found Ruth May for him. She represented him while he was in the USA working.

Macmillan & Co. Ltd.
28th November 1950

Walter Macken, Esq.,
c/o Miss Ruth May,
83 Perry Street,
New York.

Dear Macken,

Thank you for your letter telling me that the moguls of Broadway
have ordered you to New York immediately. I know you must have
arrived safely, because you are one of the most fortunate men I have
met in a life-time. I have two further pieces of good news to give
you, one of which you may have already heard from the New York
Macmillan Company. I had a letter from Mr Latham this morning
to say that 'Rain on the Wind' has been chosen by the Literary Guild
for May of next year. This means a fantastically large circulation,
and a considerable sum of money for you, so that that cottage in
Connemara should now be within reach.

The other piece of good news is that the 'Reprint Society' here,
which distributes a book a month to 170,000 readers, has chosen
'Rain on the Wind' for distribution some time in 1952. The royalty
payable on these copies, which are supplied to members at a reduced
rate, is 2d, which will mean for you a minimum of £1,300. You will
have to start thinking of consulting a tax expert to make sure that
these payments are spread as much as possible.

I look forward to hearing news of how you are getting on in
New York. I begin to think that you bring good fortune, and that the
play is bound to be a success.

Yours sincerely,

Lovat Dickson

My father wrote an article for the Reprint Book Society magazine,
in England, around this time. This article summarises a lot of what
was going on in his life for the past ten years, but also demonstrates
his self-effacing humour:

The town of Galway in which I was born is divided into two distinct
halves, the townspeople and the Claddagh people. I was a townie
but I always admired the tall men of the Claddagh with their
black boats and their blue gansies. They seemed to me always to be

superior beings in every way. Some of their sons were at school with us, brainy boys with scholarships.

One always seemed conscious of the Claddagh in Galway. If you went for a walk along the promenade you would see the black sails on the bay. Any house in the town with an extra storey could view the Bay, always there would be the black boat coming or going on it. Someday, I said, I will try and write about the Claddagh and what it means. That was in the palmy days when you knew you were going to be a writer although you had nothing concrete to back it up except a scarifying short story written at the age of twelve which had actually been turned down by a well-known English newspaper. Imagine! I have never forgiven that newspaper. At seventeen the Abbey Theatre refused to put on a three-act masterpiece, and had the colossal nerve to return it, actually pointing out what was wrong with it. The only thing that was wrong with it that I saw was that it was written in longhand, all two hundred and fifty pages of it and that was the third writing. That was the time I abandoned writing for good.

I had the misfortune to be born with another talent, for the stage. I decided to indulge this when a cynical world couldn't see what it was missing, so while still struggling hard at school, throwing off education like a duck's feather, I became part of the small Gaelic Theatre in Galway where people had the vanity to produce plays in a dead language called Irish. The plays were good, only the best translated into Irish. Nobody much came to see them but we had a wonderful time trying to be concise in a spoken language, while thinking in basic English. The fact that original plays written in English were translated into Irish was a wonderful method of finding out the real meaning of the author's intention. I recommend to the student of Shakespeare trying to translate him into another tongue. He'll know exactly what he meant or he will end up in a lunatic asylum.

The writing business cropped up again when I made the discovery that I could actually type with three fingers. The art of typewriting was acquired by taking the portable typewriter in the theatre to pieces and putting it back together again.

First one had to get married because one loved the girl and her father didn't love me. Two happy years in London trying to sell insurance to people who spoke English with peculiar accents, totally unlike the correct way of speaking we Irish use. Two pounds ten a week and the slow acquisition of the gift of the gab. Those were lovely times, when Devon baskets were a shilling, cheese cakes two pence halfpenny, and turkeys nine bob a head.

We left London with a son and a second-hand typewriter so now there was really no excuse left. Went back to the first love, the Gaelic Theatre, and experimented to heart's content on account of being the boss. The most extraordinary plays found themselves being translated into Irish. In order to be original the boss had to write a few plays in Irish himself. The three-act plays earned him the colossal sum of £45. Decided that Irish was grand, but if you must eat then it would have to be in English. So wrote a play for the Abbey and a novel and another play and then, feeling that time was up, went and became a member of the Abbey Theatre players after eight years in Galway. Away from it all, one began to see the black sails on the waters of the bay at home.

One made comparisons between this poor metropolis and the place at home and I think that it was out of this bit of homesickness that the image of 'Rain on the Wind' grew. It had been tinkered with before in a play in Irish called 'Oighreacht na Mara' (Heritage of the Sea) which you will never read unless you have the Gaeilge. One found one had to abandon the Abbey Theatre to write the book, and having no money left had to go and act in a play on Broadway to try and keep the wolf away. Anyhow it was done.

For me it was a sincere effort to picture the background of a place I like, peopled by people I admire. I don't know what you will think of it, but some of the little people at home I like, liked it, and what was better still, got a kick out of it. The fact that you are reading it is incidental, pleasantly so, but incidental, because it was written for the little men at home, and that may be you too, because I think that should be the highest ambition of all of us, in these peculiar days, to be little men at home and let the atomaniacs [*those who write automatically with no feelings*] get on with it.

In New York, they were met by the producer Michael Grace, who had booked them into a hotel. When Michael told his brother Peter and his wife Marjory that they were in New York, they insisted on meeting my parents. (Peter was the chief executive of Grace Corporation, a multi-national company with thousands of employees.) They insisted my father and mother stay with them at their large house in Manhasset, Long Island. It was to this address that Lovat Dickson's next letter was sent, containing exciting news:

7th December 1950

Walter Macken Esq.,
c/o Michael Grace Esq.,
Tullaroan,
Manhasset,
Long Island.

Dear Macken,

Thank you for your letter of November 29th telling me of your call to the New York Macmillan office. By the same mail I had a letter from Mr Latham giving me his account of the visit and of the lunch you had at the office on the day following.

I gather from Mr Latham's letter that he told you the terms of the Literary Guild contract. This carries a guarantee of $30,000 on account of a royalty of 15 cents per copy and the guarantee covers a sale of 200,000 copies. The New York Macmillan office are entitled to half that amount, so that $15,000 will be transferred to us here. Under the terms of our contract with you, we are entitled to keep 20% commission on your one-half share of the proceeds, but my fellow directors are all of the opinion that we should try and help you as much as possible at this early stage of your career, and we propose therefore to keep only 10% of this amount, and 10% on the ordinary trade sale made in America. I hope this will please you.

Alas the Double Taxation Agreement between the United States and Éire has not yet been signed, so that you will not be able to claim exemption from tax, but perhaps by the time the money has been received the Agreement will have been signed. It has been on the point of signature for a long time, but something seems to be holding it up in Washington.

Miss Ruth May [*Dad's agent*] tells me that you not only have a large house, but a Cadillac car and chauffeur put at your disposal in America. You are doing very well, and I shall hope for a letter when you have the time telling me what you think of it all.

With all good wishes,
Lovat Dickson

Lovat Dickson wrote a further letter to my father in Long Island at the end of that same month:

29th December 1950

Dear Macken,

Thank you so much for your letter of December 20th, which I received when the office opened again after the Christmas holidays. I can well understand your feeling of unattachedness at being separated from your family for the first time this Christmas, and that feeling must have been especially accentuated by the rather brilliant gloss given to Christmas festivities in New York. I hope that rehearsals have started by now, and that your feeling of homesickness is mitigated to some extent by your work.

If the play settles in for a long run, I will enter a subscription for you to the airmail edition of 'The Times' which I believe arrives in New York within twelve hours of issue. 'The Times' isn't always right, and its Irish news is not as full as you would wish, but I dare say it will serve if you read it in conjunction with the American papers. I am sending you two copies of 'Rain on the Wind' and 'Mungo's Mansion'. Just let me know if you want any more.

With all best wishes for the New Year.

Yours sincerely,

Lovat Dickson

The King of Friday's Men had to be tested in smaller theatres in provincial areas, including Boston, New Haven and Rhode Island, before coming to Broadway and it was due at the Playhouse Theatre in New York on 21 February. My parents wrote to us regularly and here my grandmother replied to them in January 1951:

31 Ardpatrick Road,
Cabra.
January 24th 1951

Dear Peggy and Wally,

I received your letter. I'm glad you are both keeping well, you are sure getting some travelling around. However, we will not feel now until February then into May [*sic*] and you'll be home soon after that.

The boys are keeping fine, Thank God. You need not worry about that. You will be glad to hear that Ultan has not wet his bed now for over a week. I got him to pray to St Philomena every night; as he says his prayer, I say one too. It looks like as if she answered our prayers.

Let us know about the play. I keep on wondering how it will go over there. There is not much to write about, we never see anybody, nobody calls. The weather today is mild but there is no drying out as there is no breeze to dry the clothes. The girls in the chemist were asking for you, of course envying you, wishing they were in your place. I cannot think of anything else to say at the moment. Glad to know you are both keeping well. There was a small bomb thrown at the British Embassy here, because the British had sent Dutch army men to the north to be trained.

    Wally Óg will write tonight,

    Love Mother

On 29 January 1951, *The King of Friday's Men* opened in a Boston theatre. The cast included Rex O'Malley as Gaisceen, Maggie Mc-Namara as Una Brehony, Norma Crane as Maura Pender, and Frederic Tozere as Caesar French. The stage manager was Windsor Lewis. When my father was in these places, he was invited to give public talks, and he gave one in Boston on 11 February at the Copley Plaza Hotel, the subject was 'The Abbey Theatre and Present Day Ireland'.

While they were in America, my parents met up with what they called 'the aunts', my grandfather Walter S. Macken's sisters, who had all emigrated to the USA. Sabina Walsh, whose mother Margaret was one of my grandfather's older sisters, phoned them while they were in Boston and wrote them a letter to follow up her phone call:

162 Dermott Avenue,
Rockville Centre NY.
February 11th 1951

Dear Walter,

I was so delighted when I spoke to you on the phone that I fear I was a trifle incoherent. I know how joyful Mother would be. She was sceptical about you being in America. She planned to write but is too excited.

    Walter do not fear bombardment by your cousins here, as by and large they are not clannish. I am the exception – and also I know how very much it means to Mother. We anticipate seeing you and knowing you when you come to New York. In preference to staying at a hotel, you could stay here with us. We would love it and I think Peggy might prefer the suburban atmosphere to the metropolitan. Contact us when you arrive here. We will await your call eagerly.

Yours sincerely,
Sabina Walsh

P.S. This just occurred to me for clarification.
Walter Stephen Macken
Mary Jane Rodgers (grandparents)
Mary, Kate, Pat,
1883 Margaret (Sabina's mother)
Birdie, Nannie
Tom
1888 Walter – (your father –)
Michael
John (and Hannah (John's first wife)) (my godparents).

My parents were delighted to meet the aunts. Sabina organised a party and they all came to meet my mother and father. Many years later I learned that there was great anticipation among the aunts about meeting their brother's son. One of them told Sabina afterwards: 'He is a disappointment, he is nothing like his father, he is not as handsome or as outgoing as his father was, nor is he as good a singer.' Of course she never told my father this. It was a great experience for my parents to meet them and they became great friends with Sabina and her husband.

News came in February 1951 that a Dutch edition of *I Am Alone* had been published and on 21 February 1951, *The King of Friday's Men* opened at the Playhouse Theatre. My father felt it would be a flop; he watched as the cast was chopped and changed after each venue, trying to improve its prospects. The reviews of the play were harsh; here is an extract from one:

'The King of Friday's Men' (by Michael Molloy, produced by Michael Grace) is about as Irish as plays come – even out of Dublin's famous Abbey Theatre. It is a gaudily romantic period piece about a homely 18th century shillelagh fighter who turns up in the west of Ireland just as a great landlord is about to seize a pretty young peasant girl for his pleasure. When the girl (Maggie McNamara) pretends love for the brawny shillelagh-swinging Dowd (Walter Macken), he cheerfully whips the landlord's entire press gang. But though Dowd eventually wins the girl's love, the landlord schemes so that he does not win the girl.

A swashbuckling stage piece about the Ireland that ran more to liquor than to leprechauns, 'The King of Friday's Men' has some of the old Irish gift for words, while Dowd has some of the mighty human dimensions of folklore. And actor Macken, who first played the part at the Abbey, brings real vigour to it, and the smack and caress of Irish speech. But the play's snatches of racy prose do not offset its stretches of lumpish play-writing. Too often both untidy and old fashioned, it closed after four performances.

The letter telling him that the play was closing came from Michael Grace.

The King of Friday's Men Company.
February 23rd 1951

Dear Mr Macken,

This is the advise you that 'The King of Friday's Men' will terminate its run at the playhouse theatre on Friday night, February 23rd 1951.
Yours very truly,
Michael Grace

However, despite this play's failure, the excitement generated by my father's performance on the American stage generated two substantial offers:

Western Union to Walter Macken,
c/o Michael Grace, Manhasset NY.

Dear Mr Macken,

Cecil Beaton anxious to be in touch with you immediately regarding 'Gainsborough Girls'. Interested in you for part of 'Gainsborough'. Rehearsals in April, play to be produced Duke of Yorks London. Sherek producing no director yet. He wants to get script to you. As he is sailing Friday, time is of the essence. Would you call him tonight Sherry Netherlands Eldorado 5 – 2800 and call me tomorrow Plaza 9 – 7500 and let me know results of your conversation.
    Edie Van Cleve, Music Corporation of America

The second one involved a film company:

Congratulations by Western Union,
Burbank, California.
Walter Macken,
c/o King of Friday's Men Company, Playhouse Theatre.

Congratulations on your splendid performance. We have starring role in our next production which might be suitable for you. Please advise who we should contact for business negotiations. We urge that you delay any commitments until you have investigated our proposition.
    William Cagney of Cagney Productions INC, Burbank, California.

It must have been difficult for my father to turn down these kinds of opportunities. I think he phoned about both the theatre offer and the film offer. My mother told me how they received an invitation from a Hollywood production company and, when they accepted, a large limousine arrived outside their hotel to take them to the New York offices. The Hollywood moguls were determined to persuade my father to go to Hollywood. My mother's memory of the scene was very clear:

> He was surrounded by these small men in expensive suits chomping on cigars and offering him huge amounts of money to sign a contract. All I could see was him shaking his head to all of them, obviously refusing them. I was afraid he would be tempted and that he would actually take up their offers. They came over to me and they asked me what could they do. They explained that they were offering him substantial money terms and they would provide a house and they would fly the two boys over. My mother asked them then: 'Well what did Walter say, when you made these offers to him?' They looked shocked, 'Walter says that he is in the middle of a novel and he has to go home to Galway to finish it, can't you persuade him, Mrs Macken, it's a good offer.'
>
> 'No,' I told them, 'once Walter makes up his mind, that's it, there will be no change.' I was so pleased that he had made that decision, I dreaded the idea of going to live in Hollywood and I felt that his writing would suffer.'

The studio offered him a seven year contract on a salary of $40,000 a year and a free house and for that they wanted to give him starring roles in movies and promised that he would also be involved in writing scripts. I think it was an extremely brave decision but he had watched how Hollywood had previously dealt with writers and he knew from his friendship with Liam O'Flaherty that writers were not particularly valued. He was halfway into his fourth novel

– *The Bogman* – and he wanted to get back to finish writing it. The producers were shocked when he turned down their offer. They might have understood it if he had been going back to work at the Abbey, but when he told them he planned to go back to live in Galway and become a full-time writer, that was beyond their comprehension.

13

LIFE IN OUGHTERARD – WRITING AND FISHING

With the Hollywood meetings over and the play finished, my father and mother made plans to return home. I think that the Grace family bought their tickets for the liner. March was a bad time to cross the Atlantic and my poor mother was never a good sailor. It was so rough that she was confined to her cabin for the entire three-week voyage and could barely eat anything. I don't know whether they landed in Cobh or Southampton. When they arrived in Dublin, my father went to a garage, bought a new black Ford Anglia and drove to Galway. We knew they were coming home, but we were not sure of the date and there were no phones in houses then. All I remember is sitting on the footpath with my friend Paddy Mervin and, looking up, I saw a car approaching. I could see my father was driving and my mother sat proudly beside him. We were thrilled that they were home.

They must have written to Marjory Grace to thank her for her hospitality as she wrote back to them quite soon after they arrived home:

Gracefield.
April 24th 1951

Dear Wally and Peggy,

Thank you for your very welcome letters and I'm sorry the voyage home was so rough. I've heard about the North Atlantic in winter and I guess you got it at its worst.

I'm afraid after a trip like that we'll never get you to America again. But we miss you both so much, I hope the next visit will be real soon. But Peggy, bring the boys this time and we'll all have lots of fun. Everything is well here and I should say that everyone is well. My Peter was home for two weeks and is now back in South America again for the past four weeks. I'm hoping he'll get home very soon and be able to stay at home peacefully for a long time.

I wish I had more news of Michael to give you but the most I know is that he has fired most of his office and Patsy (whatever her name is with the British accent) is now his secretary. He is working again on his Fatima movie and I hope something comes out of it. He was away on vacation for a week but he is home now.

The children are all well, thank God, and growing every minute it seems. I wish I had some snaps of you, I'm so angry at myself for not taking any pictures while you were here. Please pray for us as I do for you both. God bless and love from,

Margie

While in America, my father and mother had been contacted by their former best man and woman, Gary McEoin and his wife Josephine. The following note from Gary was among my father's papers:

La Hacienda,
20 Vesey Street, New York.

April 27th 1951

Jo and I were as mad as hell that you never got in touch with us after promising you would when we called you on the telephone. But we are so happy at seeing merit recognised, especially when it is of the Irish and by the foreigner, that I am writing to you anyway to say God prosper and keep it up.

As for us, a lot of things have changed around us one way or another, but we haven't changed so much you'd notice since you were last staying with us.

Beir bua agus beannacht,

Gearóid Mac Eoin

Despite his rejection of the offers from Hollywood, after my father had returned to Ireland an agent from the William Morris Agency, Joe Magee, began to write to him about various offers of work:

William Morris Agency,
1740 Broadway,
New York.
April 30th 1951

Dear Wally,

I thought you might be interested in seeing the enclosed review [*of 'Rain on the Wind'*] which appeared in the 'New York Times'. It will come as no surprise to you that you are a smash hit. I am looking forward to reading it.

I hope things go well for you and Mrs Macken. I envy you the peace and quiet and leisure of Ireland.

With best wishes to you and Mrs Macken,

Cordially,

Joe Magee

Judging from the following letter, I think my father must have written to Macmillan telling them of his plan to work as a full-time writer in the west of Ireland:

16th May 1951

Dear Macken,

After I had your letter of April 30th, I wrote to Mr Latham asking him when the Literary Guild settled their account, and he answered me today that in the case of a selection, payment is made 90 days from the date on which the Guild first begins to distribute the book.

Since 'Rain on the Wind' was the May selection, payment is due about the 1st of August, and the money will probably, therefore be here at the end of that month. Your share of the payment will be somewhere around $13,000 – about £4,700. I thought you would like to have this information for the future plans of which you speak in your letter of April 30th.

Yours sincerely,
Lovat Dickson

Some weeks after Joe Magee's letter, a cable came from America with another offer to go to Hollywood for a movie part:

May 24th 1951

James Cagney Picture around June 1st four to five weeks asking if you can test in London immediately asking soonest be free leave for Hollywood also need age height where possible – reach quickest by wire or phone –
Joe Magee

Joe followed up the cable with an explanatory letter:

May 24th 1951

Dear Walter,

In explanation of my cable to you today, Cagney Productions is interested in you for a movie titled 'Bugles in the Afternoon'. The picture would be made in Hollywood commencing around June 1st. They would need you for four to five weeks.

If you are interested and can get free for this, they would like the following information: age, weight, height and where you could reached by wire or phone. Would you be agreeable to testing in London immediately? How many days before June 1st could you leave Ireland?

If you are available and interested, please cable us collect as soon as possible.

With best wishes to you and Peggy,

Sincerely,

Joe Magee

Five days later there came another cable from Magee:

29th May 1951

Plans changed Cagney Picture, would you come to Hollywood direct arriving no later than Thursday May 31, with deal subject to test and interview on arrival. Terms approximately $1,500 weekly on three to four week guarantee, plus round trip transportation for one only, if not acceptable after interview Cagney still willing to pay round trip transportation plus expenses if you got picture wife and children could follow later your expense advise immediately.

Magee

My father wrote in pen at the bottom of this cable – 'impossible'. He sent a cable back to Joe Magee once again stating that his wife and children must be included if he was to go:

Can test. Free fly Hollywood June 13. Conditions wife and two sons accompany. Age 36, height 5 ft 11 inches weight 186 lbs. Quickest wire Ardpatrick Road.

Macken

Hollywood did not respond positively to that request and so he did not go. As far as he was concerned, he was working towards creating a life where he could live full-time as a writer. He was incredibly disciplined and he immediately began finishing *The Bogman*. By 8 June he had written to Macmillan to tell them that he had finished the manuscript and received an encouraging reply:

Macmillan & Co. Ltd.
8th June 1951

Dear Macken,

I'm delighted to hear that you have finished 'The Bogman' and that the manuscript is on its way to us. We will look forward very much indeed to reading it, and I will get in touch with you as soon as several of us have read it and I can send you an opinion. I haven't any doubt that you have made a good job of it.

Yours sincerely,
Lovat Dickson

Joe Magee then wrote to my father about his rejection of the offer from Cagney productions:

June 12th 1951

Dear Wally,

I certainly understand your inability to drop everything and fly the ocean at Hollywood's command at such short notice. I am glad also that you understand my position as disinterested and unbelieving passer-on of information and mad requests.

Even though you missed this one, I felt certain another one would come along and just today we had further indication of such a possibility. The Cagney Productions have requested that we get some stills and background information for them, so if you have any pictures you might happen to have from the Abbey plus a full list of your theatrical past history, I should appreciate it. They have several other pictures scheduled and would like to think about you for them.

Let us hope we have more notice next time.

With best wishes to you and Peggy,

Sincerely,

William Morris Agency,

Joe Magee

An interesting letter arrived shortly after this from Virginia Patterson of Macmillan Company in New York. My father had obviously written to them about Hollywood's demands:

Macmillan Company,
60 Fifth Avenue,
New York.
June 19th 1951

Dear Mr Macken,

Mary and I got a good hearty laugh out of your account of the Royal Command from the screwballs, Hollywood division. You must really think Americans are really nuts. The next time you come over I am going to make a point of introducing you to some bank tellers, supermarket checkers, window box gardeners and train conductors.

I also enjoyed your comments about the review in *Time*!

Jay Tower always asks about you when I see her, and I report the titbits from your letters.

No, we are not sweltering, having had lots of very wet rain, but I suppose the streets will start to steam any minute. Ah, lucky you and Peggy in Ireland.

As ever, sincerely yours,
Virginia H. Patterson
Publicity Director

In 1951 my father became determined to find somewhere for us to live in the Galway area. He loved Galway and for him, it was the only place he wanted to live. He went to see a Galway auctioneer and eventually he was brought to see a house four miles from Oughterard. It was called 'Gort na Ganiv' and was owned by a lady called Countess Ruth Metaxa. My father decided there and then to buy it. It was going to cost £3,000. He rang Macmillan in London and they agreed by cable to pay him an advance on future royalties so he could buy the house:

15/06/51
London
We will advance three thousand on account of royalties writing – Macmillan.

Here then is the letter written the same day to my father:

15th June 1951

Dear Macken,

Thank you for your letter of June 13th. The house you have in mind sounds most attractive and I am so glad that you have found a place which suits you so exactly. I hope that the deal is going through without any hitch, and that you will soon be established there.

We are quite prepared to advance you £3,000 on account of your royalties so that you can complete the purchase whenever it suits you. As I gather from your letter that you are rather anxious about this matter, I have telegraphed you today confirming what I have said above.

Yours ever,
Lovat Dickson

He came back to Ardpatrick Road and told us all that he had bought a new house in Oughterard and gave vivid descriptions of the grounds, the beautiful shrubs and flowers, a hard tennis court, a forest and a boathouse on the lake. When his description ended, he still had not told us anything about the house itself. It became clear then that he had not actually taken more than a cursory look inside the house, he just loved the location and for him it was perfection.

My father received a letter from the Countess in June:

Gort na Ganiv,
Oughterard.
11.6.51

Dear Mr Macken,

I went to Moon's yesterday and I asked them for carpet prices to the size as those seen here by you. The prices were fantastic and I asked them to assess mine at today's values considering their age, etc. – would you consider the enclosed a fair price to charge? – an answer by return would oblige as time is passing and the cabbages and lettuces are in.

Yours sincerely,
Ruth Metaxa

Carpets:

Axminster	£30	Green
Wilson	£35	Blue
Axminster	£18	Green
Indian	£30	
	£113	

I realise that those carpets that my father bought from the Countess in 1951 are probably the same ones that I have in my house in Menlo to this day!

A further letter came from Countess Metaxa:

Gort na Ganiv.
20.6.51

Dear Mr Macken,

I understand from Mr Joyce that you might be interested in the carpets of the above, if you or your wife could call and see if you want anything in the furniture left, I would be glad as I am single-handed here; I'm going into a very small bungalow which I can't have until December. I will not need the large carpets or linoleum which were made specifically for the large rooms here – and I have to make plans for storage of same. Mr Joyce said you might be willing to put the annex at my disposal to store my stuff until December; as you wouldn't require, he thought, all the rooms at first – I shall be in Dublin on Tuesday evening next at the Gresham Hotel – could you or your wife meet me there to solve these difficulties of mine? It would perhaps save some time. I have just been reading your wife's account of my daughter's wedding [*written for the 'Connacht Tribune'*], it has made me wish to meet her again.

Yours sincerely,
Ruth Metaxa

While all this excitement was going on, my father had completed the novel he had started before the American adventure. His new novel, *The Bogman*, told the story of a young seventeen-year-old boy Cahal Kinsella who arrives at the train station in Ballinasloe, but there is no one to meet him as his only relative, his grandfather Barney, didn't bother to come to the station. Cahal is the bastard son of Barney's daughter and has been in an industrial school since he was young. Despite the harsh regime imposed by his grandfather, Cahal is glad to have somewhere to lay his head and to be living with a relative.

The novel's setting is confined to a small farming community in East Galway and is based on my father's memories of working there every summer with his Uncle Frank and his wife. It is also a tribute to his father who was in the industrial school from the age of nine to fifteen.

My father deliberately chose to make his principal character a songwriter or ballad-maker. Each chapter had a song at the beginning, and he wrote melodies for these, but sadly these have been lost. Here is the one he wrote for Chapter 23:

> The soft breeze will blow,
> Where the water hens play,
> The rushes will sigh at the turn of the day,
> The heron will call and the curlew cry
> By the free roamin' Ree in the evenan
> Ori ó, I will be,
> Far away, but I will see
> The wings of the swallows caressing the Ree
> When I'm closin' me eyes in the evenan.

The Bogman portrays a close community which doesn't really

accept this young man into their midst and he antagonises them
in the way he reacts to them. His publishers liked it:

Macmillan & Co. Ltd.
26th June 1951

Dear Macken,

I have not yet finished 'The Bogman', but I hope to do so by tomorrow. I cannot, however, even at this stage, refrain from sending you
a private note to say how magnificently I think you have done it.
It is immeasurably the best book you have yet written, and I hope,
indeed I am sure, that all my colleagues will agree with that view,
when I can write you officially about it.
  Yours sincerely,
  Lovat Dickson

P.S. Are you the author of the verse at the head of each chapter?
Don't tell me you are a poet – as well as actor, novelist, playwright,
angler!

The following day he wrote an official letter accepting the novel:

Macmillan & Co. Ltd.
27th June 1951

Dear Macken,

I am so happy to be able to tell you that we have now read 'The
Bogman', and we are all delighted with it. It strikes us all as being
the best book you have yet done. We are so glad to add still another
book of yours to our list. May it be the precursor of many more!
  I see that we have paid you the same royalties on the previous
books, but my fellow directors feel that we should improve the
royalty scale now, and we are suggesting to you 15% to 5,000 and

20% after. I hope you will be pleased with this suggestion. If you will let me know that you are, we will prepare an Agreement right away and send it to you for signature.

Have you a duplicate of the MS which we can send to the New York Macmillan Company? I am sure that they will be most anxious to do the book. They can wait for proofs, but they would much prefer to have an earlier sight of the MS. There are a number of important things about which I would like to talk to you, and I wish it were possible for you to come over to London soon. It would suit us here best if you could come for a couple of days in the two week period beginning July 9th.

I shall look forward to hearing from you, and I hope very much that it will be possible. Meanwhile congratulations from all of us here on 'The Bogman' – a very fine piece of work.

Yours sincerely,
Lovat Dickson

One other letter came from Mr Dickson concerning the ballads:

Macmillan & Co. Ltd.
29th June 1951

Dear Macken,

Your letter of June 27th has crossed mine of the same date. I thought all the ballads at the head of the chapters were delightful, most evocative of the Irish scene, and most musical to the inner ear. There were one or two which I thought especially good. I think we should mention in the prelims that the ballads are your own work. I will look forward to hearing you sing them one day.

Yours sincerely,
Lovat Dickson

During these summer months, my father received a series of letters from the English theatre director, Michael Powell. Michael Powell was one of the best theatre directors in Britain in the 1950s, he went on to make a number of very important films later on in his career. Obviously he had heard good reports of my father's acting and so he invited him to star in his next production scheduled for London's West End – *Heloise And Abelard* written by James Forsyth:

Milnton House,
Dumfriesshire.

My dear Macken,

I am delighted at your decision to concentrate on sea-trout: partly for selfish reasons, partly because I like to meet a man who doesn't need Hollywood, but whom Hollywood needs. Also sea-trout are good eating and catching them is good for the soul. We must talk about the two plays. Also about your career and Siobhan's [*Siobhan McKenna*], for which I feel partly responsible. Tell me your own movements during the next six weeks and I will arrange to meet you wherever you may be. I am free and of a restless disposition.

My regards to your wife. I am looking forward to meeting her again if she is just as attractive with her hair up.

Yours sincerely,
Michael Powell

A second letter from Powell arrived a short time later, where he makes fun of Jimmy Cagney's expectations that my father would drop everything and fly to Hollywood when asked:

Dear Mr Macken,

This is a country of two Roberts: the Bruce and the Burns. It is a country of long glens running up into the Galloway Hills, which are full of lochs and streams. John Buchan, in '39 Steps', described it well. The people are hard-working, practical, and a thought close

295

[*close-knit*]. Burns with his warmth and leaping imagination would have been happier in the Highlands and Islands than he was among his own folk. Does Burns interest you?

Jimmy Cagney ought to know better: he and his brother founded Cagney Productions: he claims to have Irish blood. The only way to answer his cable would be:

'Have gone fishing, please wish me luck?'

The 'please' is very important: it will appeal to them with the disarming old world flavour. I want to talk to you about both plays. Do you fly? Come and stay the week-end. Can your wife come, too? Fly to Glasgow and I will meet you at the airport. You only have to wire the flight number. I will return you to the airport on Monday when I fly to London.

Does this savour too much of Cagney Prods?

Michael Powell

I have a third letter from Michael Powell and it's obvious he decided to visit them at their new home in Oughterard:

Great Southern Hotel,
Killarney.

Dear Mr Macken,

I hope that the play arrived and that you read it: and that if you read it, you liked it. I wrote to Mr Elliman that I would like to put a play at the Gaiety but I haven't seen him yet. I don't think Kerry is comparable to Galway. My regards to your wife: I hope she forgives me for calling so unceremoniously. My address in London is:

146 Piccadilly WI.

Yours sincerely,

Michael Powell

Powell wrote to him again in June:

Somewhere in Orkney.
22–6–51

We saw the sun sink into the sea last night from the highest hill in Westray. It isn't very high. Time 10.39. It was the longest day of course. This is written on a steamer, feeling our way through fog to Sunday. Do you know the Orkneys? Very Norse.

I return to London about July 1st. It might be a good idea if you would come over to London to meet Forsyth. I would like his approval on Abelard [*his choice of my father to play this role*]. Then we could have a business-like talk and settle dates. If impossible for you to come I will send him over to see you. I can't leave London that week (expenses paid by me of course) – Answer to 146 Piccadilly, please, I will get it on my return.

I saw Siobhan in London but did not see 'Ghosts'. What a wonderful girl she is.

I hope by now you are a landed man.

My regards to your wife,

Yours sincerely,

Michael Powell

In July, my father went to London to see Macmillan, Michael Powell and James Forsyth. His letters were addressed to Ardpatrick Road so it seems likely that we did not move to Gort na Ganiv until either the end of July or the beginning of August. He was staying in his sister, Eileen's house and wrote to my mother:

18 Bourn Avenue,
Hillingdon Heath,
Uxbridge,
Middlesex.
Weds. 11 July 1951

My darling,

I suppose you got my wire yesterday. I can nearly feel your depression coming over here to meet me. There is only compensation as far as I can see that every time I am away from you, particularly for a long time I realise how much I really love you. What a confession from a middle-aged man. I can see no charm in woman unless you are around. This waiting around was practically unavoidable as I will tell you. The Macmillan business was all right. I can't quite understand why they wanted to see me. Some vague talk about income tax, but nothing important enough to have brought me over.

When I first came, I rang Michael Powell's secretary. She asked me if I could come to lunch with himself and Forsyth on Tuesday, I said yes. Then when I got to Macmillans they wanted me to go to lunch with them on Tuesday at their office. This I gather was an honour. So I dumped Powell's lunch. This caused confusion. Powell was a bit annoyed. Cheltenham is 90 miles from London, near Stratford-on-Avon where he's going to the Shakespeare plays. Anyhow Monday I met Mark and Heath (at Macmillans), after that I met Forsyth and had tea with him until six. He seems to be a very nice man with a strong Scottish burr in his voice. After that I went to Dickson's flat. His wife and son were away in a cottage he has near Isle of Wright. I had dinner with him – cold salmon – and I stayed talking with him until 10.30 when I got a bus out to Bourn Avenue (I had wired them). Got here at 11.30 and was talking to them until 1.30. I slept very little.

I thought about my wife. I dozed for an hour or two. I got up at 6.30. I shaved and went to mass with mother. I got into town at 12.00 I signed contract, etc. [*This is either the contract for the play or the contract for 'The Bogman'.*]

I heard from Powell. He said that he had to go back immediately to Cheltenham and he had to be there at 5. I said that was too bad but I couldn't do anything about it – that Macmillans were my bread and butter and I said if he liked we could call the whole deal off. He said could I call to his flat after the lunch for a minute. I said yes.

So I went to lunch with Harold Macmillan [*who became prime minister in 1957*], his son Maurice, Lovat Dickson and a Professor of Philosophy from London University. He reads a lot of heavy stuff for Macmillans, I gather. It was a stiff enough lunch. Conservatives depress me a little. Very nice of course. The best news of all is what I'm enclosing. Dickson gave me this. He shouldn't have given it to me or even told me about the name J.C. Squires. He is Sir John Squires and he is Macmillans' senior reader. His report is why there are all in a flutter about 'The Bogman'.

Don't show the report to Olive [*Gibson, a close friend*] or anybody. Dickson made me swear I'd show it to nobody but you. He would be excommunicated from the business if it was known he smuggled it out of the office. I enjoyed the evening with Dickson enormously. You'll like him. I've more or less settled that he will be bringing his wife and son over to us next August 12 months.

Anyhow I went over to Powell's flat afterwards. James Forsyth was there, no wives around. Powell only stayed for ten minutes. He asked me if I would go to Stratford to see three plays – 'Richard II', 'Henry IV' and 'Henry VI'. He would drive me back Saturday night after the play. I thought a while and then said 'Yes'. It's the only way of pinning him down and finding out what he is like. Besides I would like to go to Stratford and see a few Shakespearean plays and having seen them would be able to see what their standards are like.

London is the same as ever – I might enjoy it a bit if you were with me, but it's driving the lesson deeper and deeper about how right we were right to go back to Gort na Ganiv. If we do come and do a play here, I'd say it would be the very last. If it should prove unbearable to us then we would cry halt. If 'The Bogman' does well there won't be any need anymore.

You know I love you. I only know myself how really deep it is when I am away from you. I don't know why I'm sure but there you are. I think of you a lot and I get quite excited when I think of getting back to you. Don't be too lonely. I will write to you again and should be home on Sunday at 12.00 It's like an evening star in the distance. Powell will be lucky if I don't call off the plays. That's the way I feel now. Tell Wally Óg and Chicken that I love them. I will see you on Sunday, Thank God and love you.

    Your husband,

    Wally

Every time I read my father's letters, I get a clearer idea of what he really believed about acting versus writing. My mother told me that when he was giving a talk in Boston or New York, he told his audience: 'I love my writing, but I lust after the theatre.' There is little doubt that if had a choice, he would concentrate totally on writing and would not have acted any more. Unfortunately, economic circumstances resulted in his having to work as an actor a few times during the 1950s and into the 1960s.

Here is another letter written by my father to my mother and posted on the 15 July 1951:

The George Hotel,

Shipston-on-Stour,

Warickshire.

My darling,

You can see the kind of country this is from the name of the town. It is some miles from Stratford-on-Avon. Everything is 'on', 'over' or 'under' something else. It is the Cotswold country. Small villages with houses built with black beams and small leaded windows, it's very pretty. I got here yesterday at 5 p.m. It took three hours from London to get here. Michael Powell was to be at the station. Of course he wasn't but I hardly expected him to be so it didn't matter. He arrived fifteen minutes later. His wife was with him. She seems to be just like himself going into long silences. I think they are very well matched.

We went to see 'Richard II' last night. We had been at the

producer Anthony Quayle's house beforehand. I will tell you about that again. Michael Redgrave was doing the part of Richard. I thought he was terrible. I didn't think much of the whole outfit. I'll talk about that when I get back.

I got up early this morning and went looking for a Catholic Church – but they were all Protestant, Baptist, or Friends of Presbyterian. I had been at mass in Brompton Oratory in London yesterday morning at 7.30 a.m. It is not far from Michael Powell's flat. It's in Kensington. I stayed there Wednesday night. Nobody in it except James Forsyth. James is very nice. I still like Powell. He has a wonderful library. Most of the books you would want to read. I'm not sorry I came now. It's interesting country and so 'English'.

Needless to say, I am looking forward to going home, even though it is only Ardpatrick Road. I hope you haven't missed me too much. I'm dying to see you again. Give my love to the two sons. Are they mad at me? It won't be long now, when you get this letter, I will practically be there.

You have all my love,
Your husband,
Wally

The contract for *Heloise and Abelard* arrived in September. Rehearsals for the play began on 26 September. My father told me that the rehearsals were painful as the weather was hot and they were wearing heavy costumes. The tour commenced in Southsea on 22 October and then the play would open three weeks later in the West End. His salary was to be £50 a week along with expenses. The play ran for about four weeks in the Duke of York Theatre in the West End and then my father returned home. More opportunities for acting roles kept coming to his door. One company wanted him to play a part in Seán O'Casey's play, *Purple Dust*, in America, then came a telegram asking him to take the part of a gentle gunman in a film due to be made at Ealing

Studios, but this fell through. He also went back to the Abbey at some stage during the 1950s to play the part of Bartley in a revival of *The King of Friday's Men*.

14

DAILY LIFE IN THE 1950s

When I read about the 'depressing' 1950s I cannot believe it. For us living in Oughterard the 1950s were a never-to-be-forgotten period. For my father in particular, it was a wonderful era. *Rain on the Wind* being published in 1950 had allowed him to give up a weekly wage packet and concentrate on earning his living as a writer. It was (and still is!) very difficult to rely totally on writing to earn a living. My mother often told me how hard my father found living without the security of a weekly wage packet.

I think that we moved to Oughterard either the end of July or the beginning of August 1951. As a boy of seven, the journey seemed to me to be very long. We set off from Ardpatrick Road very early in the morning and it took hours to reach Galway. Then the final part of the journey to Oughterard and the trip out the narrow road to Glann, the name of the area where we lived, seemed to take forever to my mind. I seem to remember that when we drove into Gort na Ganiv, it was about 2 a.m.

I will never forget that first morning waking up in Gort na Ganiv. I got up, dressed and walked out the back door. The sun was shining, and I began to explore. There were two sheds at the back of the house and then through the bushes, I spotted a sort of path running up through the hedges. I pushed my way through and discovered the path lead up to a concrete tennis court. There was even a little tennis pavilion where spectators could sit and drink lemonade and watch the matches. Behind the tennis court, the path led to a gateway to our own forest. It looked huge to me, it was about an acre with a wide range of trees. I even noticed one tree that was bent down towards the ground in such a way that you could sit on it and ride it like you were riding a horse.

After I had explored the forest, I turned my attention to the orchard which stretched back towards the house. There were almost a hundred fruit trees, cooking apples and eating apples, pears, rows of raspberries and a bed of strawberries. There was a huge lawn in front of the house and then to the right-hand side there were hidden gardens that we called the Upper and Lower Glades. It was a wonderful place for a young boy to grow up.

My father soon established his own daily pattern in Gort na Ganiv. We got up every morning at about 7 a.m. My father and mother, coming out of their bedroom coughing, would wake me up – they were both very heavy smokers. There was a washing and shaving routine and then we set off for morning mass in Oughterard. My parents were daily mass-goers and so we always went to 8 a.m. mass. After mass, we went to the local shop where my father bought the *Irish Press*. We were back at home about 8.40 a.m. and then had breakfast. My father read the newspaper from cover to cover and then he left us in the kitchen. He went into what we called the living-room, where he had his typewriter on the large table, and closed the door. He walked around the table smoking cigarettes and working out what he was going to write.

In my memory, I see myself and my mother waiting anxiously in the kitchen. My mother would actually be saying a few prayers to herself aloud, but I have no memory of my brother being there during these morning sessions. When we heard the typewriter going my mother would say a prayer of thanks! My father typed for maybe half an hour or three-quarters of an hour. Then he would open the door and call out – 'Peggy'. My mother went in to listen to him reading the piece he had just written. She was his first audience and he always watched her keenly to see her reaction. When Peter died in *Rain on the Wind*, she cried. 'Ah,' my father said, 'it's working.'

He then worked in the garden during the afternoon and there was always a walk. In those first months, my mother was often too busy to accompany him and so I was his walking companion. We would leave the house and walk up the road a bit until we came to what was called the old road to Oughterard, and there were wonderful views of Lough Corrib and the islands stretching towards the horizon. My mother always had lunch ready at 1.30 p.m. and tea at 6.30 p.m. At night, my parents sat in the living-room, reading books.

There was a huge amount of hard work to do with the gardens. My father, with help from local men, built concrete footpaths right around them. We sowed vegetables and of course he went fishing on Lough Corrib. He spent his first season on the lake in 1951–52 going out with local man, Paddy Mons. Once the season began on 14 February, they tackled the lake most days and were sometimes called 'bellmen', because they used long lines attached to a plain wooden rod. On top of each of the rods there was a little bell and when a fish struck their bait, the bell rang.

They used a small version of a Corrib boat, called a punt, suitable for one person.

There was a pattern to their fishing season. The first few months was called the 'bricín' season. As bait, they used small little fish, 'minnows', which were readily available in the streams right around Lough Corrib and kept alive in a tin can until they were used. Professional fishermen earned a living from the lake – when they caught fish they brought them into local dealers in Oughterard and the fish were picked up by train and taken from Oughterard to Galway and from Galway to Dublin and could be on sale in Billingsgate, London, the following day.

By the second season, my father had his own boat and knew the best fishing areas in the lake and I would go with him. As soon as I hooked my first trout and landed it, I was hooked on the sport. I often fished on school days with my father's consent and he wrote letters of regret to the school principal. The season was as follows: bricín fishing from February through March; fly fishing March/April; dapping with the Mayfly to the end of May; then fishing for the summer salmon (grilse) in June/July and Harry and Daddy Long Leg dapping in August /September.

Before leaving Dublin, my father had completed *The Bogman*, which had been very well received by the publishers. Once he had finished writing *The Bogman*, he began writing what would become his best known play – *Home is the Hero*. It was first staged by the Abbey Players at the Queen's Theatre, Pearse Street, Dublin on 28 July 1952 (they had moved because of the fire at their own theatre). The kernel of *Home is the Hero* is the story of Paddo O'Reilly who was imprisoned for five years for the manslaughter of a neighbour, killed in a drunken rage. As the play opens, the family are anxiously waiting for him to come home. It's clear the family had a difficult time while he was away in prison and had to take in two lodgers, an old drinking friend of Paddo's, Dovetail, and his wife Bid. Also in the house is Paddo's son, Willie, who has a lame leg and taught himself to become a cobbler, and his daughter Josie, who has smart alecky boyfriend, Manchester Monaghan. Under the influence of Bid, his wife Daylia has begun to take an odd sup of alcohol.

The play opens with Dovetail excited about his friend coming home and he wants to make sure that there is a big welcoming party for him at the station. Paddo avoids the crowds and comes quietly into the house. Paddo is a different man to the man who went away and wants nothing to do with Dovetail or any of his friends. He objects to his wife drinking and he is shocked to find out that Dovetail and his wife are actually living with them. He is very angry when he learns that Josie is seeing Manchester Monaghan and he is equally horrified to find out that Willie is going with Lilly Green, the daughter of the man he killed. That original Abbey Theatre production was the most successful run of one of his plays and ran for seventeen weeks. Up to the 1960s and the arrival of Brian Friel's plays, it held the record for the longest-running play in the Abbey.

Reviews for *The Bogman* in both England and America seemed to suggest it was destined to be successful, but there was disappointment again at home, as once again this new novel was banned. My father was deeply hurt; again the basis on which it was banned seemed to be that there is some suggestion of a sexual encounter between a traveller wife and Cahal. And of course at the end of the novel, Cahal leaves his wife and goes away with his true love Máire – an unmarried woman.

I talked to my father once about *The Bogman* and what he was aiming to do with the story, as he had planned to write a sequel. He asked me what I would do about the ending of *The Bogman* and I said that I would kill off the old woman.

'Ah,' he told me, 'that's where you are wrong, I plan to kill off the young woman.'

The success of *Home is the Hero* led to talk of it being staged in America and there were a lot of conversations and letters and telegrams about it. Finally in January of 1954, a concrete proposal was made when the Theatre Guild in New York decided to produce it:

The Theatre Guild,
23 West 53rd St,
New York.

Directors: Therese Helburn Laurence Langner, Armenia Marshall
January 18th 1954

Dear Walter Macken,

Again you must forgive me for being so long in answering your letter. We had our cast fairly well lined up but were delayed and then disappointed by the director. It is now so late that we think it is unwise to open this season.

We now think it would be much wiser to open early next fall with the chance of a long run. We can set the director now for an early date and would like to go into rehearsal around the middle or the end of August, opening out of town in September and coming in to New York at the end of September or early in October. This will also give us the chance to get the right theatre for New York.

We all very much want you to play Paddo, and I hope this will make it easier for you to do so, since it will give you time perhaps to finish your book, dispose of your sons and to get away without too much difficulty.

We are trying to communicate with Miss May, but she has not yet returned from Europe. If she is abroad now, perhaps you will see her. We are also contacting Joe Magee and advising him of our change of plan and our desire to have you with us in September, but please let me hear from you direct as soon as possible.

I hope you will be able to come. I personally can think of no one who would be as right for the part as you are.

Sincerely,

Therese Helburn

Good fortune came in March 1954, when the US Treasury Service decided to pay back the taxes he had paid in 1951–52, and he received a cheque for $6,202.78.

He completed the manuscript of his fifth novel, *Sunset on the Window Panes*, which he had begun in spring 1953. The principal character is Bart O'Breen, a tough young fellow who always gets into trouble. The world he creates come alive on the pages so much so that you think you actually know the people.

His friend Lovat Dickson loved it:

Macmillan & Co. Ltd.
11th March 1954

Dear Walter,

I should know better after twenty-two years of publishing, but after reading half 'Sunset on the Window Panes', last night, I cannot refrain this morning from writing you a note to say that I think you have really pulled it off this time. I read until the early hours of this morning, and found myself to be completely gripped throughout. It seems to me to be far the best book you have written, and I cannot tell you how delighted I am. All this is most irregular. I should wait until several readers and Directors have read it and give you the consensus of all their views. However, it is impossible to control my enthusiasm, and you are the man to whom I want to impart it.

There are so many things I would like to talk to you in connection with this book: the title for instance, the American market, possible serial rights, time of publication, and a host of other things. I wonder is there any chance of you and Peggy coming to London for a few days? If it is a matter of finances, let me know and I will see what my fellow Directors think of that. If it is a matter of leaving the boys, then I will understand if you cannot make it and will write about everything – though how much I should prefer to talk to you.

Yours ever,

Rache Lovat Dickson

From this time on Lovat Dickson starts using his popular name Rache, when signing letters to my father. He was so enthusiastic about the new novel that he wrote a follow-up letter the following day:

Dear Walter,

I finished 'Sunset on the Window Panes' at an early hour this morning. It was a tremendous finish. I do congratulate you. I think it is a wonderful story and will be remembered for a long time. The title is absolutely right, of course, the end of the story makes that clear.

I wish I could convey to you how much moved I have been by this story. It had a tremendous effect on me, and I think it will have on all its readers. The characterisation is so consistent: one sees so at the end looking back. I cannot suggest a change throughout the book except that part in Chapter 19 where Breeda tears up Bart's letter and throws it into the sea and then the pieces come together again to form the 'tumbled words and sentences' and you get a further bit of Bart's story. I do not think I would have the end of this chapter, but this is a point we can talk about.

The MS will now be read by my colleague, Thomas Mark, and he will prepare it for the printer. Meanwhile we will be getting a contract ready and will send it to you for signature.

Yours ever,

Rache Lovat Dickson

Meanwhile the Theatre Guild was making arrangements for the staging of *Home is the Hero* on Broadway. It was very common to get telegrams rather than phone calls when someone in America wanted to contact my father. The following was one such telegram, which was sent on 4 June 1954:

Worthington Minor directing Hero, he and we want you for Paddo could you hold yourself available to start rehearsals on either August 15 or 22. Do you know Dinah Sheridan age and ability and can she play with Irish accent, who played Dovetail there and any other suggestions besides Barry Fitzgerald, please reply immediately. Will confirm definitely within two weeks also could you airmail photo of Irish stage set. Thanks and greetings – Therese Helman

Following on this invitation, my father agreed to go to New York, because a week or so later, on 15 June, the following piece appeared in the *New York Times*:

Temporarily stymied in getting a leading man for Walter Macken's Irish drama, 'Home is the Hero,' the Theatre Guild is furtively eyeing an ace up its sleeve to solve the problem. It is trying to persuade the author to portray the chief role, for which Thomas Mitchell was last mentioned. An actor since his salad days, Mr Macken gave a sample of his histrionic ability in the swashbuckling lead in Michael J. Molloy's, 'The King of Friday's Men' seen here briefly in 1951.

If all the loose ends are tried up firmly, count on 'Home is the Hero' being the Guild's first local entry of the 1954–55 season. One thing is set though, C. Worthington Minor, who hasn't been associated with the Broadway stage since 1940, will grip the directorial reins.

My Dad wrote to Sabina Walsh on 12 July to tell her that he and Peggy would be in New York on 15 August and he hoped to see her and her family when they arrived. He told her that Cyril Cusack had invited him to go to Paris in July to play the part of the old man in *The Playboy of the Western World* at an international theatre festival. He declined the invitation as he told Sabina in his second letter, sent to her at the end of July:

Gort na Ganiv,
Oughterard,
Co. Galway.
July 28th 1954

My dear Sabina,

I didn't go to Paris. I didn't like the play. Instead, Peggy and myself and the two boys went on a tour of Switzerland and Italy. We had a marvellous time, used all our money. Otherwise I would hardly be going to act in New York even if it is in my own play. We expect to fly over on the 14th of August. Rehearsals are to start on the 16th. When we meet you can expound all the great mystery. My agents have booked a room for us in a hotel. I don't know where as yet but will get in touch with you.

   With regards to Peter and the family.
   Sincerely,
   Walter

PS. By the way the play is my own play – 'Home is the Hero' and it's to be directed by C. Worthington Minor – do you know of him?

Another telegram came from the Theatre Guild, this time spelling out that the play would open in Westport on 23 August, with a New York opening shortly afterwards.

My father received two letters from actors in August wondering was there any chance they could be offered a part in the Broadway production: Brian O'Higgins who had played the part of Paddo in the Abbey wondered if he could act as understudy to my father, while Jack McGowran, another Abbey actor, who was finding it difficult to get work, asked to be considered for the part of Willie. A letter came from my father's theatre agent, Joe Magee, posted on 12 July:

William Morris Agency.

Dear Walter,

It was good to get your nice letter and we are all looking forward to your arrival. Rehearsals begin in New York about 10 a.m. on August 16th and continue for two weeks. Then you open at the Westport County Playhouse, Westport, Connecticut for a one week try-out there the week of August 30th, then either to New York for the Broadway opening tentatively set for September 30th.
    Best wishes,
    Joe Magee

My father wrote a rough note to himself, names of people that he would like to meet: Lee Strasberg, Julian Compton and Clifford Odets [*prominent American theatre people*]. In a second letter, Joe Magee suggested that my parents could rent his apartment for $200 a month. I do not know whether they did that although it strikes me that it was probable. While they were in Westport, they met another first cousin, Rita Joyce, for the first time and she became a good friend of theirs.

The play opened in Westport on 30 August and among the cast was Glenda Farrell as Daylia, Richard Lupino as Willie, Peggy Ann Garner as Josie, Frances Fuller (Worthington Minor's wife) as Mrs Greene, J. Pat O'Malley as Dovetail and Christopher Plummer as Manchester Monaghan. My mother told me how Chris Plummer regularly sat her down to talk at him so that he could learn a proper Irish accent.

The play opened at the Booth Theatre on Broadway on 22 September.

My parents were in America from 14 August until nearly the end of November. Wally Óg and I primarily stayed with our relatives in Galway; I think we spent some time with the Kennys in Salthill and the rest of the time with the Lohans in Woodquay; both families were relations of my mothers. Every week my father wrote and included a US dollar for me.

When they returned to Galway my father began a period of great productivity and he wrote the following article analysing his work which I found among his papers:

I believed that my first work would set the world on fire. I knew that first novels rarely became best sellers (outside of America) but I now know that each writer considers himself a special case. It's the egotism that keeps you going. In few other professions is your ego in for the mangling it's due to receive just when you think everything is lovely.

Your poor ould ego is due to be kicked and battered and despised and spat upon and sat upon and jumped on from a height. So at the time when you think everything is going to be fine, you wake up and find you are farther back than when you started. You will never again have that untarnished beautiful knowledge that everything you write is perfect and is going to be greeted warmly immediately it is released.

When my first play and my first novel had been launched with moderate success, about one millionth of what it deserved. I had to sit down and set to, considerably shaken, feeling that my faith in myself was on very unsolid ground. I wrote two novels containing almost a million words. I knew they were trash before anybody told me. They told me. My second published novel was on the cautious way back. I believe I have steadily improved since that. I believe this cautiously, keeping my fingers crossed as I think it. I am now very critical of what I put down. My fractured ego is recovering. It will never be the same. It will always show the marks.

I believed that the people among whom I was born in my own home town were the people to write about. They weren't people who were well off. They had to struggle for their food, their clothes and their relaxation. I was interested in everything about them and me and where we lived. But would other people in other lands be interested in me and my people. I didn't really give a damn. They were, because people are the same everywhere, as delightfully unpredictable in a Galway street as they are in a small town in America or England or France. So you put your money on the people you know and they will win out. I still believe this, that a writer should write about the things and the people he knows. He should write so that the people he knows would get a kick out of what he writes if they ever bothered to read what he writes about them, which they probably won't.

Once a writer starts writing so that people in a foreign place get a kick out of what he is writing about his own people, he is on the way out. He is getting tired. It is easy for a writer to get tired in Ireland. People in Ireland have very little respect for Irish writers. They write them off. They ban their books. Three of my novels are banned in Ireland. I can't tell you what a hurtful thing this is. You are supposed to be artistic and laugh it off. A good joke. You are supposed to talk about clodhoppers and jumping Jesuses and craw thumpers, but I must confess (is this literary weakness) to be hurt and bewildered every time they ban one of my books.

You are writing for your own people. What's going to happen if they stop your own people from reading you. Is your writing as they say indecent and/or obscene or is this in their own minds, or are they reading excerpts out of context like picking out the dirty bits from the Bible. I don't know.

But I still believe that you should write for and about your own people. I believed writing would be a great adventure. I still believe this. Once you have reached the stage of reason where you can let your mind wander over a story, and be stuck with it and can't go on. Day after day, month after month and you see no resolution. And then in the middle of the night when you awake from the tail end of a dream, or when you are out walking on a city street, or catching trout on a lake, it comes into your mind, so clear and so real, the solution you wanted, that quite likely you will say out loud, I have it! I have it! And if there is somebody with you looking at you with wide eyes it will be a bit of an anti-climax to try and explain what you mean, you probably won't, but there is a great river of joy inside you that lasts until the next depression. The next depression begins when you have to sit down and write out what your brain has already written.

You will find many excuses to avoid this writing business. The weather will be heavy or there will be a few jobs to do around the house, or the fishing will at that point become particularly good and you just have to go and get a few fish while they are on the take, or you have a cold coming or you don't feel so well or you have some urgent books to read that must be read at once. There are a million excuses but eventually you will have to be drawn to that typewriter and when you sit down and get going, you will wonder why you have been fighting so hard against the inevitable, and why is it that each time you get away from it, you have the same struggle to get back with it. At times like this you so envy the writers you read about in interviews who go to their studies each morning at six o'clock and work steadily until breakfast time at nine. Then back to work at ten and quit at one, having completed six solid hours of writing.

They never deviate from this, four to six hours a day. You can envy those writers and pray that you may emulate them because after the first fine rapture is over, every instinct you have will be crying out for you to go the contrary way. I think you will have more fun being contrairy [*sic*] if that's bad advice, I can't help it. I'm sticking with it. Apart from all that, you know yourself in your own head where you are going, and nobody can stop you from going there. You know when you are good and when you are bad. Deep down in you, you know all the answers and you will keep sending them out until your well is dried and that will be when you are six feet under or a handful of ashes scattered on a hill.

Details of his earnings from the American production of *Home is the Hero* were sent to him as follows:

Dramatists Guild,
6 East 39th St.,
New York.

Gentlemen,

Enclosed is the statement and our check covering the balance due to Mr Walter Macken on 'Home is the Hero'. The check is made out to his agent, Miss Ruth May Bendukov at the instruction of Mr Macken. The check represents the following:

Sept 5 Westport	$875.61	Gross	$11,756.10
Sept 25 NY	$621.47	Gross	$ 9,214.72
Oct 2 NY	$675.30	Gross	$ 9,752.99
Oct 9 NY	$701.64	Gross	$10,106.41
Oct 16 NY	$958.29	Gross	$12,582.94
Total			$3,832.31
Less advance			$2,100.00
			$1,732.31 (check enclosed)

Statements for the Westport engagement were sent to Miss May, statements for Sept 25th and Oct 2nd were sent to the Dramatists Guild and I enclose statements for Oct 9 and 16.

If any further information is needed, let me know.

Sincerely yours,

Margaret Becher (Bookkeeper)

In November, my father wrote a letter to Sabina Walsh, his first cousin in New York:

Gort na Ganiv.
November 13th 1954

Dear Sabina,

Peggy is of course completely ruined on me. My counter-reformation assaults are moving very slowly. We have had to give up window shopping. Anything she sees under £50 – she just scoffs at it. We haven't got the new car yet. We gave up the old Ford and decided to buy a small car for Wally Óg. We did and now we are stuck with it because Wally Óg can't get insurance cover until April when he will be 17. But we managed to put the fix in and got him a licence.

All the days are passing in a sort of Celtic Dream. My old typewriter gave up the ghost at last and it takes years to get a new one – so I have a great excuse for not working. I'm afraid that new typewriter will turn up any day now. Ruth May has been fired. I have a new agent now [*Don Congdon*] and he is panting to perform and I have nothing for him to sell … The station is of course not a station [*station mass due to be held in our house*]. They call it that. The main purpose is to say mass in homes that are far away from churches so that the old and the feeble may have a chance to get mass and Holy Communion either in their own homes or in the homes of a neighbour. It is a terrific privilege for us that he will say mass in our home. It will never happen again because it is principally a privilege of the poor. I told the priest that I could always qualify under that heading, but it is decent of him to grant us the opportunity.

The people of the neighbourhood, five or six families come to the mass and they get a cup of tea afterwards. If you are not joking about coming, I can't tell you how pleased we would be to see you. I have sent you page proofs copies of 'Sunset on the Window Panes'.

All my love,
Walter

It's not clear why my father changed his American agent at this point.

My father's cousin, Rita Joyce wrote long and detailed letters to my father and mother. Here is one of my father's replies:

Gort na Ganiv.
January 25th 1955

Dear Rita,

Thank you for your letter. I'm glad you liked the book [*he had sent her a copy of 'Sunset on the Window Panes'*] and pleased you wrote and said so. It's encouraging to know that here and there; there are a few people who like what I'm trying to say.

We are very pleased to get home. It's wonderful to sink into the old routine and watch the elements. We had a very bad winter since we came home, rain and floods and recently snow and frost, with pipes bursting and cars sliding. We are not used to weather like that so we are not geared up for it like Americans. Now the weather is grand and mild and there seems to be a suspicion of spring in the air. Very soon we will be on the lake fishing for trout and I will have to be resisting the temptation to fish unless I have done enough to earn our daily bread. I'm sure all around you is lovely in the spring with all those woods ready to burst.

Give our love to your mother and the rest of the family we didn't meet. I don't know when, if ever, we will get to America again, but I am sure (no matter what your mother says) that even if it is twenty years she will still be there to chat us.

> All the best from the lot of us,
> Yours sincerely,
> Walter

In the summer of 1955, there came great news from his new American agent, Don Congdon:

> Harold Matson Company,
> 30 Rockefeller Plaza,
> New York 20.
> June 22nd 1955
>
> Dear Walter,
>
> I'm delighted to report that Randy Williams of Macmillan wants to go ahead with a collection of short stories. He says: 'We've read them with interest and genuine enthusiasm and while some are considerably better than others, that's as might be expected in a collection of short stories.' He says that he has worked out a plan for all the stories we have sent along. I am asking him for a formal list for the record. This I'll send along to you when I get it.
>
> The terms offered are $750 advance on signing, royalties of 10% on the list price to 5,000 copies, 12 and a half percent on the next 2,500 and 15% thereafter. If you're agreeable I'll forward the contract. They also want to have an option on your next novel. I hope that's all okay with you.
>
> Yours sincerely,
> Don Congdon

More concrete news came in August 1955:

> The Macmillan Company,
> New York.
> August 11th 1955

Dear Mr Macken,

Before we proceed to place your book of short stories, we should like to know in what order you would like to have the various stories appear in the book. For your convenience, these are the names of the stories:

The Proud Man, Gaeglers and the Wild Geese,
The Young Turk, Duck Soup,
Green Hills, The Curragh Race,
Barney's Maggie, The Fair Lady,
The Gauger, The Wasteland,
The Atheist, Tuesday's Children,
Hallmarked, The Lady And The Tom,
The Eyes of The Cat, Foreign Fish,
The Sailor, The King,
The Hurling Match,
The Boy and the Brace, The River.

We are a little disturbed at the title you have selected – namely, 'Tales of a Citie'. The title is quite clear when one reads your dedication, but we are wondering whether it has in itself enough inherent appeal to capture the interest of a prospective buyer.

I talked to Mr Don Congdon about this and he thought that probably it didn't make much difference what the title was, the book being a collection of short stories. Some of us rather liked the title 'The Green Hills and Other Stories' and others liked the title 'The Proud Man and other stories'. Perhaps it does not make any difference, and we shall use the title you have suggested, unless on further thought you wish to make a change.

We are delighted indeed to have the privilege to publishing these stories and are most happy to have you back on our list of authors.

With kindest regards to you and Mrs Macken,

R. De Wilton

The year 1955 was a productive one as regards publishing – *Sunset on the Window Panes* was published and now a book of short stories, *The Green Hills and Other Stories*, was accepted and his new play, *Twilight of a Warrior*, was about to open in the Abbey Theatre and was going to be published as well. A letter came from Lovat Dickson at the end of August:

Macmillan & Co. Ltd.,
London.

Dear Walter,

Thank you for your letter of August 24th. Yes it will be fine if you send us the book of short stories when they are in proof. It will do splendidly if you get an amended script from the Abbey Theatre of 'Twilight of a Warrior' when they have rehearsed and have made their cuts. We will go ahead and try and get a London production for you. It's a wonderful idea for a play, and should just appeal at this moment.
Yours ever,
Rache Lovat Dickson

In my father's letters to Rita Joyce there is interesting news:

Gort na Ganiv.
Dec. 23rd 1955

Dear Rita,

Many thanks for your letter and card. It was kind of you to remember us. We were reading about the hurricane there with you and felt sorry remembering what the last one we experienced was like. My pen has been pretty slow for the past year. I wrote a new play called 'Twilight of a Warrior'. It was produced in the Abbey Theatre in Dublin for a few weeks. It was very well received – adding enormously to my reputation but not a lot to my purse – and perhaps that's the best way. It will be published in the New Year and I will send you a copy.

I have a collection of short stories being published in the US in the New Year called 'The Green Hills'. You would be able to get a copy of that more quickly from your bookseller than I could get it to you. It is being published by the Macmillan Company. I hope when you have read it you will tell me which stories appealed most to you.

My eldest son Wally Óg will be going to University next year. At the moment (this is his 5th choice) he intends to study for his Master of Arts and after that to do an exam for the Diplomatic Service. I don't think this is his final choice but he has until next October to decide. We are very well Thank God but it is very doubtful if you will see us in America in the foreseeable future. I have given up acting altogether and am endeavouring to live solely on the pen. It saves a lot of wear and tear on the body. So I'm afraid you will have to take a trip over to see us. That's a more likely proposition. However, if we do get to New York, we won't fail to go and see you. Tell your mother we send her our love and think of her often.

Sabina Walsh spent a week with us when she was in Europe last year. We had good fun. It's a pity you don't know one another better but sure that's the way it is with close relations – the further apart they are the better it suits them and that has been going since the creation of the world. It's the same way with ourselves. This Xmas is a bit sad for us. Just when the play started in Dublin, we had to rush back from the first night to get to the bedside of the eldest child of Peggy's sister, Annette.

We watched her die for three hours. She was only 14, but the behaviour of Peggy's sister and her husband in their terrible trial was a wonderful pointer for the strength imparted by our faith. It wasn't that they weren't heartbroken – they were and are – but they got the grace of fortitude. How awful if would be to have nothing to fall back on! We are setting up a Christmas tree for them and having them all out to our house – in a rather futile effort to induce forgetfulness.

We loved Christmas in New York the first time we were there. The whole world seemed to be lit up. But then of course we were separated from the lads and that wasn't so good. So long, write again when you have time. Peggy sends her love to you and to your Mother and the lovely rosary beads always bring her to our minds.

God bless,

Yours sincerely,

Walter

My father also wrote to his American cousin Sabina about the death of Annette Lohan:

Gort na Ganiv.
Dec. 23rd 1955

My dear Sabina,

We were very relieved to get your letter, but sorry to hear about all the trouble [*Sabina had been ill*] and hope with the help of God that it is all now past – that you will recover your strength in the shortest possible time. We had a spot of trouble ourselves – not directly – you remember Peggy's sister May – the tactless one!

Well my play was on at the Abbey in November and we went up for the first night, but on the way we heard that their eldest child, Annette, 14, was in hospital for an operation. That was Monday (the 21st November). We came back from Dublin on Wednesday at 3 p.m. and spent from then until 5 p.m. watching poor little Annette die. She was only sick for one week. If she had recovered, she would have been a semi-invalid for all her life – she had some sort of blockage in her intestines. Anyhow she suffered a lot of agony before she died. Even when one knows there is a logical theological reason for children to suffer before death – it is very hard to watch it. But out of this tragedy came the light from May of all people and her husband, Mick – incredible fortitude that could only come from deep faith.

It was a revelation to me. Not that they weren't heartbroken but the way they took it! This all happened just a month ago. It seems much longer. We are having them all out here for Christmas, putting up a tree and inducing Santa Claus to pay a call in the hope that they might help them get over Xmas.

Do you remember Jimmy Joyce and Alma? Their baby – a girl – was very sickly when she was born but the doctors got to her in time. Jimmy got an attack of gall bladder and when they brought him in they discovered a TB patch on his lung. They haven't told him yet.

I go to visit him every day. In six weeks if he shows no sign of improvement they will just have to tell him. Dr Seán Maguire told me. Alma knows but there is great stuff in that woman. I don't know why I'm telling you all this tale of woe but I just thought it might help to console you with your own troubles. Tell Big Pete I was asking for him, all the best to you and Pete and Stephen and I hope that 1956 will bring us all together again.

All my love,
Walter

We had the Lohan's out for Christmas 1955 and, from that time on, they became regular visitors to Gort na Ganiv. The father of the house, Mick Lohan, began fishing regularly with us on Sundays and sometimes on Thursday afternoons.

Twilight of a Warrior was first staged in the Abbey Theatre on Monday 21 November 1955. It was very realistic contemporary play as it tackled a very modern theme for that period in Ireland. The father of the house, an old IRA man, Dacey Adams is a successful businessman who suggests that his daughter Elva visit one of his old haunts, Toobreena, where he had staged a successful ambush. The play opens when Elva arrives back at her home with a new boyfriend, Abel, a young farmer Elva met at Toobreena. Elva has been engaged a number of times before and her father believes that this new boyfriend will be as easy to dismiss as the previous ones.

Living in the house with Dacey is his brother Affy, who is a bit of a drunk; his sister Gubby, who spends her time criticising everyone; Dacey's wife Nessa; and their son Ross, a poet. Dacey married into the business and is, to a degree, under an obligation to his wife and her family. This new man coming into their lives causes friction, he is not afraid to face Dacey.

It struck me that the hostility between Dacey and Elva's boyfriend is a bit like the way that my mother's father regarded my father as not being good enough for his daughter. Even the way that Dacey spells out for his daughter what she would be facing her if she was to marry Abel – having to go back to live in a backward small farm where she would have to work to the bone – reminds me of my grandfather's attitude to my mother marrying a thirty-shilling-a-week actor.

15

MAJOR LIFE CHANGES
IN THE LATE 1950S

The year 1956 was a very important one in our lives. It started well with some good news from Don Congdon in New York:

Harold Matson Company.
January 4th 1956

Dear Walter,

The deal has finally gone through with Kraft Theatre, and they're going to do 'Home is the Hero', a live hour television show, tentatively scheduled for January 25th for a fee of $1,500. The contract should be along soon for your signature. I hope this may stir up a little interest in the motion picture rights, incidently.
   Very best wishes for the New Year to you and Mrs Macken.
   Sincerely,
   Don Congdon

Ann Thomas, the actress, wrote to my father about the televising of the play:

Of course to do any full-length play in 50 minutes is a chore, while we who knew the play hated to see so much cut out. The review I read – all those who saw it – thought it most superior television. The cast was as follows:

Brian Donlevy as Paddo	Anthony Perkins as Willie
Glenda Farrell as Daylia	Loretta Leverese as Josie
Dennis Patrick as Manchester	Pat O'Malley as Dovetail
Ann Thomas as Bid	

We were directed by a new young director called William Graham. Anthony Perkins, son of the late Osgood Perkins, was a mumbling actor. He speaks so low, we couldn't hear him in the scenes – no matter the mike picked him up – as a result all the rest of us were told we were yelling. Brian Donlevy did a remarkable job in one week – nice fellow to work with too.

My father wrote to Sabina in February 1956, to let her know that they were hoping and praying that her husband, Peter, would get a job with the Grace Corporation:

Gort na Ganiv.
Feb. 21st 1956

Dear Sabina,

It was good to hear from you. Please don't leave us in a vacuum as regards Peter and the Graces. I think he would have scope with them. They have such wide interests. If it's the right thing for him, he will get into it. They would be very lucky to get hold of him but anyhow we will pray like mad that he will get whatever makes him happy.

I have one piece of good news for a change. You remember me telling you that Jimmy Joyce had TB and that he didn't know it. Well he was in bed for six weeks and then they told him to go home and remain in bed for two months. So he got fed up and went off to a clinic in London where they examined him and told him that he never had TB. He had an allergy and this allergy collapsed the lung.

All our love and best wishes from Walter and Peggy.

In the spring of 1956, there was a dramatic change in our family. During my brother's last year in school 1955–56, we sensed a change in his life. Our parents had handed deep religious convictions on to both of us and there was no doubt that he had a religious vocation. The usual pattern in those days, would be for him to either join and study for the diocesan clergy or else study for the priesthood with an order such as the Jesuits. The Jesuits in our school were aware of his deep attachment to religion and were sure that he would choose them.

However, a new secular organisation called 'Opus Dei' had recently been established in Dublin and then it moved to places outside of the capital, like Galway. Opus Dei was founded by a young Spanish priest, José Maria Escríva, in the 1930s in direct opposition to the Community Party who were actively recruiting young people all over Spain.

One of their first recruits in Galway was a member of the Irish army at Renmore, Dick Mulcahy. Their second was Oliver Powell, a member of the well-known music shop family and Walter Macken Óg was their third. He was seventeen in 1955 and began to attend retreats and meditations at their small flat, just off Domnick Street, during his final year at school.

It did not come as a surprise to us when, in the spring of 1956, he told us that he was going to join 'the work', as they called it. He explained the primary thrust of Opus Dei was to offer ordinary people the chance to sanctify their lives by dedicating their working lives to God. The majority of their members were lay people.

There were both men and women in Opus Dei and different categories of member also. To become numeries, members dedicated their lives to God and took the same vows as priests – poverty, chastity and obedience. They lived together in communal houses, usually residences for university students in Ireland. Members could also become supernumeries, living ordinary lives, with marriage and children, but still dedicating their lives and work to God. Only 5% of the numeries were selected to become priests.

I think it was hard for my parents to come to terms with the idea that their son was joining a religious organisation, but would not become a priest. I remember my mother telling me:

> Through his years at school as you know, your brother always came in first in his class, now in the Christmas of 1955, he came third – he was really upset and disturbed, looking to make his mind up about joining the Opus Dei.

My brother formally joined Opus Dei on 25 March 1956 and our lives changed. From that point, the organisation took precedence over his family life. My father's original plan was that my brother and I would both go to university in Galway, but this was not the plan that Opus Dei had for my brother. Once he had finished his exams in June, he went off to a retreat centre, leaving home almost overnight. He did not return to the house for some time and this was very difficult for my mother in particular. I can remember her crying in the kitchen as we laid the table for meals. Having spent the summer going to courses and retreats, my brother went to Nullamore University Residence in Milltown, County Dublin, and began a BA in University College, Dublin.

I became like an only child. I was the person my mother talked to when my father was working, and while out walking, working in the garden or fishing, I was my father's principal companion.

This letter to Sabina portrays what was going on in our lives. In a letter to my father she had invited us as a family to come to stay with them in a villa in the south of France, but we were unable to go:

Gort na Ganiv.
May 29th 1956

My dear Sabina,

We were very pleased to get your letter today and more than pleased that you will be within striking distance of us during the summer. There are a number of reasons I'm afraid that we won't be able to fit in with your plans: – viz – We have already arranged our vacation in Cork from June 16th to June 30th. This is paid for. While we are away for the 2 weeks, Peggy's sister May and her family are taking over the house here and her other sister, Joan is taking over their house in Woodquay. All this is already arranged and unalterable. This takes care of any free money I might have had this year.

As you can imagine I haven't made a lot of money this year, so in order to live next year we have to be tight this year. Maybe next year, I will make a lot of money. So I can only afford to take the 2 weeks we are taking away from my work.

I am just finishing a novel ['*Sullivan*'] but there won't be any money out of that for some time – I have been writing it for nearly a year and in that time have only got one short story on the market.

Then we love you and Peter too much to endanger our friendship by living on top of you at a time when it would weigh on the peasant pride of W. Macken. Can you understand that? It's psychological and unfortunate but I honestly have to work and here, at home is the only place I can work.

Apart from that we couldn't leave the place here. We have no help and it would go wild. Also Wally Óg only partly belongs to us now – he is not permitted to come on holidays with us (I will explain this mysterious sentence when we meet) and as we will be reluctantly leaving him behind when we go to Cork, we couldn't do it for longer than that.

We spent two weeks in Ballylickey House Hotel in West Cork. There was a river full of white trout running through the hotel grounds but we could not get the fish to take any kind of fly. In the south, the white trout tended to be caught at night. We did go fishing on Lough Gougane Barra one day and we caught some small brown trout. The main thing was to be away and spend time by the sea, swimming and relaxing. It was our first holiday without Wally Óg and it was strange not to have him with us. My father finished his letter inviting Sabina and her family to come over and visit us during the summer, but they did not come.

When we arrived back home, my father resumed writing *Sullivan*. He took a break from his writing in July, going over to BBC Radio in London to take part in a radio production of *King of Friday's Men*. There was a brief note from John McNulty, posted end of June:

New York.
June 30th

Dear Walter,

This is one of our funniest magazines from a pictorial point of view, if you or the two boys like it, I'll be pleased to put in a subscription for you.

Faith had a story in last week's 'New Yorker'. Be sure and watch out for it. It's called 'A Man's Country' and it is about Ireland.
Love to all,
McNulty

It was in 1956 that my father's first book of short stories, *The Green Hills and Other Stories*, was published. He introduced it with the following description:

The title of this book could be 'Tales of a Citie' because it is about the people who inhabit the city, with history which most old towns possess as their background, and the struggle for existence which is eternal as their foreground. All cities have their hinterland. The hinterland of this one is wild and beautiful; so the lives of the people are wild and beautiful.

From the city you will meet Gaelgoirs, a bad do-gooder, The Turk – a city boy, a pub keeper; also a bookmaker, a poet, a doctor, a tinker, a dog, an angry fisherman, a handicapped child and a regal distiller of illicit whiskey. From the hinterland you will meet a farmer, a pensions' inspector, an old athlete, a lover, a Connemara pony, an aristocrat, a murderer and a policeman.

All these and the people and places and the drama that surrounds them go to make up a living land and all the created land is enriched by the bones of the people and when you know the people, you know the place:

Everyman is indebted to his home town,
He may sneer at it; jeer at it, rail at it or
Be secretly proud of it.
Righteous when you fault it:
Incensed when a stranger does so
You cannot get away from it
It bred part of you –
So this book is dedicated to
My home town – The City of the Tribes.

The publication of *The Green Hills and Other Stories* in 1956 proved that he was a master of the short story form. Many of his stories were published in various magazines during the 1950s including *The New Yorker*, *Argosy* and *Saturday Evening Post* in America.

Sullivan, my father's sixth novel, was completed and posted to both Macmillan of London and to his American agent in July:

Macmillan & Co. Ltd.
4th July 1956

Dear Walter,

Thank you for your letter of July 1st. I am so glad to hear that you all had such a good holiday. The contract for 'Sullivan' is just being arranged by the Accounts Department. We are bettering the royalties we offered you on 'Sunset on the Window Panes' – and are suggesting 15% to 10,000 and 17 and a half percent thereafter. I hope you will think this is satisfactory. We won't send the manuscript to the printer until you let us have Chapter 29. I am simply wondering whether Chapter 29 is not really missing that you simply numbered the chapter after 28 as chapter 30. I notice chapter 28 finishes on page 249 and chapter 30 begins on Page 250.

I am so glad that you like the cover design for 'The Green Hills'. I think it has a marvellous tone too. It is to be published tomorrow. You already have your six author's copies so all I need offer here is my heartfelt wishes for its success.

I am going on my summer holidays on Friday July 20th and I see that you and Peggy will be in London from July 23rd to July 30th. That is a great disappointment. It would have been so nice to have an evening or two together, but it looks out of the question. Anyone in the office will be glad to see you and I do hope you will come in. I do not return from holiday until August 8th.

Yours ever,
Lovat Dickson

Reaction to *Sullivan* was not very positive. Even his American agent, Don Congdon raised doubts about some parts of the novel:

Harold Matson Company,
30 Rockefeller Plaza,
New York 20.

July 11th 1956

Dear Walter,

I caught the lapse in the numbering of the chapters as I was finishing the novel over the weekend. I was halfway through the novel when I received your note which is why I cabled you immediately … I simply looked at the numbered chapters and noted that one seemed to be missing. As soon as I'd read through the chapters, it was clear that the manuscript was intact.

I like the novel very much, and particularly the background of the stage, and the zest by which you draw Sullivan. I did feel that the novel let [*the reader*] down a little when Sullivan got to New York, and somehow I wanted to have Bernie Taylor more in the end of the book She seems to me to be as strong a character as Pie and Sullivan, and to have her wait off-stage so long, to have her give up and wait for Sullivan to work things out, while understandable in character motivation, was a little unsatisfactory to me as a reader.

I also found it difficult to believe that Sullivan would stay in America; he seemed to be firmly rooted in Ireland, and so it was only a matter of time until he decided to go back to Ireland. I'm not suggesting that a big reunion scene between Sullivan and Bernie would have been preferable, but it did seem to me that his resolution in finding himself ought to take place on stage among the three of them. I say this also in the knowledge that you can stage a conflict such as this so beautifully.

I've sent the novel over to De Wilton at Macmillans and hope to hear from him soon. It seems to me that the novel has a possibility with the magazines in a condensed version over ever. I don't suppose you have an extra carbon copy that's legible, that I could use for this, by any chance? Lacking this, I'll try and get the novel from Macmillans for a couple of months when they've made up their minds about it and show it to several editors.

Sincerely,
Don Congdon

A post card came from Sabina in France. It was from a famous resort in the south, Juan les Pins. My father wrote back to her:

Gort na Ganiv.
July 18th 1956

My dear Sabina,

Hope this finds you. When you settle down somewhere, let us know. I have the page proofs of the books of short stories that I want to send you. I have finished the new novel called 'Sullivan' and both publishers are pleased with it, so if it is a real success, I will buy Juan les Pins. Peggy and I are off to London July 24, back August 1st, a play on BBC Third Programme. It will be a break. We enjoyed our two weeks in Cork, very beautiful, very quiet.

Fr McCullagh wants to know if we have any chance of seeing you at all this year. I said I hoped so. Is that enough of a hint? Peggy will pass out if we don't get to see all of you somehow – any chance?

Hope the lads are enjoying the trip. Give them our best. You know we love you and desire to see you.

Walter and family

John McNulty came to visit us quite a few times during the 1950s and he was a great help to my father when he was in New York both with *The King of Friday's Men* in 1951 and with his own play, *Home is the Hero* in 1954. On 29 July 1956, John McNulty sadly died from a heart attack at his home in Rhode Island. He was only sixty.

My father wrote to Wally Óg in July when he returned from taking part in the BBC radio production of *King of Friday's Men*:

Gort na Ganiv.
July 31st 1956

My dear Wally Óg,

Thanks for your letter. We got back last night arriving in Galway at about 7.30. It was a tough week. Up at 6.30 a.m. each morning to walk 2 miles to mass, rush to get a bus into London at 8.30 a.m. Rehearsing from 10.30–5.30 and on Sunday (God forgive me) practically all day.

We didn't have a flight booked yesterday, so we went out to the airport and tried out on stand-by; and with help of Our Lady a couple didn't turn up and we got their seats on the plane. The plane was two hours late but we didn't mind, Mick and May had been out to the house and brought Nigger [*our black retriever dog*] into Woodquay.

Have tried to light the adjectival Aga twice and it went out both times. I hope you are happy. Anybody who asked me where Wally Óg was I replied carefully that himself and a few other lads had rented a 300-acre castle in Meath for a few weeks, so now they know that we are all millionaires [*probably Lismullen – which Opus Dei later converted into a major retreat centre*].

All the best, we will be looking forward to seeing you. We enjoyed London. We had a lot of fun at the rehearsals. There were a lot of ex-Abbey people in the cast so it wasn't too bad. A good laugh! But I'm so happy to be home again. Your mother will write (I hope!). Anything you want ask!

Love,
Your ould fella

My father always included news of what was happening in his life in his letters to his relatives in America:

Gort na Ganiv.
September 14th 1956

Dear Rita,

Many thanks for your letter and the cuttings. I'm very pleased that you liked the stories. They got good reviews in the USA and in England as well. It all goes to prove that people are the same everywhere. Writing stories about the people in Galway is just writing about stories about humanity in general, if all men could truly recognise the truth of that we would be all brothers and true Christians – no thought of segregation, or apartheid or the other names men think up for intolerance and lack of charity. That may be an over-simplification but it has a shade of truth somewhere.

I'm delighted to hear that your mother is well. Pity we can't meet for a chat. But who knows. No chance of you and your mother coming on a visit to Ireland, I suppose. Would that be too painful for her? Suppose all that travelling around would be too hard on her. Maybe we will get to the USA again but at the moment, there's no sign of it.

Wally Óg, eldest son, is off to College this year. Probably Dublin, he will start studying for his MA. Languages and the Humanities seem to be his bent. After that, journalism or the Diplomatic Corps – he doesn't know which yet, Ultan, 13, we will have still have for a few years more, Thank God.

Something that might interest you. Windsor Lewis – he directs plays on Broadway and he stage-managed the first play I acted in over there – called to see us a few weeks ago with his wife Barbara Bel Geddes. They loved the land so much that they bought a house down the road from us. It's a beautiful property, built on the shores of the lake, lying in 56 acres of woods and shrubs. They hope to come and live here for a year, next April, bringing their two girls. They should be happy in it because they will be living in a welter of beauty. They will stir us up anyway in case we become too somnolent.

'Twilight of a Warrior', the play I wrote last year will be published in England in November. I won't forget to send you a copy. No publisher in the US yet until we can get it put on stage there. Up to this they complain bitterly that it's too 'good' to take a chance on. You can judge it for yourself when you get a copy.

The new novel is called 'Sullivan'. It's all about an actor (by a strange coincidence) who starts acting in a small town in the West of Ireland and deals with his life in Dublin, London and New York.

All the best to your mother, family and yourself. Thanks again for your letter.

Sincerely,

Walter

There was another letter from his American agent, Don Congdon about *Sullivan* at the end of September:

Harold Matson Company,
30 Rockefeller Plaza,
New York 20.
September 26th 1956

Dear Walter,

I had lunch with the Macmillan people, John Budlong and R.L. De Wilton last Friday at which time we discussed 'Sullivan'. They made an offer to do the novel contingent on a revision, and the letter embodying the terms and their criticism is enclosed herewith.

The letter is largely self-explanatory. I think if you brought off a satisfactory revision that I could improve the royalty terms which seem to me to be very low. The other terms seem to be reasonable in view of their dissatisfaction with the last third of the novel.

As you know, I too felt disappointed with the section taken up with Sullivan's being in America and I also felt that Bernie need to be brought into the ending since she was such an appealing character in the earlier part of the book.

I'll say no more until you let me know what you want to do about Macmillan's offer and the revision. If you decide that you don't want to change the book for them, they have said that they would have to reject it and they hate like hell to do it because they have real enthusiasm for your and your writing. They have continued to advertize the short story collection, incidentally, even though their sales to date are just under 3,000 copies. I don't mention this to influence your decision concerning a revision, but only to confirm their present faith in you and their hopes to continue publishing your books.

If you'd like to submit the novel elsewhere, of course I will be glad to do so.

Yours,

Don Congdon

The following is the detailed letter that Macmillan sent to Don Congdon, which he forwarded to my father:

At luncheon you asked that I wrote to you about our and our readers' reactions to the novel. They are substantially what Mr Budlong and I conveyed to you. Here is the consensus of those reactions.

All knowing Mr Macken's 'Rain on the Wind' and 'The Bogman', and knowing also his experience as a playwright and actor, feel that he could do a first rate novel about the theatre. Everybody who read the manuscript of 'Sullivan' thought at the beginning and well on into the story that he was definitely on his way to bringing it off. Up until the change of scene to America, the novel has vitality, excellent scenes, and convincing characterisation and detail.

There was only one real criticism of the first part, and that was the handling of the marriage of Sullivan and Bernie. The situation seems a bit contrived, as one reader put it, 'to clear the decks for Macken, the marriage serves to get the sex problem pretty much out of the way, and yet Bernie is to all intents and purposes eliminated from the story'.

From that point on it was thought that Sullivan's character suffers and that there is not enough seriousness in his portrayal. It isn't clear just what Mr Macken is trying to do with his main character. I have a definite feeling that the story begins to bog down and fall apart soon after the arrival in New York, in the main because Mr Macken allots too much space to the critical discussion of the theatre as he found it, to a large degree, probably, from his own experience. Macken's criticism is doubtless true, and deserved, so far as it goes – but one cannot help seeing that it is one-sided, too narrow. It is here that the characterisation of Sullivan, but of all the other people, suffers. Some readers thought that this part became patently autobiographical.

Some thought that since Bernie is so important in the Irish part, so important in the beginning, so far as Sullivan is concerned, it would be only logical and desirable to have her play a definite part at the end – at least something more than a memory in Sullivan's mind. Others thought that the sacrificial element of Pi's death was too great a price to pay for arousing Sullivan from his self-centeredness; in the degree that Pi looms large in the reader's sympathy, in that degree Sullivan seems to lose. Perhaps that is a partial reason why Bernie should be of more importance at the end.

We are all convinced that with some revision, Mr Macken can make this the novel it ought to be. All our criticisms have been made because of that belief in him; and it is for that reason, too, that we have made this offer. By publishing 'Rain on the Wind', 'The Bogman' and 'The Green Hills and other Stories' we have helped to establish firmly his American reputation as an important novelist and we are sincerely solicitous that that reputation be maintained and increased.

Sincerely yours,

R.L. De Wilton

My father replied to Congdon's letter:

Gort na Ganiv.
Oct. 1st 1956

Dear Don,

Thank you for your full letter of Sept 26th. As I told you before, I am no Iron man. I'm not writing for posterity but to try and make a living, and I am quite willing to tackle the last third of the book in order to try and make it more appealing. I will even save the life of Pi (something which on reflection I like doing even if it revolts against my whole plan). However, I will endeavour to return Bernie to the fold so that everybody will be happy. One of the main reasons, I will do this is because you yourself thought it could be done even before the publishers read the book.

Before all this, however, I will have to get in touch with London Macmillans. They didn't criticise the ending at all. I will try and find out if they really would approve the changes of if they want the book to remain as it is. If they like it to remain as it is, that means there will probably have to be two versions, but that's all worry for the future. One point on which I cannot change is the marriage of Bernie and Sullivan. I was not dodging sex in that. All that is based on a lot of life and a lot of truth and it is something that will just have to take it as it stands or no deal.

Since I haven't a copy of the MS, would you arrange to have the final chapters returned to me, that is the chapters before Sullivan's trip to America and all the subsequent ones.

All the best,
Sincerely,
Walter Macken

That same day, my father wrote a letter to Lovat Dickson in London:

Gort na Ganiv.
Oct. 1st 1956

Dear Rache,

Would you read the enclosed and please tell me something honestly.

Would you or your colleagues and your readers agree with the criticisms therein contained? Would you agree that the book should be revised as suggested?

I wouldn't consider the revision but Don Congdon when he read the MS before submitting it to the publishers, wrote almost the same criticisms, and writers are not in this business for their health but let us say to be guided by sale-ability, or are they?

I don't know, I am a bit confused. I remember what you made me do with 'Rain on the Wind' and how solid your advice proved to be in the long run.

So I am hoping you will clear up the confusion and tell me what you think.

With all the best wishes,
Sincerely,
Walter Macken

Don Congdon replied to his letter first:

Dear Walter,

I thought your letter was a damned good one in answer to De Wilton's and I passed on two of the pertinent paragraphs to him to mull over. He called me this morning to say that he liked your letter and your reaction, too, and asked if he should go ahead and make a contract. I said, yes, except that we wanted the same royalties that you had on the book of short stories; I see no reason why you should accept 10% to 7,500 copies inasmuch as you're agreeable to making the changes they want.

If Macmillan of London says anything that's relative to the New York Macmillan situation, let me know right away. Macmillan is returning the novel to me and I'll send it off to you first class for the revision. De Wilton asks if you could have a more careful retyping of the manuscript when the revision is done. He says that your typing job would be difficult for the printer to set from, and there would undoubtedly be some overcharges from the composition room. As a matter of fact, I could use a carbon of the novel myself, or two copies, because I think it has a chance with the magazines, as well as offering a potential with the motion picture companies.

Yours,

Don

Lovat Dickson wrote my father a long letter of six pages. Here is an excerpt:

Dear Walter,

I have now read 'Sullivan' with great care and interest, and I find myself, up to a point, more in agreement with the criticisms which the New York Macmillan Company's readers have made than I expected to be when I wrote the other day.

In fact your letter of October 1st only asked me to tell you honestly whether I would agree with the criticisms contained in De Wilton's letter, and whether the book should be revised in the way suggested. But I think you may value it more, knowing the genuine regard we here have always shown for your literary welfare, if I tell you exactly what I think is wrong with the book – for there is something wrong – and leave it to you to decide whether to follow the American recommendations, which would certainly be the easiest way, or to follow ours, which will entail considerably more work, but which I think will produce better results in every way.

The trouble, of course, is with the character of Sullivan. He starts out admirably, but you have made him a monster of selfishness and self-centredness, defects conceivable enough in a gifted actor's make-up, but not the kind to hold a reader's sympathy throughout a long book, and assist the important process of his self-identification with the leading figure.

The three main themes in the story are Pi's devoted friendship for Sullivan; Sullivan's and Bernie's love story; and the life and difficulties of a gifted actor. I think, that you don't hold these in proper proportion, and the reason is not hard to find, nor are you wholly to blame for it. Pi's devotion to Sullivan is obviously the thread that has attracted you most, and understandably you spend most of the novel on it. Bernie and Sullivan's love is, as you describe it, merely an incident in the development of Sullivan's character; you seem to me to give it much too little emphasis and significance of its own. As you tell the story, it affects Sullivan merely by giving him nostalgic feelings for home; it represents purity as opposed to the hypocrisy and falseness of stage life; it is the distant haven to which Sullivan is eventually going to return. But to be all these things properly it should have occupied a much greater part at the centre of the novel.

Bernie is well portrayed, but you had the chance for the development of a love story which would have been of vital meaning in Sullivan's life, and it seems to me that you don't make enough of it. I do not agree with the point the Americans make that you might have made this a first-rate novel about the theatre. Somebody might one day do that, but the novel will be about people, not about the theatre, which will provide only the background. Back-stage films may be successful, but novels about actors and the theatre have to conquer an extra layer of disbelief with the reading public who find it hard to credit the real emotions of people whose profession is to display false ones. Certainly Sullivan can be a figure of absorbing interest as an actor who is at the centre of the story, but I think you have to keep down the theatre and bring out the personal off-stage side of his life. My criticism is that there is too much theatre in the book and not too little. For example, you often go into digressions about theatrical practices in which the reader suddenly ceases to see the story through the eyes of the characters and is conscious of the author writing about the theatre.

This is only the first part of the letter which went into incredible detail as to what Lovat Dickson would like to see changed. My father spent the next two months cutting and revising his MS and then resubmitted it to both the London and New York offices of Macmillan. They both accepted the revised version for publication. Thomas Mark wrote to him on 7 December:

Dear Walter Macken,

Lovat Dickson had to go to America for a few days and has asked me to write to you about 'Sullivan', as I have been getting the MS ready for the printers and had promised him to let him have my impressions of the book. As you know, I am strongly pro-Macken, but I have to admit that I have not enjoyed this work so much as your earlier novels. I liked the opening chapters, but later on I became impatient with Sullivan himself and found the whole situation difficult to believe. However, I would not attach too much importance to this reaction, for these characters who generate trouble in and around themselves without any easily acceptable reason are not new to your work, and an extra dose of the artistic temperament in Sullivan's case would no doubt explain a great deal. All the same, I think you will have to accept the fact that the ordinary reader may find it difficult to develop that feeling of sympathy and almost self-identification with the central figure which is such a help to a novel.

I did not see the uncut version, and the revised text did not strike me as being too long, except perhaps for Chapter 10 about the 'sacking' of Sullivan and his walk out the country. I should be inclined not to give the full text of the prayer at the wedding service. There are probably too many extracts from plays which one feels that nobody would have dreamed of putting on, but you may mean these to show why the pieces in which Sullivan won a great personal success were nevertheless predestined flops.

I have written a short list of passages you might like to omit or modify. I have written them down on one side of the sheet, so that you have only to write something beside them to show what you would like us to do. This will make things easier than a letter.

I hope that you and your family are flourishing. The very cold weather looks like setting in early a week or two ago, but we are having a mild spell now. You might look around to see if there is any oil on your property.

Best wishes,

Yours sincerely,

Thomas Mark

I think my father was probably hurt by all this criticism of *Sullivan*, but finally, just before Christmas 1956, he completed the final revisions and sent them off. *Sullivan* is the first of his novels where his characters spend most of their time outside of Ireland.

One of the last letters to reach us that December was one from Windsor Lewis, telling us that Barbara and himself would be coming to Ireland to live in the summer of 1957. They wanted to make sure that my father bought a Corrib boat for Barbara and that my parents had booked their two daughters into the local school for the September 1957 school term.

16

THE HISTORICAL TRILOGY

My father began to work on the first of his historical novels, *Seek the Fair Land* in 1957. I think he felt the need to write this historical trilogy as he felt there was so little published about the ordinary life of Irish people down through the centuries. The history we all learned in school concentrated on the leaders in every country, the famous kings, queens and prime ministers. Cromwell, Daniel O'Connell, Michael Collins, Charles Stewart Parnell, Pádraig Pearse, Napoleon, Julius Caesar. Meeting the Macken aunts in America and realising how little they knew about the social history of their own country led him to concentrate on how the 'ordinary man and woman' lived their lives at particular times in history. He selected three distinct eras, starting with the middle of the seventeenth century, and beginning his story with Cromwell's sacking of Drogheda in 1649. The second book began in the early part of the nineteenth century and involved his principal character leaving Connemara and going to Munster where he met Daniel O'Connell. In the third book, he planned to tackle the most difficult period of our history – 1910 to 1925.

Since he was not a professional historian he had to do a lot of solid research work, for example for the first book, he had to find out how people had lived in Drogheda in 1641 when the book starts, what kind of clothes they wore, what food they ate, how they travelled and what kind of weapons they used. He found there were almost no records of the day to day lives of ordinary people to be found in Irish libraries. He accessed some material from the Folklore Commission but otherwise most of his detailed research was done in the British Library in London. He spent the best part of six months gathering material on the basic clothes, food and housing of the Irish of that era. Then in the summer of 1957, he brought my mother and me with him to Drogheda to absorb the atmosphere of the town. From there, we made our way to Lough Sheelin, up towards County Cavan where his main character, Dominick MacMahon, spent the winter after the Drogheda siege. From Lough Sheelin, we made our way back towards Galway passing through Carrick-on-Shannon in County Leitrim and then back to Galway itself.

The next journey for the principal characters happens when they escape from Cromwell's soldiers in Galway via the River Corrib and Lough Corrib. We brought our own boat down to Galway and then travelled up Lough Corrib, through the narrow part of the Lower Lake into the deep part of the Upper Lake. From there, we went up the Maam Valley. The O'Flaherty clan brings him up through Maam Valley into the mountains until finally he reaches a mountain fastness where Murdoc, chieftain of the O'Flahertys, has his home. Murdoc gives Dominick MacMahon a piece of land to build a house. Dominick settles there, believing that he will be at peace as he has finally found his 'Fair Land'. Most of 1957 was spent researching and he began to write the book towards the end of the year, so our lives went on as normal. Wally Óg spent October

1956 to June 1957 studying Spanish and English at UCD and obtained first class honours in all his exams. Then, in the summer of 1957, he informed us that Opus Dei had decided to send him to Rome to continue his studies.

My father was asked to write an article for the theatre magazine *Playbill* in 1957, to coincide with the publication of his novel *Sullivan*:

> You who are so familiar with the sacred rites, taboos and ceremonies of the theatre in New York have no conception of the bewildering impact it can have on a starry-eyed author coming into it for the first time with his European back-ground. It is like sending a lamb into the jungle; a four year old boy to college; or presenting an infant with whiskey instead of mother's milk.
>
> I have thought a lot about it and I have come to a conclusion. Since Ellis Island is no longer in use, I think it would be a good idea if all incoming authors were confined in it for a spell, and that it be used as a sort of decompression chamber, for their enlightenment and education. While they are kept there they could be conditioned over a period of weeks by various Broadway impresarios. Naturally somebody would have to pay the impresarios but it would be worth it. The course would be intensive, without sleep, and the food would consist of coffee and hamburgers.
>
> At the end of it the foreign author would not be nearly so naïve. He would be aware of the following facts:
>
> That an angel is not altogether a pure spirit.
>
> That a turkey is not a bird which he used to eat roasted at Christmas.
>
> Other things which could be disentangled for him are this business about the producer and director. He would have to find out that unlike the British Isles, a producer doesn't direct and that a director doesn't produce. He would discover that a producer is somewhat like a market gardener, who finds the lettuce, but that even if it is of the

same colour, this lettuce doesn't go well in salad. The director is the fellow who does all the work and all the cursing.

He should be taught that even if a play is taking in $12,000 a week at the box office, it is still a dead duck (another inedible bird).

Further, he should know, that if, instead of paying the price of the scenery for his play, they gave the money to the author, he could go home and build three or four five-bed roomed houses in a sylvan setting, or that he could afford to buy a thatched cottage on the American millionaires' island in Killarney.

He should know that under his contract he possesses almost dictatorial powers to hire and fire, and that nobody but nobody can talk him into changing a line in his play if he doesn't wish; that nevertheless, as sure as a turkey isn't a turkey or a duck a duck, he will be talked into more changes than a cash register in Woolworths.

He will be informed that a play doctor is not an actor with an MD degree who takes out an appendix in his spare time, but a sinister, unseen character, who descends like a hurricane and departs leaving destruction in his wake.

He will be taught to assess people who are waiting for the cat to jump and that the cat is also a mythical animal with temporarily sheathed claws.

He must be warned that even if critics tear the guts out of him, they don't really mean any harm, and that no, he had never assaulted their mothers, that it was all purely impersonal for his own good; to teach him how to smile with a crack in it, so that he would be a better and a wiser man at the end of it all.

These are only a few suggestions. Any other alien author is heartily welcome to add to the subjects in the course. And what's going to happen at the end of it all, when the student staggers wearily, white-faced and pie-eyed into the open air, under the statue of Liberty. I'll tell you what will happen. The poor fool is going to stick out his neck anyhow!

I remember my father saying to me: 'When you write a play, it has to go through a whole series of people before reaching an audience

– producers/directors, actors but when you write a novel or a short story there is no one between you the writer and the reader.'

Windsor Lewis, his wife Barbara Bel Geddes and their two daughters – Susan (12) and Betsy (8) – came to live in Oughterard in May 1957. Windsor had been to a tennis coach at Forest Lawns in California and as we had a hard tennis court, he spent many hours during the summer playing, against me primarily. Barbara Bel Geddes was at the height of her career in those years and in 1958, during her period living in Oughterard, she went to Hollywood to co-star in Alfred Hitchcock's famous film, *Vertigo*, she played the wife of Jimmy Stewart's character who was obsessed with Kim Novak's character.

I think Windsor Lewis and his wife Barbara thought that they could continue to live in the peace and serenity of Oughterard, despite Barbara's success. They had seen how we lived and how successful my father was in terms of writing and they thought that the house they had bought and the fifty-six acres of land would offer them the opportunity to escape from Hollywood. Their plan was that Windsor would write and Barbara would concentrate on her painting. Their two girls went to school at Taylor's Hill in Galway, where my mother had started her schooling. We were all driven into school in the morning and we came home on the bus from Galway to Oughterard. I had just moved into second year in the Jess (St Ignatius College, Galway) and so of course, I was beginning to have an interest in girls.

However, I think that Windsor and Barbara soon began to realise that there were drawbacks to living in Oughterard if you wanted to continue a career as a major actress. It was so difficult at that time for anyone in Hollywood to contact her as the phones were manual, you lifted the handset and twirled a handle and then the postmistress in Oughterard answered you. If you asked her to phone Los Angeles, she would find this very difficult and would tell you just how expensive it was to phone LA. In the summer of 1958, they returned to America.

My father had begun writing *Seek the Fair Land* but an unexpected diversion arose. There had been talk about the possibility of establishing an Irish Film Industry for many years, and now Seán Lemass, as the Fianna Fáil Minister for Industry and Commerce, made money available to build a film studio in Bray, County Wicklow. It was agreed that three popular plays from the Abbey Theatre repertoire would be filmed, including *Home is the Hero*. My father was persuaded to sell the film rights for the small sum of £1,000 and then one of the producers, Louis Elliman, wrote to my father asking if he would be willing to play the part of Paddo in the film. Henry Keating wrote the screenplay and they sent it to my father for his approval.

Once my father approved of the screenplay and agreed to take on the part, the other producer, Emmet Dalton, wrote to him:

Emmet Dalton Ltd.,
Independent Film Producers,
1 Bank Chambers,
25 Jermyn Street,
London SW1.
24th March 1958

Dear Mr Macken,

Louis Elliman has been with me and passed me a copy of your letter which was a relief to me, because I was doubtful about your accept-ance of our screen adaptation of your play. My company is producing these Abbey plays in association with an American Company and I have so many people to please that at times it becomes difficult.

I am attaching for your information, the details of our produc-tion and the dates we need you in Dublin. My production manager, Ronnie Lilis, will be in Ireland from next Friday and he can be reached at Ardmore Studios, Bray, telephone number Bray 3490, would you please confirm with him. Your contract will be issued in due course from Dublin.

Thank you for your co-operation,

Emmet Dalton

The letter included the details of his engagement with the film:

1. Part of Paddo O'Reilly

2. Period of engagement: – Four weeks commencing Monday 14th April made up of:

One week location shooting commencing 14th April

Three weeks studio shooting commencing 21st April

3. Script discussion with Director/Costuming etc.

Mr Macken will be required in Dublin not later than 9th April

4. Salary

Mr Macken will be paid at a rate of £15 for each shooting day, either on location or in the studio, with a guarantee of £200 cover-ing 12 days shooting and the pre-production period.

5. The company will pay for Mr Macken's transportation from Galway to Bray and the return journey at the expiry of the engage-ment.

6. Accommodation

The company will provide, at their cost, hotel accommodation at Bray, during the period of the engagement.

There was considerable correspondence between my father and mother while he was away filming. My mother, who was not able to drive, would cycle into Oughterard, a distance of some four miles, both to go to mass and to get some of our shopping. Local grocer Dermot Joyce delivered food and groceries to our house. Another couple who helped us out during this time was the manager of the local factory, Peter Gant. Peter and his wife Betty would also take us into Galway a few times each week and sometimes, as a treat, we would go to the cinema.

While my father worked away on *Seek the Fair Land*, there was a letter from Terese Sacco, his new editor at Macmillan of London, concerning his plays. *Twilight of a Warrior* had been staged in Stockholm, while the Norwegians staged *Home is the Hero* twice in Oslo. The Australians were broadcasting *Mungo's Mansion* and planned to do *Twilight of a Warrior*. South African radio had broadcast *Twilight* in Africaans. She also told him that BBC TV were broadcasting their version of *Home is the Hero* on BBC TV on Sunday 27 July starring Eddie Byrne as Paddo, Peggy Marshall as Daylia and Donal Donnelly as Willie.

As a direct result of my father's work on *Home is the Hero*, the film, he made two new friends – Arthur Kennedy who played the part of Willie and the director Fielder Cook. My father worked very hard on that film – he told us that running through the narrow streets of northside Dublin was exhausting. When he was running for the same shot for about the sixth time, some of the local urchins shouted after him: 'Hey mistah, who do you think you are – Ronnie Delaney is it?' My father, Fielder and Arthur Kennedy got on very well and I got the distinct impression that the script was practically re-written on a daily basis. The completed film was previewed in America in January 1959 and received good reviews. It previewed in Dublin on Tuesday 17 February 1959 and my father was invited to attend. When he agreed to attend, he received the following letter from Louis Elliman:

Dear Walter,

Thanks for yours of February 6th. I am very glad you are able to come to Dublin for 'Home is the Hero' and if there is anything we can do to enhance you in the eyes of your son then rest assured we will do it. Seriously we would like your opinion on the picture and as requested, we are sending an invitation to Dr Macken of Phibsborough.
Hope to see you in the morning,
All good wishes,
Louis Elliman

There was a lot of optimism that this was the beginning of a completely new Irish film industry, and it was exactly that.

Fielder Cook wrote my parents a lovely letter that month:

Dear Wally,

I know it seems a monstrous thing that we haven't written since God knows how long. But things have been turning over. Sally has a 'little watermelon' in the oven and by now (8 months), it's bigger than a truck of grapefruit, also far lovelier. I have been busy with TV and I'm getting a play ready for August rehearsals. I'm sure I wrote you about it – 'A Cook for Mrs General' – Bill Travers, a lovely English actor, is our star.

Most important immediate news is that 'Home is the Hero' opened to lovely notices except for the 'New York Times'. I'm sending you a batch of them with this letter. Don Wall and I sat and watched and we cried like a baby. It is a fine film but I'm sure what he and I felt was homesickness for dear Ireland and my lovely friends. Sally and I miss you greatly. Also we have had no word from you about 'The Voices of Doolin' or anything since summer. So please write. I read part of your novel over again before lending it to a friend who loved it. We agree that you are the hope of Ireland and of Irish letters.

All happiness and love to you and all the family,
Fielder and Sally Cook

Seek the Fair Land had been accepted for publication by both Macmillan of London and Macmillan of New York and then came great news from the managing editor of Macmillan of New York:

The Macmillan Company,
60 Fifth Avenue,
New York.
February 18th 1959

Dear Walter,

It's with more pleasure than I can tell you that I am sending you this cable:

'Delighted tell you Literary Guild has chosen "Seek the Fair Land" as August selection. Must have by return article approximately thousand words about background of book development of story characters etc., similar to "Rain on the Wind" article – deadline March First – Congratulations.'

Actually the offer came through while I was in the Mid-West on a short trip last week, so that I am afraid I was one of the last to know about it. But it's wonderful news just the same, and at the cost of sounding immodest, I predicted this would happen when I first read the book. It's a grand piece of work, in some ways your best, I think, and what has happened to date is solid confirmation that a number of people think so.

Well every bit of fortune has its attendant problems, and yours is in the form of work. I know you won't let down our friend, John Beecroft, at the Literary Guild, who really needs the background article by the first of March. Since you did something similar for 'Rain on the Wind', I'm sure you don't need a further briefing from me. But because it might be helpful to see how the Guild is doing these things currently, I am sending you a copy of 'Wings', their magazine. So much for the publicity part.

Now Mr Beecroft has made a further suggestion which I think is wise, not only from his point of view but from our own, concerning American publication. Here's what he says:

> We feel the book needs a foreword explaining the political situation and the seriousness of the Cromwell campaign in Ireland with some reference made to the determined effort to stamp out the Catholic Church and the significance of the Oath of Allegiance.

He also felt a map was needed. Now Don has mentioned that you had prepared a sketch or two which Macmillans in London think highly of. We look forward to seeing these just as soon as possible, so that we can determine whether they will fill the bill.

Mr John P. Budlong completed his letter telling my father that he was resigning from Macmillan to move to a new job in McGraw–Hill and he wished my father all the best in his work.

Don Congdon, his American agent, explained in a letter that the selection by the Literary Guild meant a guaranteed payment of $30,000 of which half went to the publisher, meaning that my father would earn at least $15,000 and Congdon believed that if the book sold well it could earn him something like $20,000.

Terese Sacco had news of the publication of my father's books in Polish and Russian. The Polish publisher decided to publish *Sullivan* and planned to publish 10,000 copies of the novel in paperback. They offered to pay a royalty of 5% but they wanted to pay in the Polish currency of zlotys. Terese advised that the best way to make use of the money would be to spend a holiday in Poland. On 4 March, she wrote that they had heard from the Russian publisher:

> We are pleased to inform you that Publishers of Foreign Books in Moscow have recently published your collection of short stories, 'The Green Hills'. We are sending you by air (registered) four copies of your book. We wish you good health and creative success.
> (signed) Pavel Czurvikov
> The Director

The Soviet Union was not a signatory of the Berne Convention so it did not pay royalties for its publication of books by foreign authors. However, the two translators of the work began to write regularly to my father and over the next few years, they translated many of his books into Russian. They wrote to him regularly and he explained what he meant by phrases that were purely Irish slang, not really the King's English!

The extraordinary friendship which my father developed with the two Russian translators is illustrated somewhat in the following letter they wrote to him in March 1959:

Moscow.
March 30th 1959

Dear Mr Macken,

We thank you very much for the books which Messers MacMillan & Co. Ltd. sent us on your request and which we have already received.

We admire 'Rain on the Wind' very much. We started translating it into Russian already half a year ago, and have almost completed the translation. We will advise you if and when it is published. We are now studying the play [*probably 'Home is the Hero'*] and its possibilities here.

We are sending you today under separate cover a copy of 'Green Hills' and a copy of one of our leading magazines – 'Ogoneki' – also containing some of your stories.

The portrait on the cover was copied from a small photograph on the jacket of 'Green Hills'. We are not very sure of the resemblance. If the artist has done a poor job of it we hope you wouldn't mind it very much. Please send us a good picture of yourself for any future editions.

We would like you to know that your stories were very favourably reviewed by the press. An article in 'Literaturnaya Garesta' of March 3 says in conclusion:

Walter Macken is a new name for Soviet readers. The publication of these stories is most welcome as the author is undoubtedly a real artist who draws his characters with liveliness truth and beauty and he has an excellent eye for the dramatic incidents of life.

Sincerely yours,
Vera Ganoba and Nanina Nizovovc

My father received a really nice letter from his new editor in Macmillan in New York, Al Hart:

The Macmillan Company,
Sixty-Fifth Avenue,
New York.
March 5th 1959

Dear Walter Macken,

You can imagine with what pleasure I forwarded to Don Congdon your file copies of your contract together with our check for your advance. I would have been extremely glad, in the normal course of events, to have been your American editor for 'Seek the Fair Land'; as it is with a whopping Literary Guild bonanza to signalize the beginnings of our relationship, I'm positively euphoric. Congratulations and don't spend it all in one place!

You may well not remember this but I do, vividly and with warmth; after your performance at the Westport Playhouse in 'Home is the Hero', you repaired to my house in Weston along with Randy Williams and John Budlong. I remember being impressed by your sparkle after a long and gruelling day, and I was sorry when the time came to deliver you to your hotel. And although you didn't know it, I was engaged in silent prayer that we would make it, for my gas indicator (petrol to you) registered zero.

I have just returned from a six week trip to Paris and London, and nothing would have pleased me more than to have seen you in Ireland, but my crowded schedule absolutely prohibited this. I did, however, have a very pleasant session with Lovat Dickson who had just returned from seeing you, and I felt closer by at least that much.

Please feel free to communicate directly with me whenever you like on any subject whatsoever. Bear in mind that I'm here to be used. You may be sure that I'll keep you posted as I shepherd your new book through the machinery here.

Best regards,
Al Hart

Lovat Dickson who had helped him along throughout his writing career was delighted when my father presented him with the original drawings he had made and which had been included in the original hardback edition of *Seek The Fair Land*. Dickson writes to thank him for this:

London.
31st March 1959

My dear Walter,

Thank you so much for your letter and for a generous thought that pleases me enormously. I do like the drawing very much indeed, and I would be very proud to own it, though I think it should hang on the walls of Gort na Ganiv. However, I know you mean what you say, and I therefore accept it with the greatest pleasure. I will have a proof carefully pulled by hand for you, and what is more I will have it framed, and I will bring it to you when I come, as I hope to do, at the end of June.

I do thank you very much for what you have written. You are one of half a dozen authors whom it has given me the greatest pleasure and pride to work with in my long life of work, and I think I have learned more from you than I have from the others about integrity.

Yours ever,
Rache Lovat Dickson

The following article appeared in the Literary Guild Magazine about *Seek the Fair Land*:

John Beecroft presents the August selection:

The Irish have always been wondrous weavers of tales. This book by Walter Macken is a marvellous story. Several years ago the Guild used 'Rain on the Wind' by the same author. It was a good story, but not nearly as spellbinding as this book.

In 'Seek the Fair Land' Macken tells the story of Dominick, a man who was determined to survive the trouble and sorrows that beset Ireland. First he had thought he was secure in the city of Drogheda. Once, when Drogheda was besieged and he hid Murdoc, an Irish clansman, Murdoc told him he should not stay in towns, and that if Dominick ever needed security, to get out to the hills, to seek the high country.

Dominick helped Murdoc escape through a secret passage that led from his home to the river. A few years later Drogheda was again besieged – this time by Cromwell's army. Their purpose was to put down all insurrection in Ireland, and everyone in Dominick's city was to be killed. Luck was with Dominick; he survived the slaughter and with his two children, Peter and Mary Ann escaped through the same secret passage from his home to the river.

A man with two children could not move easily through a country infested with English soldiers. Their escape was further slowed by Father Sebastian, whom the English had wounded and left to die, and whom Dominick added to his party. Dominick's son, Peter had suffered such shock during the siege that he had become dumb. The priest's devotion to the children made the party of four a solid unit.

Finally after many adventures, they reached the town of Galway. Life was easier there, but Dominick soon got into trouble and again had to get out of town quickly. In the escape he found himself in company with Columba Dorsi, a wealthy woman of Galway who had refused to pay tribute to the English invaders. To Columba the escape in the boat and over the wild land was an entertainment – to Dominick and his family it was a life and death matter. Dominick, in spite of himself, was attracted to Columba [*I don't know where he got this idea – it isn't in the book at all!*] and Columba liked Dominick and his children.

When they reached their 'fair land' Dominick found that Murdoc had inherited the domain of his uncle and was now living in high feudal style in the castle. Murdoc welcomed Dominick and his children and remembered that he owed him his life and gave Dominick land to build a house. Columba settled in the castle as guest of Murdoc. Though he had reached the 'fair land' in the shelter of the hills, the life of adventure was not over for Dominick. Also he realised that Mary Ann was becoming a woman ready to marry – and he was astonished as everyone when Peter, his son, miraculously found he could speak.

'Seek the Fair Land' is superb story-telling. It is grand reading, and a novel with a message marked by faith and an abiding love.

My father wrote the following introductory note for the novel in the same copy of the Literary Guild magazine, *Wings*:

Many years ago, shortly after the last war, I read an account of battles long ago, and migrations of peoples, and it struck me how like it was to the age we are living in. At the time I was reading, Europe was torn apart, from the Channel Islands to the Urals. Few people had homes over their heads, or jobs or work or clothes or enough to eat. The whole of the Continent was sundered; and yet one knew that all this would pass, that people would survive, and in our own lifetime there would be adults to whom all this great cataclysm was merely history. How do we know this? Simply because it happened before.

Similarly, in a period in the lives of my own people, I saw a time in the seventeenth century when the Irish were living the history of all peoples. This was the dark night of the Irish soul, and it was to last a long time in the midst of Cromwellian brutality, persecution, and all the well-known satellites and camp followers of conquerors – famine, disease and pestilence. All this was not important. What was important was that the ordinary people, some of them, managed to survive it and pass on their own indomitable courage, hope, and faith to their children.

So this is the story of Dominick, a small man who, although much bereaved, snatched his daughter Mary Ann, his son Peter, and a wounded priest Sebastian from the massacre of Drogheda, and set out with them to find the fair land. It takes them a long time, right across the middle of a war-torn and hungry land, where the black horsemen ride at will, accompanied by wolves. Such a flight involves many hazards, requires courage and tenacity. They will meet with treachery, the friendship of the giant Murdoc, the sadism of Coote, who belongs to all terror-stricken epochs. They will be sheltered and will escape from walled towns. They will meet the ordinary people, living out their lives in terrible times, and they will find the fair land, where the mountains raise themselves from the hard earth and try to impart to man a little of their own strength and fortitude. They will find the fair land, but the fair land itself is a place that does not give itself easily, so they will have to fight for that too.

And all this is the story of how Dominick does so. Always people have been seeking the fair land. America was made what it is because people weren't satisfied with what they had and set out to find it. Some of them found it: some of them didn't. When it wasn't in the east, they looked to the west; and when it wasn't there, they went north or south. Even now, with a world where there are not too many wars, there are people still searching. If they seek long enough, they will find it.

This is the story of how Dominick found it.

In the same magazine, there is a paragraph about my father's life written by the editor of the magazine:

He has appeared several times as an actor in the United States. People ask him how he can be a writer as well as an actor. The truth is, Mr Macken simultaneously goes about his daily life and thinks books. 'Research in Ireland,' he assures us, 'mainly means talk.' He believes that his 'research' has taken a lifetime of observing, listening and questioning.

My father got a letter from one member of the staff of Macmillan in London in April 1959:

Dear Mr Macken,

On reading 'Seek the Fair Land' in the proofs recently and becoming whole-heartedly involved with your wonderful characters and plot, I had a sneaking suspicion that Sir Charles Coote was a regrettably familiar figure to me. Indeed on visiting my mother's house this weekend, I found his portrait hanging on the wall and he appears to have been an ancestor of mine. I thought you might be interested to see a photograph of this portrait together with the epitaph written below it which I always understood was on his tomb.

I am very interested to know whether in fact Sir Charles Coote was murdered in the way described in the book, if you know by any chance whether this was his epitaph and if so where is he buried? [*I think my father's dramatic description of Sir Charles Coote's murder by Murdoc came from his imagination – the historical fact appears to be that he died of a fever in his bed.*]

My mother's family still lives in Ireland and the name Coote has appeared more than once in the family tree. I must say I am rather hesitant about writing to you as your feelings are so obviously engaged on the other side (and small wonder!) but I thought you would be intrigued to hear that Macmillans was unwittingly harbouring a descendent of the villain of your book.

It is possible that Independent Television may want to interview you on their Bookman programme. Would you consider making a trip to London should they decide to televise you on publication? (This last question is in my business capacity as assistant to Mr White in advertising.)

Yours sincerely,

Elizabeth Romyn (Mrs)

Terese Sacco, who became his principal editor instead of Lovat Dickson, wrote to him on 28 May about a statement she had received from the Russian publishers of *The Green Hills*:

'You know, of course, that the Soviet Union does not take part in international arrangements with regards to author's royalties. It is therefore, as you will understand, very difficult for us to enter into negotiations with your firm regarding Mr Macken's royalties. We have nothing against the author but we cannot deviate from our principles.'

I consider the last sentence a minor masterpiece. I think I shall have a principal that forbids me to pay my rent – while generously holding no ill will towards the landlord. I suppose there must be some happy medium between the 'Reader's Digest' and Russia?

All good wishes,

As ever,

Terese

My father received an invitation to attend the Berlin Film Festival as the leading actor in *Home is the Hero*, but he decided not to attend. He did not see any purpose in attending such a festival.

In October, news came of the success of *Seek the Fair Land* from Don Congdon:

October 6th 1959

Dear Walter,

Al Hart has just reported the following in connection with trade sales of 'Seek the Fair Land':

'As I think you know, our first printing was 12,500 copies. As of today we have disposed of 8,000 copies including presentations. My guess is that the first printing will be exhausted early next year.'

When I've got more news towards the end of fall, I'll report again.

Yours,

Don

Now that the first historical novel was published and launched, work had begun on the second volume. A bit of a diversion came on 13 October 1959, when a different publisher, the World Publishing Company, was interested in commissioning my father to write a full-length adult biography of Daniel O'Connell. They were anxious to tie my father to a contract to write the biography and they were willing to pay him an advance of $4,000. The man from this new publishing company, Thomas P. Coffey, had actually worked with Macmillan before joining the World Publishing Company.

However, Al Hart did not want to lose Walter Macken to the World Publishing Company and he was willing to pay an advance of $5,000 either on a biography or else on a fictional work where Daniel O'Connell's life would be the a background to it. With prompting from Don Congdon, the letter commissioning the novel came from Al Hart on 30 December 1959:

Dear Don,

We will be happy to offer you a contract for the unwritten and untitled novel by Walter Macken based on the life of Daniel O'Connell.

We are willing to pay an advance of $5,000 on signing, against a royalty of 10% on the first 10,000 copies and 15% thereafter, with a reverter to 10% in any year after the first year of publication in which sales fall below 1,000 copies.

We would like to suggest that the manuscript not exceed 120,000 words in length, and we would like to include a delivery date to be determined by the author. All other clauses would be similar to those that obtained in our contract for 'Seek the Fair Land'.

If you can let us know before the end of next week that you ap-prove, I will ask to have the contract drawn up for Walter's signature before I leave for London. Incidentally, I hope to see him while I'm over there.

Many thanks for your friendly cooperation, and have yourself a hell of a 1960.

Best,

Al Hart

17

TEARS OVER
THE SILENT PEOPLE

This contract helped my father to begin work on the second novel of his historical trilogy, *The Silent People*, with its guaranteed advance. He began exhaustive research on that period of Irish history to gather the material needed for the background. He did quite a lot of research in London, and Lovat Dickson (as can be seen in the letter below) arranged for him to look up the Daniel O'Connell files in the offices of the *Times* in London. He also read a lot of material about the famine, both in London libraries and at home, particularly in the Folklore Commission files. When my father was reading the vivid descriptions of what happened to people during the famine years, the terrible deaths they suffered from disease and starvation, my mother would find him in tears.

The following letter came from his American agent:

Harold Matson Company.
February 16th 1960

Dear Walter,

Thanks for your good letter of the 12th. It seems to me that your letter, which I quoted to Al Hart, was very clear on the point as to whether it would be based on O'Connell or not. I think the contract title is simply for a frame of reference. If you like, in the contract why don't you change it to 'The Era Of O'Connell', and initial it.

As to the length – I think 120,000 words will allow you a little more than 'Seek the Fair Land' length. I don't think you should be too concerned about the length, however, because even if the novel runs to 150,000 words, I don't believe Macmillan will kick if the novel holds up in that length. The business of inserting a maximum length is simply a point of control in the negotiation of terms, but I have not as yet found a publisher to insist that an author cut when they felt the novel held up in the length in which the author submitted it.

Yours,
Don Congdon

An interesting letter arrived from Lovat Dickson the following month:

Macmillan and Co. Ltd.
2nd March 1960

Dear Walter,

I heard from Mark that you were to be over here the week after Easter and wanted to consult the files of 'The Times' about Daniel O'Connor.

I spoke to A.P. Ryan, the Assistant Editor and he will be only too glad to be of every assistance to you. He tells me that 'The Times' has some remarkably interesting material on O'Connor, some of which has never been published.

There is some connection between their famous correspondent Russell and O'Connor, and he told some amusing stories in this connection. He would like you to write to him about a fortnight before you come, just saying when you will be calling in, and he will

do everything to be of assistance to you. You will find him a most
likeable and intelligent man.

I look forward to seeing you then too, and I hope you and Peggy
will set aside an evening for dinner with us.

Yours ever,

Lovat Dickson

It was unusual for Lovat Dickson to get a name completely
wrong, but he had clearly mixed up the names O'Connor and
O'Connell.

An interesting letter came from Fielder Cook on 17 March:

Dear Mackens,

This note comes only to say we love you and miss you all and need
to hear from you soon. I've been working on television, getting a
play ready for Broadway next season that I own and will direct, if
it comes out properly and gets on. I'm getting a fierce itch for new
lands, especially Ireland, and if everything dies around here this
summer, as is quite likely, I'm determined to take off and land in
Shannon. Seems to me I could find a way to live a month over there
at less cost than sitting home. Anyway, that's the insidious reasoning
I'm using to get away.

No word on 'Hero' yet. From what we can find out, they plan to
release it in May, but nothing definite. I was most disappointed when
they released the Fitzgerald and Julie Harris two films first. Both
got good reviews everywhere but the 'Times'; the first did okay, the
second (Julie's) died fast. I went to see the Fitzgerald one which was
pretty awful. Couldn't face going to 'The Poacher's Daughter'. From
what I can gather, they released these two [films] as Fitzgerald and
Julie's marquee name value is much higher than Arthur Kennedy's.
The Abbey Players was the strong draw in all three films, but as
they (the theatre managers) could advertise them in all three films,
they took the two with the biggest 'star' names. Quality is never

discussed in the film market here, only what is likely to get them into the theatres.

I gave your lovely book to some friends who enjoyed it immensely and asked that I wrote you of their pleasure. Please let me know how it did and what you are on now. People ask me and I can't tell them anything. We are so respectful of your very fine talent.

I know you made the right decision not to come to New York to act in the play that was offered to you, but I must admit it would have been a real greatness to have you and Peggy here. You mentioned in the letter that you might possibly bang away at a play? If this happened please write details when it's proper to do so.

Come to think of it, my friend Ultan should be big enough now to act in the parts you turn down, so next time why don't you send him and say it's you. These idiots over here wouldn't know the difference and he might even put you to shame.

So a good night to you all and every wish for your health and happiness. Write when you have a moment; it will reassure us that all is well and you haven't been eaten by a druid.

Fielder and Sally

There was another short note from Fielder in May:

Dear Walter and all the Mackens,

Your letter was so welcome, and we love and miss you all something fierce. Just the morning before the mail brought a letter from Phillip O'Flynn with a pile of reviews too, and we were most overjoyed at the reception. My next prayer is that it does really great business. It would give me great pleasure as this is the exact reverse of what the English film boys think possible, but far more importantly, I want to hit Elliman and Dalton with my plan for a movie of 'Rain on the Wind'. I have thought, and I have decided, and now it must happen. It is a beautiful picture, and it must be done in Ireland, nowhere else. The best first step would be for 'Hero' to be a financial smash. The rare thing everyone hopes for, but it occasionally happens, write me how the film does.

No change with us. I am most anxious for news of your book and I just assume we are to get the second copy printed view [*sic*] airmail for my anticipation is great.

I do miss Ireland, Wally, muchly. And so far as I can see we have absolutely nothing in common. But love, health and good fortune to you all. I'm, in a bit of a rush now, but I wanted to answer your note soon. Please write all news and gossip of Connemara. And look after it for me until I get back.

Your friend,
Fielder

For the next few years, our annual holiday was usually spent wherever my brother was studying. So in June/July of 1960, we visited Rome. I think we spent about two weeks there. I remember visiting places like the Via Veneto, the Vatican and St Peter's Basilica. My brother was living at the head house of Opus Dei in Rome, where the founder, José Maria Escríva, also lived. My father made reference to the trip in this letter to Rita Joyce:

Gort na Ganiv.
July 11th 1960

Dear Rita,

Thank you for your card and letter. We were in Rome seeing our eldest son who is studying there and had a wonderful time in the sun of Italy. Back to the frost and the cold north wind, it is hard to get back to work again. I'm glad you liked the book [*Rita had written to him about reading 'Seek the Fair Land'*], the Joyces were very big shots at one time. They owned all the land on the north-west shore of Lough Corrib. The whole of Connemara is still filled with Joyces. You should come and see it sometime. I hope your mother is very well. I had one or two chances of going back to the US since but they all seem to coincide with my work and that has to come first.

Hope we will all meet again soon. Tell your mother we were asking for her. While we were in Rome, we did a vigil in St Peter's in front of the body of Saint Pius X, so we hope that all our relatives will benefit. With most sincerely wishes to you all for 1960.

Yours,
Walter

My father continued his intensive work on his second historical novel and also wrote short stories, many of which were being published in magazines like *The New Yorker*, *The Saturday Evening Post* and *Argosy*, and Macmillan put together enough stories to go to make up a new short story collection. Lovat Dickson wrote to my father in December 1960:

Macmillan & Co. Ltd.,
London.
9th December 1960

Dear Walter,

We have now chosen the following twelve stories to be included in the short story book – they are 'Patter O'Rourke, No Medal For Matt, The Conjugator, The Red Rager, The Match Maiden, The Big Fish, This Was My Day, Light In The Valley, Solo and the Nine Irons, Solo and the Sinner, Solo and the Simpleton and The Lion', but our cast off of these would make a book of only 144 pages, which is much too short. As you know, we have other stories of yours here, but we feel rather lukewarm about them, and it would be foolish to put them in simply to bring the book up to a reasonable length.

If you have nothing else that might go in, what I would like to suggest to you, and I hope you will consider it seriously, is that you write a long story about 20,000 words in length that could be used as the title story. This would add substance and balance to the book, and I think you would work well at this length, where you would have more elbow room to develop your plot and characters and not be working within the strict and rather suffocating confines of a magazine story. If you could pull off something good, it would make an admirable lynch-pin for the collection and the variation in tone and length would set off the shorter stories.

What do you think? I am loath to deflect you from the novel you are working on at present, but if this collection is to be a success then I think we must have a good, long story to strengthen it, and not weaken it by taking the easy way out and adding the other less good stories we already have just to make weight. Will you let me know how you feel about this?

All good wishes to you and Peggy,

Yours ever,

Lovat Dickson

While these letters from Lovat Dickson are revealing, it is such a pity that I was never able to get my father's responses. Because of Lovat Dickson's advice, my father sat down in the period between December 1960 and February 1961 and wrote one of his most powerful stories, 'God Made Sunday' and this became the title story of his second short story collection.

As previously mentioned, my parents took holidays to visit my brother. He spent three years studying in Rome and secured a PhD in Philosophy. He had to defend his thesis in both Latin and Italian. In autumn 1960, Opus Dei sent him to Pamplona University in Spain to study for an Arts Degree – Opus Dei had founded the university.

For Christmas 1960, my parents decided that we would visit my brother at Pamplona, even though I did not want to leave home for Christmas and protested. The plan was to spend Christmas itself at Lourdes and then to take a train to Pamplona. Being at Lourdes in the winter is a very different experience from being there during the pilgrimage season. The only people there were the local French people and I felt a spiritual presence at the Grotto and at the midnight mass in the church. Of course, there was no turkey or ham for our Christmas dinner; instead we were offered some game bird! We made our way to Pamplona, passing through San Sebastian on our way. Pamplona is a nice small city and we saw lots of my brother who seemed very happy in the university and had discovered a new talent for singing folk songs at concerts – he was called Wally, The Irish Singer.

My father's first letter of 1961 refers to the trip to Pamplona:

Gort na Ganiv.
Jan. 13th 1961

Dear Rita,

Many thanks for your card and letter of December 20th.

We were in Spain for Christmas so just got your letter yesterday when we came home. My eldest son is attending the University of Pamplona, having just done three years in Rome where he got his Doctorate in Philosophy – summa cum laude (terrible the way we boast about our children). He will be three years in Spain where he is taking an arts degree in journalism. So we went to spend some time with him, staying at Lourdes on the way for midnight mass.

The play I wrote in the fall was not successful. Nobody but myself and a wonderful actor seemed to understand what it was about [*probably 'Voices of Doolin' which only ran for about a week in the Gaiety with Cyril Cusack as the lead actor*]. However, it was a good play and some day its merit might be seen.

I am writing the story of the little people of Ireland in three books; the first one was 'Seek the Fair Land' (did you read that one?), the next one that I'm writing now is about the people in the Daniel O'Connell period. I've been at it for 2 years and the 3rd one will be the people in the freedom period from 1901 to 1921. So I have plenty to do.

I'm glad your mother is well. Tell her we send her our warm greetings. Pity we can't all meet again but then 3,000 miles is a lot of miles.

With all best wishes from me to you.

Most sincerely,

Walter

In January 1961, the film of *Home is the Hero* was finally released in America to mixed reviews and, despite Fielder Cook's hopes for it, it was not very successful.

My father was working hard: between 9 December and early February he wrote the title story for the new collection, 'God Made Sunday'. The story is based on an island off the west coast – I think he was probably thinking of Inisheer (one of the Aran Islands), an Irish-speaking island. The principal character, Colman Fury is a fisherman whose first language is Irish. Each summer a red-haired stranger, Pól, came to visit the island. He was a successful writer of novels and did not believe in God. He used to go fishing with Colman and one day he asked him, 'Why do you believe in God?' Colman was stunned, and said that if he needed an answer to that question, he should talk to the priest, but Pól insisted he wanted to find out why Colman believed. He kept pestering him until finally Colman agreed that during the long winter months he would sit down, write his life story, and in this way explain to Pól how he came to believe in God.

Colman does not write his life story in conventional chapters, instead he uses the days of the week: his first chapter is Monday, second is Tuesday and so on. His father and brothers were drowned at sea on a Monday, he learned to make a boat on Tuesday and fell in love with Caitriona on a Wednesday. The style is extraordinarily simple and Macmillan loved the story:

London.
21st February 1961

Dear Walter,

Three of us here have now read 'God Made Sunday'. It is first class. Many congratulations. The monumental, but poetic, effect comes off splendidly and the method of writing you have chosen admirably sets off the simplicity of the theme. The only problem you set us now is that of avoiding anti-climax with the shorter stories, which will be overshadowed by this one.

There were only literal corrections to be made in the MS, as you obviously do not intend that quotation marks should be used for the characters' speeches. If you like we will have it re-typed as you ask so that you may have a copy for Don Congdon; alternatively you may care to wait until the story is in galleys, and we will arrange for him to be sent an extra set of these. That would save some expense for you. Let me know what you think.

We think that the stories to follow 'God Made Sunday', which will of course be the first and title story, might go in this order, 'Patter O'Rourke, The Big Fish, Solo And The Nine Irons, The Match Maiden, The Conjugator, Solo and the Simpleton, Light in the Valley, This Was My Day, Solo and the Sinner, No Medal for Matt, The Red Rager, The Lion'. Does this suit you? If so we will send the copy to the printers. So very pleased about all of this.

Yours ever,
Rache Lovat Dickson

In July, Terese Sacco wrote to my father to update him on the publication of *God Made Sunday*:

London.
13th July 1961

Dear Walter,

Here are galleys of 'God Made Sunday', two sets and the manuscript. Will you please correct the marked set and return it to me. I see that despite our instructions, they have not yet left a gap after 'Sunday' in the first story, though this may be intentional. [*My father had asked that there be a blank page after Sunday to illustrate that Colman never got to write Sunday but the publishers on both sides of the Atlantic ignored this request.*]

We had better mark it again in the galleys. I have just heard from Al Hart and will be sending him galleys straight away. He asks if there is any news of the next book in the trilogy, by which I presume he means your book on Daniel O'Connell. All that I know is that you are working hard on this at present, but if at some time you could spare us a note on the project as a whole, i.e. 'Seek the Fair Land', the O'Connell book and the next proposed volume, this would be terribly helpful to us, and no doubt to Al Hart, in dealing with any enquiries we receive when we start publicising the O'Connell book.

After some hard thinking we have decided to delay the publication of 'God Made Sunday' until January. Because of printer's holidays, we could not hope to set the publication date before mid-November now, and that would be a bad time to bring out a volume of short stories. The booksellers will have spent their Christmas allocations, and there are so many books jostling in the autumn catalogues for the reviewers' space that we feel 'God Made Sunday' might be overlooked in the journals, and that it would probably be better to launch in January when people still have their book tokens to spend and when reviewers will have more space and leisure to deal with it properly. I will of course be letting Al Hart know about this when I write. Perhaps we can coincide publication with them now.

All good wishes to you both,

Yours ever,

Teresa

In the autumn of 1961, while my brother was still at university in Spain, I began my own university course in Galway, studying science, much to the astonishment of my parents. In September of 1961, a London theatre agent, Roy Fox, began to try to get my father roles in television or film; this again was probably to provide some financial security. One ATV (Associated Television) part fell through and then at the end of October, the director of the film version of Brendan Behan's *The Quare Fellow*, Arthur Dreifus, asked to meet him. My father met him on 29 October at the Shelbourne Hotel in Dublin and was offered the leading role of Regan, the prison warden. He would be starring with Patrick McGoohan and Sylvia Syms. The money wasn't too bad, he would be paid £900 for the six week shoot and any day over that he would be paid £75 a day.

My father had a wardrobe fitting on Wednesday 8 November and they began shooting the film, primarily filmed at Kilmainham jail, on Thursday 9 November. They did a few studio shots in Ardmore. The original play did not have any kind of a romance in it, but of course Hollywood had to introduce the idea of the young warden, Patrick McGoohan having an affair with the young wife of the condemned man, played by Sylvia Syms. My father enjoyed the experience. Brendan Behan had been recruited by the film company to sing the title song, 'The Auld Triangle'. Behan was keen to meet my father, but he would arrive on set drunk and my father avoided him. As far as I know, they never met. Others actors in the film included Harry Brogan, Eric Gorman, T.P. McKenna, Eddie Golden, Pat Layde, Michael Hennessy and Charlie Roberts.

Good news about *God Made Sunday* came from Don Congdon

on 15 November. *Good Housekeeping* the well-known American monthly magazine decided to publish a condensed version of the story in their March issue, they were paying $4,000 for the right to do so.

On 28 December, Terese Sacco wrote to him with good news about the German publication of *God Made Sunday* by Rex Verlag, while another German firm, Herder, decided they would like to publish a German edition of *Seek the Fair Land*.

My father's work on his second historical novel, *The Silent People*, took almost three years. He had begun his research in 1959 and finally finished the manuscript by the end of 1961. He set out to tell the story of a descendent of Dominick MacMahon, Dualta Duane, who begins his life in the small village of Clonbur on the northern side of Lough Corrib. At the beginning of the novel Dualta is a carefree seventeen-year-old, when suddenly his life is changed by an encounter with the son of a local landlord. He strikes the landlord's son and is forced to go on the run. He escapes across the lake to the Glann side, where he is helped by a local family and sets off for Galway with a young man from the house, Paidí.

The two boys make their way to Kerry where they are employed as farm labourers. Dualta becomes involved with the Whiteboys through Cuan McCarthy and is chosen to infiltrate the house of the local landlord Wilcock. He gets a job in the house, but he falls in love with Wilcock's daughter, Una, and when the night comes for the Whiteboys' raid, his loyalties are torn. Eventually he flees over the mountains with Cuan, finally reaching County Clare. There Dualta decides to settle down, gets himself a small-holding and begins to work on the farm. Meanwhile Una arrives in the same village to take up a job as a teacher. She has converted to Catholicism and so has been disowned by her parents. The pair fall in love and marry, but then the famine strikes the village.

Dualta decides to emigrate to America with Una and their baby, but the last moment, they change their mind and instead head back to Connemara, where they are determined to make a new life for themselves.

The publishers in England and the America both liked the book, but agreed that it was too long. Once my father had cut it, its publication got a green light. Terese Sacco wrote: 'I thought "The Silent People" very impressive indeed. It is a powerful book.' The only letter I have from a publisher about the book is from some time after its publication, but gives an indication of its success:

The Macmillan Company.
April 18th 1963

Dear Walter,

It occurs to me that I've never told you what we did by way of advertising 'The Silent People'. Briefly, we took ads in the 'New York Times' Book Review, the 'Boston Herald', the 'San Francisco Chronicle', the 'Chicago Tribune' and 'The New Yorker'. To date our sales total just over 5700 copies.
  Best,
  Al Hart Jr

The Silent People got very positive reviews all over the world and, like the other historical novels, has remained in print with Pan Books, the paperback imprint of Macmillan, up to the present day.

For Christmas 1961, we visited Spain again, as my father explained in this letter to Rita Joyce:

Gort na Ganiv.
Jan. 11th 1962

Dear Rita,

Many thanks for your card and your letter.

We have just returned from Spain where we were visiting my eldest son (24) who is studying in the University of Pamplona. We had a pleasant time wandering around Spain and spent a few nice days in Paris on the way back. My youngest son, Ultan is studying science – a strange animal in our family of the humanities. But he likes it. Says it avoids speculation – working on known facts, etc. I spent two months in Dublin acting in a film, made enough money to go to Spain. Did you read 'Seek the Fair Land'? It was a Literary Guild choice in the US last year. It's one of three. The next one is called 'The Silent People', it will be published at the end of this year maybe. I have a book of short stories coming out in April called 'God Made Sunday', thirteen tales. 'God Made Sunday' is a long tale, a sort of novella. I think you might like it.

Tell your mother we were asking for her and hope she is well. I wish we could all get the chance to meet again. Life is so short. I'm afraid we will have to wait for Heaven, so it is worthwhile making sure we get there.

Peggy sends her best wishes,
Yours sincerely,
Walter

Anthony Havelock Allen, a producer from Liger Films Ltd., the company who was producing *The Quare Fellow*, wrote to my father at the end of February to tell him they needed to do some post-synchronisation work for the film and asked him would it be possible for him to come over to London to do the recording. At the same time, BBC Radio made a request to feature *Rain on the Wind* as their book of the week on Woman's Hour. When Macmillan and Woman's Hour discovered he was coming over to work on the film, they asked him to drop into BBC to do an audition for narrator of the book on their programme. As these negotiations went on, my father wrote a most interesting letter to my brother concerning his mother's recent death. My brother had obviously written to him to say that he felt no sense of loss owing to the death of our grandmother.

Gort na Ganiv.
March 8th 1962

My dear Wall,

You were nearly spot on for your mother's birthday. I will try and explain why you felt no deep sense of loss for your granny's death. In the first place grandchildren only see their parents' parents when they are old. You probably remember Granny when she looked after you in Dublin. She was nearly sixty then, not able to do as much work without getting tired, impatient and irritable. You saw her very few times after that. It would be very difficult to form an attachment for a person you saw only a few times in your life, and at other times only heard about.

Apart from this my mother left home to work in Galway when she was about 14. Her mother was dead. Her father was a very bad-tempered old man (it seemed to me) I don't remember any tears at all when he died. I don't remember my mother crying for him. All her brothers and sisters emigrated to America when they were 16. She never knew the older ones, never even saw them. In these circumstances I think my mother grew up sadly lacking in love. She married my father and had only 3 or 4 years of life with him when he was killed, so she was simply deprived of the only one who really loved her, so she had to carry on bringing up three children on very little money in adverse circumstances.

I think she was incapable of showing love or expressing it. She just didn't know how. She had no practice. I think my father was the great love of her life. Even when I was quite big, I used to hear her crying for him in the night. I could never get close, in love, to my mother even though I always desperately wanted to. I'm sure she loved us just as much as I love you and Ultan but she was incapable of expressing it. In the odd way that I have of expressing it, to both of you. But I have the feeling that you both know I love you and that my whole life revolves around Peggy and yourselves.

But there is no doubt that my mother loved God. If she didn't why am I trying to this day to be a good Christian? If my mother did nothing else for me but make me a lover of daily mass (as she did) as far as I am concerned her whole life was worthwhile. The last twenty years of her life was filled with religion. You might not approve of the different rosary beads, prayer books, medals, etc., but everyone goes to heaven in their own way and this pious sentimental way was her way – all the streams of 1/– and 2/– postal orders that bloomed out from her to all the various societies and congregations. This was her way.

Her death was remarkable. She always wanted to die with the nuns. Last year she wanted to go to a home, nobody approved. There was a two-year waiting list. She wrote herself and got a place straight away with the Little Sisters of the Poor. After two months (mainly owing to a troublesome and interfering talk of a certain visitor), she became dissatisfied and wanted to go home. However, she had a fall and couldn't leave. While she was well she went to mass and Holy Communion in the Church of the Home every morning.

Then a resident priest brought her communion whenever she needed it once she became bed-ridden. She got Extreme Unction on two occasions. She died most peacefully unconscious from a clot that travelled to her brain, as the Angelus bell was ringing and the nuns were gathered around her bed reciting the prayers of the dead. It seemed to me to be a blueprint for a happy death.

Her requiem mass was most simple. A Spanish priest (oddly enough) said the mass most devoutly. Some of the other residents tottered in and the little nuns sang the responses. Somehow I felt it was impossible to feel sad at this simple and moving ceremony. Another great thing when we knelt for Holy Communion, my sister Birdie knelt beside me. Before she died, mother had made a reconciliation with Birdie and my other sister Eileen. Now I expect mother will bring Birdie back completely. She was buried in the Catholic Cemetery at Kensal Rise, filled with Irish, Poles, Italians and Spaniards.

I tell you this but I don't give a picture of my mother. I remember her as she was when we were young. Anything else doesn't matter. You have to get behind the human foibles and weaknesses of all of us to get to the inner man. That's what God sees. I don't believe my mother really knew what a mortal sin was – not to mind indulging in them. We have a strong conviction that she is in heaven (with her Walter) and if you want to prove this – just try her out to see if she is not able to help you.

Don't feel puzzled about not feeling anything. Just try and pray for her and ask her for a few favours, and you will find that you will get to know her better now than you did before. If only we could see one another's souls instead of the behaviour of the shell, how wonderful the world would be.

Having met the little Sisters of the Poor and seen them at work and the things they do so cheerfully, professionally and lovingly, I have no words to describe the wonder of their vocation. The Church is marvellous. It really provides for everybody.

You have all my love,

Your father

I remember many times when my Granny was visiting us that my father seemed unable to communicate with her. My mother told me that she found whenever Granny Macken visited us, it was always she who talked to Granny. My father seemed incapable of communicating with her. I got on very well with her myself, we would often have great conversations especially when she was taking care of us back in the 1950s.

By spring of 1962, BBC Radio was anxious to audition my father for the reading of his novel on Woman's Hour. He arranged to go to the BBC for the audition on Monday 9 April, the day before he was going to do the voice-over work for *The Quare Fellow*. He did a successful audition for BBC and was invited to come over to London to make the broadcasts. They ran the serial for two weeks, from Monday 30 April to Friday 11 May. My father did the first week's reading live and recorded the second week's instalment in the afternoon of the first week. He was paid about £4–4–0 per episode. But they also gave him over night subsistence and paid for his airfare. He received hundreds of letters from all over Britain and the producer wrote this very complimentary letter:

The British Broadcasting Corporation,
London.
17th May 1962

Dear Walter,

I have a large pile of letters on my desk marked 'Rain on the Wind'. I'll just give you a random selection of comments:

'I cried buckets …'

'A hundred thousand blessings on Walter Macken for his enthralling reading. God bless his work.'

'I wish he would go on reading "Rain on the Wind" forever.'

'The story and voice combined uplifts the mind, appeals to the best in one, even affecting the subconscious …'

Again and again listeners want their thanks conveyed to you for a 'perfect, wonderful, magnificent' serial. N.B. – they are all saving up to buy the book!

I was so glad to know that you felt it was worthwhile; I enjoyed our sessions tremendously.

Once more, our warmest thanks for all the pleasure you have given us.

All best wishes,

Yours,

Genevieve Eckenstein (Woman's Hour)

As a direct result of his reading on Woman's Hour, Macmillan were asked by many booksellers to reprint the book. It had been out of print for five years and so they decided to do a new edition of it. Something else is revealed in Lovat Dickson's letter to my father:

Macmillan & Co. Ltd.,
London.
4th June 1962

Dear Walter,

Thank you for your letter of June 2nd, and for counter-signing the copy of my letter of May 31st about royalties on the reprint of 'Rain on the Wind'.

I am so pleased to hear about Wally Óg and I know how pleased you and Peggy will be. Jonathan [*Lovat's son*] is writing [*taking*] his finals this week, but I will write and tell him. It will really be wonderful if Wally is able to celebrate his first mass in Oughterard.

Yours ever,

Rache Lovat Dickson

My brother was selected by Opus Dei to be ordained as a priest in August 1962. He had already completed his studies in philosophy and theology, but now he had to go through a whole series of minor orders so that he could join the other members of the Opus Dei who were due to be ordained on Sunday 5 August. There was tremendous excitement in our house as we planned that Wally Óg would return to Oughterard to say his first mass on Sunday 12 August and we would have a party at home that day for all our friends.

My father summarised what his plans for the summer were in the following letter to Sabina Walsh:

Gort na Ganiv.
June 26th 1962

My dear Sabina,

My apologies for putting the wrong stamp on Peggy's letter, I probably sent it by sail. I didn't tell you how pleased we would be to see Peter and yourself at the ordination. The date we have (liable to change) is August 12th in Madrid. We spend a few days with Wally Óg in Spain and then get back here in time for him to say his first Solemn Mass in Oughterard Church on August 19th, with a reception for all the guests in the house here after mass.

He hasn't had time to write to us. He is finishing his Arts Degree, knocking off the last theology exams and then had to get all the minor orders, tonsure, sub-deacon, deacon conferred on him inside a month. But the 12th was the last date he gave us. It's probably right but if it isn't we will let you know. Dearly as we would love to have you sleep in our house – we have no beds left. Will I book you in a room in a hotel here in Oughterard, or would you prefer a more comfortable one in Galway?

My love to you all. I'm painting the house from front to back for the last month. We are getting a new roof put on next week, so we are up to our eyes, but our joy in Wally Óg's ordination would be complete if you were both around.

Most sincerely,
Walter

My father wrote a follow-up letter to Sabina and Peter in July:

Gort na Ganiv.
July 21st 1962

My dear Sabina and Peter,

Cannot tell you how delighted we are that you are going to be at Wally Óg's ordination. It fills the cup for us. I'll look after the Galway end for you, hotel, car, etc., and I will give you all the gen when we meet.

We are flying into Madrid at about 8.15 p.m. on Thursday the 2nd of August. I don't know where we will be staying. Wally Óg is looking around for a hotel for us. We have arranged to fly out with Wally Óg on Monday 6th. He wants to get home and see Ireland. He will only be home for a week after the ordination and then will have to depart again, destination unknown for the moment.

We have all the arrangements made for the mass in Oughterard on the 12th – High Mass at 11.30 and then the reception here in the house afterwards. We'll have about 80 people, and if the day is fine it will be grand; we can park them all outside and feed them. Anyhow it will be fun. We are going to have great laughs. It's marvellous that Wally Óg will have 5 relations at his ordination.

He started getting all the minor orders conferred on him last Wednesday – tonsure, etc. He had a beautiful moustache which he had been nursing for 2 years. It was his only regret having to lose it.

I cannot tell you how we are looking forward to seeing you both again. This was a great year for us – our 25th wedding anniversary last February and our son a priest in the same year. My mother died in London in January. That was the only sadness. She would have been so pleased.

All our love,
See you in Spain,
Walter

It was my first time visiting Madrid and my brother's ordination was fantastic. It was a wonderful experience to be standing in St Michael's Basilica and watching my brother join almost a hundred other men as they waited to have the hand of the bishop laid on them. When it actually came to the moment, we watched as he moved, knelt in front of the bishop and his hand laid on him. I sensed the presence of the Holy Spirit in that moment.

The following day we flew back, I think to Shannon, and from there made our way to Galway. There was a lot of preparation to get ready for his big day, Sunday 12 August.

All the family friends were there and I spent the time taking photographs. Looking at those photographs now, I think my mother looks incredibly sad.

After his week at home, my brother went to Barcelona and my father wrote to him at the end of August:

Gort na Ganiv.
August 28th 1962

Dear Wall,

We got your card today. Very pleased. We were beginning to imagine all sorts of things when we hadn't heard from you. We forget that you are grown up and well able to look after yourself.

... It is still a bit like a dream that we saw you are ordained, attended your masses, saw you in a cassock, I suppose you get used to it in time. Nothing of note has happened here. I'm trying to work. I find the trouble about a writer's brain is that it can only think of a certain amount, absorb it, colour it and deliver it. There is no use being impatient with your mind while it is trying to 'create' it will only do it in its own good time, and forcing it is no help at all ...

The coloured slides Ultan took came out quite well. If you are ever at home again, you can have a look at them, also most of the snaps he took in Madrid. I will get copies done and send you one or two to see …

We went to a reception for Cardinal Browne in UCG the day after we left you in Dublin. The Bishop [*Michael Brown of Galway*] was there and singled me out in a loud voice to say how much he liked 'The Silent People'. He had got a loan of the page proofs from Canon McCullagh.

You have all our love,
Your father

My father probably started to work on the third historical novel at this stage and in the autumn of 1962, *The Quare Fellow* was released. My father received terrific reviews. Dilys Powell in *The Sunday Times* picked him out as the star of the film, in the *Daily Mirror*, critic Dick Richards said: 'But the most memorable performance is that of Walter Macken. He is a veteran warder who is sickened by the system of capital punishment. Macken's honest playing will surely leave many people wondering whether execution may be a worse offence than the original crime.'

My father received a nice letter from the director of *The Quare Fellow*:

17 Denmark Avenue,
Wimbledon.

My dear Wally,

Now that the dear old picture has been exposed in a few countries – and I have been there at the various premieres and showings – the score is clear. You have walked away with the top honours for which I want to thank you – and congratulate you, all at the same time. I might have had some severe disagreements at the time about the omission of various so-called key Behan scenes, but now that the final edition has been shown, it must be said that the impact is more than expected. There are still those who decry the modifications from the original play, and are most vociferous about it.

The raves about your Regan – in New York, London, Amsterdam, Paris, etc. – are endless. I am sure you have heard of this wonderful result – which seems to make up for some of the discomfiture and pains we underwent during production. Pat McGoohan and Sylvia, too came off well. But it seems to be Wally Macken all the way – and all the others won high praise, also.

May I take this opportunity to wish you and your family Merry Christmas and a Happy New Year, and express the hope that I may soon have the privilege once again to work with you. What's new in the writings? Please let me know what 'Wally Mackens' I should add to my bookshelves.

My special love to both you and Peggy,

Arthur Dreifus

My father had a principle he stuck to every year: he never bought or sent Christmas cards and each year he wrote a long detailed letter to his cousin in America, Rita Joyce, looking back over the past year and what had happened to us during the year:

Gort na Ganiv.
January 1st 1963

Dear Rita,

Very pleased to hear from you and to know you and your mother are well, and we appreciate your good wishes. Actually 1962 was the most successful year of our lives – because our eldest son was ordained a priest in Madrid – and in comparison with that nothing else really matters. I was sure you would have known about this as I had sent a first mass card to you, but obviously you didn't get it. I'm enclosing a couple now as a memento, so that you can put the young priest in your prayers.

We celebrated our 25th anniversary in February. My mother who was 78 died in London the previous month and on August 5th my son was ordained – so you can see it was a momentous year for us. We went to Madrid for the ordination. An occasion like that is indescribable – even for me and I have the gift of the gab. The following Sunday August 12th, he sang a Solemn Mass in Oughterard Church and we held a reception in the grounds here afterwards.

We were praying for a fine day, as the weather was very bad all summer and the Lord smiled on the young priest and gave us a glorious miraculous day of sunshine – so we could feed everyone outside. It was a most happy day. My son stayed 3 days with us and then he had to go back to Barcelona. He will be working there for a year and after that we don't know where he will be sent …

Peggy thanks you for the compliments. We remember well our visits with your mother and yourself and Peggy wishes your mother to know that she still has the beautiful rosary beads your mother gave her.

You see why the other things are not important. I hope you like 'The Silent People'. I put a lot of work into it. I am now working on the 3rd book of the Trilogy. It will be called 'The Scorching Wind' and I will be a happy man when it is finished as I can become a 'contemporary' man again.

'The Quare Fellow' is not a good film. It could have been a sort of good documentary, an anti-capital punishment film but they made a mess of it introducing unnecessary material to 'improve it'. The Director was not good – he wouldn't listen to advice from anybody – but I liked my part and carried on despite everything.

I've managed to find a snapshot for you. It's a bit dark but it'll give you an idea of what your cousin the priest looks like.

With my sincere good wishes from us here and in the hope that we will all meet again soon. Life passes so fast. We always seem to be racing after it and failing to catch its tail.

Most sincerely,
Walter and family

One of the family friends who always sent us a Christmas card was the Grace Family from Long Island. It usually had a photograph of all the Grace family. Just after Christmas 1962, Margie Grace wrote to my parents:

January 15th 1963

Dear Wally,

I cannot tell you how happy the news of Walter's ordination made me. I can only imagine how thrilled you must be. But I know you both deserve this joy. I can still remember when I was trying to encourage you not to get up so early for mass when you had to be up so late at night in the theatre and you said: 'Sure it's the only worthwhile thing I do all day.' How that response thrilled me! And you'll be embarrassed to know that I've told a great many people about it.

I often wonder how you both are and would love to hear all the news about you. I have heard a great deal about the Opus Dei as a very good friend of mine is very active in it in Lima, Peru.

Our family gets bigger and older and the pace gets a bit faster every year while I get a little slower, I'm afraid. But we have so much to Thank God for and we are grateful to him for everything. Peter is in South America at the moment but his work takes him to Europe even more these days. However, he is still just as much fun as ever and when he's home the whole house vibrates.

I hear that Michael [*Peter Grace's brother Michael was the producer of 'The King of Friday's Men'*] has bought a house in Dallas, Texas, but I'm not sure if it's true.

Charley [*another of Peter's brothers, I think*], whom I'm not sure if you know, is happily married to a lovely girl with three children.

With best wishes to you,

Affectionately,

Margie Grace

My father replied to Margie's letter:

Gort na Ganiv
Jan. 22nd 1963

Dear Margie,

It was so pleasant to hear from you and to know that you are all well.
I thought you would be pleased at the news of the ordination of our
son. It was all very moving – but like all good things in life, it was
here and gone in a flash. The only good remark that was relayed to
me – by a person who knew me long ago and in whose eyes actors/
authors are damned said – 'How could a fellow like Wally Macken
have a son a priest?' I felt no resentment at this because it just echoes
my own feelings and proves conclusively that priests are chosen for
themselves – not from their parents.

We have watched all your children growing up each year in the
Christmas card you send and are filled with admiration. What a
lovely family – the boys are so big and the girls so beautiful which is
only as it should be and Peter and yourself remain unchanged. We
often think of your kindness to us and the genuine joy we got from
your family and your home.

We live quietly here beside Lough Corrib – working as hard as
ever trying to put dreams on paper and make a living from it. I don't
think I need to tell you how welcome you would be if you drop in
on us. Peggy is very well, slowing up as you say. That happens to all
of us I'm afraid.

I'm so pleased to hear about Charley. Yes we met him, the time
we were staying in 'Tullaroon' and feeling likes millionaires on
Mike's account – although from what I heard, I think that Charley
was picking up the tab. He was most charming and we are delighted
to hear about his family.

We haven't succeeded in getting to the US since. I've withdrawn
more and more from acting. I do a part in a film now and again,
when they are made in the new studios in Dublin. It's a break from

the constant torture of thinking, which is the main part and the hardest part of the old writing profession.

It doesn't embarrass me when you quote me on the daily mass. It's still my belief, only more so now. For my part I always tell about the rosary in Grace's house after dinner and everyone is handed a rosary beads, whatever religion they possess. I still have a wonderful picture of all of us kneeling down saying the rosary and the cowboy from Texas who trained Peter's horses – a most charming man, sitting on a couch with the rosary beads in his hands. So it's nice that we tell good stories about each other.

My best wishes to Peter and all the family. Peggy sends you her love and to say how pleased she was to hear from you. I hope we all meet again someday – if not here, let's hope in Heaven.

Yours most sincerely,
Wally Macken

18

THE SCORCHING WIND
COMPLETED

During the early part of 1963, my father was hard at work completing his research for *The Scorching Wind*. He went to talk to people who had lived through the War of Independence and through the Civil War. Among the people he met was Tom Barry in Cork and my mother described the meeting: 'They were describing in great detail, the ambushes they staged and the fighting they conducted against the British army, the Black and Tans and the RIC. There was one quiet man sitting beside Tom Barry and I discovered that this quiet unassuming man was actually an assassin. He talked quite calmly about killing people.' My mother noticed that although he was a small man, he had a huge right hand – his shooting hand.

They spent some time with Tom Maguire who was related to our family. He lived in Cross and when my father met him, he was in his seventies. As the commandant of the South Mayo Brigade of the IRA, he had been in charge when they ambushed a Black and Tan lorry at Carrowkennedy on the Westport to Leenane Road. As he wanted my father to experience what it was like to stage an ambush, he walked with him over the mountain and down towards Carrowkennedy and then they walked back over the mountain with some of the men who had accompanied him on the original ambush. My father found the mountain climbing tough and was out of breath, but he noticed not one of the veteran IRA men were out of breath at all.

There is no doubt that that particular research was important, but all his life he had been talking to men and women who lived through the Rising and the Civil War. Mrs O'Connor, a close family friend, told us how one of her brothers was in the IRA, and when during the Civil War her future husband came calling to her house to see her, leading a troop of the Free State soldiers, her brother, who was on the republican side, had to hide.

There were also conversations in Roundstone with Bulmer Hobson every week during the 1950s. Hobson had been a member of the IRB and had tried to stop the 1916 Rising. My father also spoke to Geraldine Dillon, married to Professor Tom Dillon and mother of the writer Eilís Dillon. Tom Dillon was the chemistry professor in University College Galway and had manufactured explosives for the IRA during the revolution, while Geraldine Dillon was a sister of Joseph Mary Plunkett, one of the executed 1916 leaders.

My father was a very fair man and tackling such a controversial period as 1916 to 1922 posed challenges. Although he was a republican at heart and tended to support Fianna Fáil and Éamon de Valera, he was determined that the story would be told from both the Free State and the republican side.

As he was working away at this third book, regular life continued. He heard from Lovat Dickson in March:

Macmillan & Co. Ltd.
8th March 1963

Dear Walter,

We have reprinted 'Rain on the Wind' and I am sending a copy
to you under separate cover. It is an offset from the last edition, so
there is really no difference, but I thought you would like to have it
for the bibliographical information on the back of the title page.

How are you? It is a long time since I have heard from you, and
I wonder have I in some way unconsciously offended you? I hope
not. My mind turns towards you and Galway and the spring makes
me think of our dapping adventures together.

My best wishes to you and Peggy,

Yours ever,

Rache Lovat Dickson

In the summer of 1963, I went off to Bilbao in Spain where I was
placed on a student work experience programme with a company
called Union Espanola de Explosivos. My job was to work in
the laboratory primarily testing various chemicals. This was the
summer that my father was writing *The Scorching Wind*. He made
some mention of it in his letters to me that summer:

> Nothing much has happened here. The old routine is still in action.
> I have finished Chapter 7 so I am still a long way from THE END.
> I miss the shouting matches very much. I cannot shout at Peggy
> now either when both of you are gone because that wouldn't be fair.
> Anyhow it's all good practice for the inevitable time when you pull
> up stakes and depart for good.

Having spent the best part of nine months in Barcelona, my brother
was now based in London and was completing the journalism

course that he had begun in Pamplona. He was now studying for his MA in media studies. He also studied in Oxford but his main job was working as a priest for the Opus Dei university residences in London. My father wrote to him on 2 August:

Seeing that next Sunday is the anniversary of your first year as a priest has set me thinking a lot about you. A man has dreams about his sons, what they will grow up to be. Even when they are small, and he is picking them up when they fall, he is wondering what will this little fellow grow up to be. I think most people would prefer their sons to be in the world. This is a form of vanity. They want to project themselves into the world when they are no longer there – to leave a mark – so in reality they are not thinking at all of their children but of themselves (a case in point is Mrs Dickson who, when she heard Jonathan was friendly some years ago with Opus Dei members was terrified in case he might have a vocation and that she would be left without grandchildren).

Anyhow the whole case was solved for me the evening of March 25th when you came home and said you were going to join The Work. I can never forget that evening. I thought that the Holy Ghost was tangible with the three of us in the room. There was a tremendous lift in the atmosphere which we desperately tried to hold on to. Impossible, but it was there and it was unforgettable. I hope you will understand when I say that even the moment of your ordination in Madrid takes second place in my mind to that. I think it is because of the first event I never had any doubts about the second and final event. Just a sort of case of holding your breath for nearly seven years until it actually occurred. It is a wonderful thing to have a son a priest; I don't think there is any human honour that is comparable to it.

Unlike his normal routine, where he would rarely write for more than an hour at a time, with his historical novels he would spend many hours writing each day. He wrote to me on 6 August:

August 1963

Nobody visited us. We have heard from nobody interesting. So pretty barren. Still having trouble with the book. I had to dump two or three chapters and start all over again – but God is good, I'll get on the right lines soon now and bash it out.

Later on in the letter he tells me:

Peggy and myself are certainly getting a foretaste of what it will be like to be living on our own and have come to the conclusion that you are an asset to the place. This information will probably horrify you.

He wrote again on 14 August:

I went to the mass on Inchagoill on Sunday. It was most moving. They had set up a bower clad altar in front of the old church. The sun shone but the lake was rough. About 500 people there. A Galway band playing the Royal Salute at the Elevation; the trumpets muted by the open, sounding soft and beautiful over the graves of all the saints there …

A very nice family staying in King's bungalow – the one near Vesta's – they are the family of Mr Dan Costigan who is the head of all the cops in Ireland. He is a daily communicant, we noticed. I met his wife and children in Inchagoill. They are very nice. The girls are blonde and pretty and intelligent and nice. They all came and played tennis here. We said it was a pity that you weren't here. You would have enjoyed meeting them and showing them around a bit.

I think I have got over the hump in the book. I'm now about one-third of the way through and if I can keep on as I am going I should have it finished by the end of October.

He completed the manuscript of *The Scorching Wind* by the end of October. A letter from Terese Sacco confirms this:

Macmillan & Co. Ltd.,
London.
30th October 1963

Dear Walter,

We are delighted to hear that we may expect the manuscript of 'The Scorching Wind' next week and we have every confidence that the marriage will be a long and happy one for this book.

We are equally delighted to hear that you are coming over in two weeks to see Wally Óg – whom I had the pleasure of meeting a couple of weeks ago.

The German edition of 'Seek the Fair Land' has come in today and I have sent you five copies under separate cover. They have printed 3,000 in hard covers and 2,000 in the usual Continental paperback edition. They now want to get their hands on 'The Scorching Wind'.

See you soon,
Yours ever,
Terese

Lovat Dickson also wrote:

Dear Walter,

I am delighted to hear that the manuscript of 'The Scorching Wind' is winging its way over here. I hope that I will have time to read it before we meet, as I hear from Wally Óg that we will do when both you and Peggy are here in mid-November. It doesn't give me much time, but I am longing to get at it.

I am sure you are sorry to bring such a long work to a close. You have been living with it now for eight years, and it must feel like losing a good friend. We can talk of all this when we meet. I am looking forward so much to seeing you both.

Yours ever,
Rache Lovat Dickson

My father and mother postponed their visit until after Christmas but Lovat Dickson wrote to him to re-assure him about the reception *The Scorching Wind* was receiving from their readers:

London.
21st November 1963

Dear Walter,

You must be worrying about 'The Scorching Wind' and I thought I should put your mind at rest by saying that we have just received on it a most favourable report. I am now going to read it myself and I hope to do that by the end of next week and I will write to you then without delay to say what I think of it.

But this much is already clear from the readers, whom we trust, judging the work of an author who has proved that he can also be trusted to turn out the goods. To them, the readers, it seems better than the two previous volumes in the trilogy, and I am delighted that this should be so.

More next week, and love to Peggy.
Yours ever,
Rache Lovat Dickson

My brother was based in London from September 1963 up until the autumn of 1964. My father wrote to him in November 1963:

Gort na Ganiv.
27th Nov. 1963

My dear Wall,

It was nice to hear you on the phone, just to know that you were there, since we have more or less forgotten what you look like! It was odd that Rache Dickson should have been there. One of the reasons

I rang you was to tell you that we were not going until January, as I had already told Rache this in a letter about the book but he got the news in first.

I'm most pleased that they liked 'The Scorching Wind'. I don't know what I would have done if they didn't. I found it the hardest book to write of all, I don't know why.

Maybe it was because I'm dealing with almost contemporary history and I know there are people around who could be hurt by what is written. Anyhow it's mainly a human story of a fight for liberty, an anonymous fight for liberty. I wanted it to have more of an impact than the first two books, since the first two were sort of introductions – and the third had to be a crushing and exciting finale.

I'll tell you one thing – no more trilogies for me. A man can only do one in a lifetime. I'm pleased to be finished. It seemed an awful long road that I started out on. I hope to have proved something – if only to myself; hoping I have a better knowledge of myself and our people and why we are as we are.

I met some wonderful people in the course of writing the book – the ordinary men who went out to fight for freedom and when it was over went back to their various jobs and got on with living. It was the greatest period of our history and then we had to smash it all with a Civil War. This was a very sad business but I had to bring it in …

Isn't it terrible about President Kennedy. The Irish took him to their hearts when he was here. They waited a while to see if he was really sincere and when they found he was, they pulled out all the stops. He was really a literate statesman and they are so rare that I suppose they must die, since apparently God permitted it to happen.

Looking forward to meeting you and seeing you,

Much love,

Your father

Good news came from Lovat Dickson soon afterwards:

2nd December 1963

Dear Walter,

I spent a pleasant weekend reading 'The Scorching Wind', and I wholeheartedly congratulate you on it. You have brought this trilogy to a triumphant close. We must now send the book to the printers in order to get estimates, and I won't write to you about royalties until we have the figures before us, but you need not worry, and I hope you will put all these matters aside now and let us settle them when you are in London in January.

I will talk to you then about the detail in the book, but there is nothing I can criticise. I have only praise for everything. Tess has been through the manuscript and has tidied up the typing and spelling, and I think she has one or two editorial queries she has to put to you when you are here. We look forward to meeting you and a discussion of your future plans now that you have this great project behind you.

Yours ever,
Rache Lovat Dickson

My father wrote a pre-Christmas letter to my brother on 11 December 1963, saying that he was looking forward to seeing him in January and then he gave the following description of our Christmas:

Christmas – as a family feast, I mean – loses some of its meaning when the family breaks up. It is grand when children are young and cursing fathers are tripping over shoes when they are playing Santa Claus first and then playing with their children's toys afterwards. God be with the days when you and Ultan used to be up at 4 a.m.

He also wrote to Rita Joyce, summarising what the family had been doing for the past year:

My dear Rita,

Many thanks for your letter. I'm glad your mother took such pleasure in the ordination of our son. He was in Barcelona since until last September. He is in London since then. We haven't had a chance to see him since he was ordained but we are hoping to go to London for a few days in January.

I just managed to get the last book of the trilogy written before Christmas. It is called 'The Scorching Wind'. The London publishers think it is even better than the other two which cheered me, because it was meant to be the climax of the trilogy – the burst into freedom. I always thought of the books as one book really, a large piece of music – agitato, dimmunondo and crescendo. I hope to have it published as one book under the title – 'The Sons Of Milesius'. Then they can be read as one. I have been 8 years writing them. It seemed a long time since I set out to write them and now that it is over, I feel a bit lost – having to winkle my way out of history back to the contemporary scene again. Still it gives one a good feeling to have accomplished something (whether good or bad) that started as a small thought so many years ago.

My other son, Ultan is still going along with science. He is doing his pass BSc this year, honours next year and MSc the following year if all goes well. Then he will presumably get married and leave the nest like all fledglings but this is life and we had lots of fun while he was here.

I'm glad you liked 'The Silent People'. That took a lot of sweat and agony – it was such a terrible period, so difficult to find any hope at all in it – and yet there must have been a little since we are here to prove the people survived. I hope you like, 'The Scorching Wind'. I read a lot for it but talked even more to people who are still alive and I hope that I captured even the tail-end of the dream and the reality of the time. It too was a sad period but somehow here and there was also laughter. I hope that when you read it, you will write to me about it.

In the meantime to your mother and yourself and all the family, our sincere good wishes and affection.

Yours,
Walter

My father wrote to my brother on 9 January 1964:

I'm glad you wangled 'The Scorching Wind' out of Macmillans and
I am also glad that you liked it and that it brought you home for a
few hours. I don't know why but it was the most difficult book I ever
tried to write. On at least 3 occasions during the writing of it, I had to
abandon what I had written and start again. I think the Irish and the
Russians are happiest when they are most oppressed. Then I wanted
this book to be a climax of the other 3 – the burst into freedom. It was
a wonderful period, but look what happened, we started to kill one
another. I wanted to bring this out in the stories of the two brothers.
It is merely an expression of the lesson that life is constantly teaching
us – when what seems to be unattainable is finally attained, it is no
longer as beautiful or as desirable as it seemed to be.

So we have to look somewhere else and strike out in anger, our
eyes filled with blood, because inside we are crying – but this is
not what I meant. This is not what we wanted. This was the Irish
Civil War, when you talk to men who were there in those days, you
can still sense their anguish, inarticulate but overpowering. Yet they
were great men, because the greater percentage of them just got on
with it and when it was over put down their guns and just went back
to their jobs, bewildered, still more or less inarticulate but inside
they know. It will be no surprise for you to hear that most of them
are very good-living men, although a few of them died still in revolt;
but God understands them.

I'm glad you noticed the absence of politics. These fellows had
no time for politics. All they were there for was to get on with the
job and go home. But they were very determined men. On this
occasion England just didn't have a chance of winning no matter
what she threw at them.

I still haven't heard from the Americans re 'The Scorching
Wind'. This stalled me for a time but now I'm now down to work

again trying to earn some bread and butter, which we are beginning
to need.

Glad that things are going well with you. I remember the day I
went alone from the pier. Even if you didn't lose one father that day,
you certainly gained a better one [*the father and founder of the work,
José Marie Escríva, becomes the father of every member*].

All my love,
Your father

During the months of January, there were some letters from Al
Hart of Macmillan in New York asking my father to consider
cutting the first seventy pages from his novel. But then at the end
of the month came good news, first in the form of a telegram:

Macmillans taking The Scorching Wind. $5,000 advance and
improved royalties. New editor Cecil Scott says pay no attention
changes Hart's letter. Letter following – Don Congdon.

Don Congdon followed up the cable with a letter the following
day:

January 30th 1964

Dear Walter,

This letter follows my cable of yesterday. Macmillan came through
a day sooner than they expected to. Cecil Scott read the novel last
night and this morning and called me, just before the end of the
working day, to say that they were delighted to make an offer on the
same terms as the last. I asked him to improve the royalties to 10%
up to 5,000 copies, twelve and a half percent to 10,000 copies and
15% thereafter. This is agreeable to Cecil and they are drawing up
the contracts.

He also said he didn't agree with Al Hart's letter to you. He thought the first seventy pages are fine just as they stand and asked me to tell you that he will be writing to you himself should there be any minor points which he would like to check with you. I'm delighted, after all this time, to have this news. The last novel, as you know, did not do well and, since Macmillan is willing to offer these terms, it is probably advantageous to you to have this third novel in the trilogy published by them.

Cecil Scott has been with the company for a long time. He is a serious editor, is most admiring of your work and is fully familiar with your record at Macmillans.

Yours,

Don Congdon

The new editor, Cecil Scott, wrote to my father on the same day as his agent Don Congdon wrote:

Macmillan and Co. Ltd.,
London.

As you must have heard by now, Al Hart has left us, and the task from now on of acting as your editor devolves on me. I look forward to it. Al made his formal adieus last Friday, and on Monday of this week, I took the manuscript of 'The Scorching Wind' home with me and read it on Monday evening and most of yesterday, Tuesday. Before I did so, I read through the correspondence between you and Al, and also with the Harold Matson office. Let us now hasten to say two things: the first is that I think Al was quite wrong in his estimate of the first seventy pages. I think they are essential to the structure of the book, and I would not change a word. The second is that I am most enthusiastic about the book. In fact I have not been thinking about anything else all day yesterday and today.

One other criticism that Al made, I feel sure, is quite unjustified. This refers to Dualta's siding with the Irish Free State. It seems to me that this was true to character in the first place, and it was also necessary in order to provide a dramatic climax.

Scott confirmed that he would be sending my father a contract for the book and also asked him to write an explanatory historical note to explain to readers about Sinn Féin and the Black and Tans, the Truce and the troubles that followed. He was so keen on the book that he wanted it to stand on its own rather than associating it with the previous two books.

The move towards publication quickened now as Macmillan of London editor Terese Sacco wrote to him to tell him that they would offer the same royalty terms for the new book as they had offered for *The Silent People*: 10% for the first 5,000 copies and 15% thereafter. She also told him that they were willing to commission the artist Seán Keating to do the cover once again, as he had done the covers of the first two books.

News came in May 1964, that Robert Hogan of Purdue University in Indiana sought permission to include *Mungo's Mansion* in an anthology of Irish plays to be published by the Devin-Adair Company of New York. There was also news that a film company, Seven Arts, decided to take out a film option on *Seek the Fair Land*.

My father and mother visited London in July of 1964 and they met producer Kenneth Hyman of Seven Arts. They got on very well with him and while he was there, Kenneth arranged for my father to do a screen test for a big Hollywood film he was about to make called *The Hill*. He thought he had a chance of getting the part but it was given to Harry Andrews – Sean Connery was the co-star. I had an impression that my father was disappointed he did not get it, as he felt the money he would earn would ease the worry about his financial situation. Although his books were very successful, the long periods of time spent researching meant that there were often periods where not much money was coming in. I don't really remember my father ever not being worried about his financial situation.

Kenneth Hyman wrote to him on 7 September:

> I enjoyed meeting with you and your wife, and hope that in the not too distant future we can all get together again.
>
> I leave for Spain on the 10th for locations on my film, 'The Hill', and return around the 12th October for five weeks Studio work. After that I hope to be able to get down to 'Seek the Fair Land' and start moving on it.

In the early part of 1964, Don Congdon wrote to him and suggested he should attempt to write a children's adventure story. He wrote a thrilling story, *Island of the Great Yellow Ox*, featuring four boys on an island off Connemara in about three months. After the serious nature of his work over the previous eight years, writing his first children's book was an enjoyable exercise. He captured the voices and dialogue of young ten-year-olds perfectly.

Terese Sacco mentioned it in her letter dated 30 October 1964:

> We are delighted to hear about 'Island of the Great Yellow Ox'. I remember you telling me about this, and we all think it is a medium to which you can bring something really fresh and exciting besides gaining you a well earned rest from historical research.
>
> I enclose the 'Cork Examiner's' encomium of 'The Scorching Wind'. You are the pride of Ireland.

In January of 1965, my father wrote his annual Christmas letter to his American cousin, Rita Joyce:

Gort na Ganiv.
Jan. 7th 1965

Dear Rita,

We were just saying that we hadn't heard from you this year, when your letter popped in. We were genuinely sorry to hear about the death of your mother. I wish you had let us know at the time it happened, we might have shared your sorrow a little. We remember her so well, so kind and so good that it emanated from her. There can be no doubt of where she is now and that must be a great consolation to you. I'll bet the place is not the same without her. It's odd how one feels the world is so much poorer a place by the death of a good person and then again, it is richer by the birth of a little baby. I'm sorry we have not had the opportunity of getting back to America to see you all again, but that's life.

I'm glad you understand what a relief it is to be finished with the trilogy. It took eight years of hard unrelenting work. I don't know how many times, I wanted to throw it all up. I felt I owed it to my country to find out as much about her as I could and then say to this generation – Look, this is how it was and what you are, the way you are! The books were moderately successful, that is I made enough on them to be able to scrape a living, but no more than that because the great majority of people are not interested in their own history, not to mind other peoples'. A film company has only taken an option on the film rights of 'Seek the Fair Land', it remains for them to take up the option – for a very modest sum, I'm afraid, if they do do it. However, all is welcome.

In order to break away from all the history and research I have spent the last few months writing a story about boys – a tale of pure invention and imagination (such a relief to not have remain inside the limits of history) called 'Island of the Great Yellow Ox'. I just finished writing it today in fact. After that I will write a new play, I hope and so on and on until invention dies in the ageing mind.

Fr Walter was changed to Dublin last September. We are off to see him this week-end. Ultan got his BSc degree last year and is now studying for honours. We are absolutely delighted that there is a chance of you coming to Ireland and seeing Galway in June. You can't let anyone else but me show you Galway so please Rita keep us informed about your trip. If it wouldn't embarrass you, we'd love to have you stay with us for the few days, sincerely, genuinely, absolutely.

We are bound to be here unless something extraordinary happens and that's not likely. Anyway we are looking forward to seeing you very much and having a chat. Peggy is immensely pleased. She took a great shine to your mother. May 1965 give you everything you want from it.

Most sincerely,
Walter

There was a note from Cecil Scott of Macmillan of New York on 28 January that they had shipped out 7,500 copies of *The Scorching Wind* so far and he anticipated that they would reach a figure of 10,000 copies by the middle of the year.

19

THE ABBEY THEATRE AND
BROWN LORD OF THE
MOUNTAIN

Every year for about ten years, members of the Repertory Abbey Theatre Company came on their summer holidays to Galway. They stayed in Spiddal and we always went to meet them and had dinner with them in a restaurant or sometimes they would come to visit us in our house. Every year they complained about how they felt the existing manager, Ernest Blythe, was ruining the theatre and they were always putting pressure on my father to do something about the management of the Abbey.

They approached the government and asked them to help set up a new governing body for the theatre and the actors requested that the government appoint my father as a replacement for Blythe as artistic advisor/manager of the theatre. In June 1965, Jack Lynch, Minister for Finance contacted my father and invited him to become one of two government representatives on the Abbey board.

Office of the Minister For Finance.
24 Meitheamh (June) 1965

A Chara,

For the reasons indicated in the attached memorandum, changes have been made to the Articles of Association of the National Theatre Society. The 25 persons who accepted invitations to become new shareholders have been selected from lists submitted by the Directors, The Arts Council and the Irish Actors Equity Association. Another feature of the reorganisation is the increase from four to five of the number of directors by the addition of a second Government representative. The nominees of the Government hold office for a term of four years and may be re-appointed.

I would be greatly obliged if you would agree to become the second Government representative on the Society's Board of Directors.

If you accept you will be allotted two hundred shares subject to the condition which applies generally to shares held by directors that on your ceasing to be a member of the Board they shall be transferred to your successor. Shares are allotted without payment.

Directors may not be paid fees but will be able to recoup out-of-pocket expenses.

Please let me know as soon as you conveniently can if you are willing to become the second Government representative on the Board.

Mise le meas,
Jack Lynch

Eventually and reluctantly, my father agreed and his acceptance of the appointment was well received by the press. This story appeared in the *Irish Independent* of 1 July 1965, as part of the *Tatler* column:

Abbey playwright, actor, author of international repute, Walter Macken is to return to the Abbey Theatre soon as a director. I learned that the Government has asked Mr Macken to become the second nominee on the Board of Directors under the recent revitalisation plan which involved the appointment of a number of shareholders. Mr Macken is willing to accept and he should be shortly joining, Ernest Blythe, Gabriel Fallon, Riobeard Ó Fearacháin and Dr Seamus Wilmot, the other Government man on the board.

Mr Macken joined the theatre in the late 40s and his first role was as a walk-on policeman in a play which he cannot now remember but he established himself as an actor of very great talent with his unforgettable portrayal of Bartley O'Dowd in M.J. Molloy's, 'King of Friday's Men'. It is a performance that is still talked about; it ranks among the greatest of the past two decades.

His plays, 'Mungo's Mansion', 'Home is the Hero', 'Twilight of a Warrior', 'Look in the Looking Glass' were all given Abbey premieres. More recently he wrote 'The Voices of Doolin' specially for Cyril Cusack. This was presented at the Dublin Theatre Festival of 1960. Mr Macken tells me he has now completed another play, with Cyril Cusack specially in mind. It is set in the west of Ireland it is called, 'The Last Gentleman' and is a straight piece dealing with the end of an era in the country's evolution. It will be presented in a Dublin theatre, as soon as Mr Cusack's other commitments leave him free and the author will direct and may also take a part.

He has also finished another book due to be published in September. Titled 'Island of the Great Yellow Ox', he says it is about children and is for children up to the age of 90.

Ernest Blythe sent a letter in July explaining the duties to be performed by an Abbey director and telling him that the Abbey Board of Directors met every two weeks on a Tuesday evening at 8 p.m. My father wrote back to him explaining that at the moment he intended to continue living in Galway as they were selling their house in Oughterard and building a new house in Menlo village near Galway city. After they had made the move to Menlo, he planned to spend some time living in Dublin. He also said he would like the Abbey to pay for him to stay in Dublin both on the Monday night and the Tuesday night so that he could get to see the latest Abbey play on stage on the Monday night.

In June of 1965, I got the results of my Science Degree. I had hoped to get high enough marks in Zoology to go on and study for an MSc, but unfortunately my marks were not high enough and so I needed to go and find a job.

My father wrote to Rita Joyce on 7 August:

Dear Rita,

So pleased to hear from you today, also the cards from the Continent. We are very glad that you loved Europe. All it amounts to is that you have to travel the world to find that people are the same everywhere, just that they use their tongues differently. Apart from that the father of all of us was Adam …

We were genuinely pleased to have you with us. We enjoyed your visit so much and we had great fun. Peggy is well, a kitchen veteran grumbling like all good GIs. Ultan is getting over the shock of his exam results. He is duly looking for a job. Once he gets something to start with, I think he will work out his life from there. One forgets how vulnerable you are at 21, although I was married by then and earning six dollars a week selling insurance to Cockneys. He is far better equipped than I was, so I'm sure he will make a go of it.

We have the house on the market but have not succeeded in selling it yet. Some people have called looking it over. This is a terrible feeling, like strangers seeing you in your underwear. It's the result of going into the market-place. Writing in a way is the same. Once you go into the market-place to sell your wares, people have a licence to throw garbage (or verbiage) at you.

We still haven't got the cottage at Menlo started, so now it won't be built until next February/March. This is frustrating – but life is filled with frustration which is good for one if only to find another way of getting around it.

I'm going to Dublin on Monday to attend my first meeting as a Director of the Abbey Theatre. I'll have to go up every two weeks. Duty is a terrible taskmaster. I don't know what will happen to my own work, but maybe it will improve under the strain – only time will tell.

Now you have all the news. All the best, thank you for your kindness and your company, and we are so happy that you enjoyed your visit to us and to Europe.

Affectionately,
Walter

My father went to the Abbey every fortnight to attend board meetings. It was just the first stage of the plan to eventually have my father replace Ernest Blythe. To do this, the government and the shareholders came up with an ingenious scheme. They appointed my father as Artistic Advisor/Assistant Manager, so that within a relatively short period, my father would have taken over the running of the theatre altogether. The letter offering my father the appointment was sent on 27 November 1965:

Dear Walter,

The Board has considered your proposed appointment as Assistant Manager and Artistic Advisor and now offers you the appointment on the following basis. The appointment is made in the hope that you will succeed the present Manager. The decision on that will be made within a year but not later than 31 December 1966.

The salary for the post was £1,350, which, when added to the £100 paid for reading scripts, brought the salary up to £1,450.00.

In the rest of the letter, Ernest Blythe spelled out exactly what my father would be doing in his new job. I think that my father would, if he followed his heart, have said no to the job but he felt under obligation to the Abbey Theatre as a national institution and to the actors with whom he had become so friendly over the years. He also thought that he might be able to do something valuable for theatre in Ireland.

Some of his worries about the future come out in a letter to Rita Joyce, written on 14 December 1965:

Dear Rita,

We got your parcel this morning as we were on our way to leave Ultan to the train. He is going to Dublin for his 12th interview looking for a job which he hasn't got yet. He is very keen on working in Ireland but there's little hope as the appointments are so limited. So in the New Year he is off to London. [*I was going to an interview for a job as a biologist with the Inland Fisheries Trust. I knew that I hadn't got that job after the interview, so I went to the offices of the 'Irish Press' and they granted me an interview – as a result of which I was offered a job as a trainee journalist with the newspaper.*]

I don't know how we can repay your thoughtfulness. All I can think of is to send you a copy of 'Island of the Great Yellow Ox', it's not being published until next March, but I wangled a copy from the publishers. Your gifts are wonderful but we love the copies of the photographs. They are really terrific and bring back memories of all the happy trips we took and the fun we had.

At the moment we are in a bit of a mess. I have accepted a job in the Abbey Theatre as Artistic Director and Assistant Manager with the view of taking over when the old man there departs. This means that we have to find a place in Dublin to live by next March. We still haven't sold this place and the cottage in Menlo is started. We will continue with it and hope to be able to retreat to it in odd times when the theatrical life becomes too much …

I'm trying to finish a book before I become involved in the Abbey but artists setting deadlines is bad business. Still you never know, it will force me to finish. We all have an ideal existence in mind. Mine would be a gently ageing bachelor in a small country cottage, kitchen, bedroom, pig, cow, 3 chickens, 2 acres of land and a spot of fishing, and just literate enough to be able to read, not literate enough to be able to write. My idea wouldn't work anyhow, I would have to have Peggy around somewhere.

Again, many thanks,
We think of you often and your families,
Most affectionately,
Walter

The book he refers to was the novel, *Brown Lord of the Mountain*. He began writing on 25 August 1965 and he completed it by 2 February 1966. Once again, my father's letters to his cousin provide us with a pen picture of what was happening to the family in February 1966. This letter, dated 12 February 1966, was sent from Gort na Ganiv as usual:

Dear Rita,

We were all so pleased to hear from you. I was very pleased that you liked the 'Yellow Ox' and that you used the poor niece as a guinea pig. The book is due to be published over here on February 22nd. I don't know when the US edition is due.

We had rather a hectic time for the past few months. Ultan was due to go to England after Christmas. He attended four interviews in Dublin during December and he was promised a job from one of the Fisheries Boards at the end of January. At the last moment he went and sought an interview with the 'Irish Press', a daily newspaper and got taken on as a trainee journalist. Most menial – running up and down with copy and making tea for the news editors – but he's taking it well. Now that he has chosen a profession, we all belatedly realise that it must have been in the blood – with his grandfather founding a newspaper and his mother editing me. He seems to love it and despite poor wages, etc., he's determined to carry on. For ourselves we are going to live in a flat in Dublin from February 25th next – the address will be 37 Marlboro Road, Donnybrook, Dublin 4.

What a change from Gort na Ganiv! However, I'm taking over in the Abbey then as Artistic Advisor and Assistant Manager. If I feel after 9 months that I can do some good there and advance the cause of it, I will stay. If not I will quit and get back to Menlo. But I'm afraid that there won't be an easy way out like that.

In the meantime I had to try and write a book with all this confusion. I finally finished it and sent it off. Only God knows what it is like. I can only hope for the best. I don't know what will happen to the writing from now on. This is also in the future and is a secret of the future. The Abbey for quite a while is going to take up a lot of my time.

We haven't sold Gort na Ganiv yet. Now that we are leaving it behind, I hope it will be sold soon so that we can make the break complete.

I think that's all the news for the moment. It's a rather odd coincidence that the four of us will be living in Dublin at the same time.

Many thanks for your letter. Write again when you have a minute.

Yours affectionately,
Walter

I began work with the *Irish Press*, early in January 1966. They had a very good system whereby every new entrant coming into the newspaper group worked as a copy-boy so that they learned on the job. They kept you at this level until a vacancy occurred for a junior journalist. For me that took eight months. I was appointed a junior sub-editor with the *Sunday Press* in August 1966. During that period, my father took on the heavy burden of being Artistic Advisor/Assistant Manger in the Abbey Theatre.

My parents lived for a few months in that flat in Marlboro Road while I had my own flat not far away. Then my mother found a house to rent, 25 Rosmeen Gardens in Dún Laoghaire, and I joined them there. Each morning I drove into Dublin, but as my father did not have to be in as early he took a bus and then picked up the car to go home. Despite the attitudes of the Abbey actors, one of my lasting memories of that period is the respect that my father had for Ernest Blythe. He told me that, but for Ernest Blythe, the Abbey Theatre would not have survived, as he was a very good businessman. While he accepted that Blythe did not rate intellectual plays very favourably, his choice of plays resulted in the Abbey keeping their audiences happy. In the six months that my father was working there, he tried to exert control over the Abbey players and he had a lot of difficulty with them. Traditionally they never had rehearsals in the morning, and my father insisted that there had to be rehearsals in the morning as well as the afternoon – morning rehearsals did not suit actors who had been out drinking the night before! He was casting plays for the Old Queens Theatre in Pearse Street (the original theatre in Abbey Street had burned down in 1951 and the company spent the next fifteen years in Old Queens Theatre) and made radical choices. He was also preparing the company to move back to Abbey Street to the brand new custom-made building which was due to open in the first week of July 1966. Although used to an independent life where he made his own decisions, now it was his job to make decisions for a group of people and to try to persuade them to work together as a team.

While Seven Arts had taken an option on *Seek the Fair Land*, a small English company took a film option on *The Scorching Wind*.

The two men involved in this company were Norman Spenser, producer, and Charles Crichton, director, and in March 1966 they came over to meet my father in Oughterard. My father asked me to sit in on those first discussions and said that as I was such a student of cinema, I might have some helpful suggestions. After that first meeting, Norman Spenser wrote my father as follows:

> Redhill Cottage,
> Denham,
> Bucks.
> March 29th, 1966,
>
> Dear Peggy and Walter,
>
> I just wanted to tell you – in writing – how very much we enjoyed our visit and how pleasant and exciting it was to meet you both. Quite apart from the pleasure and fun we have had together, it has been enormously helpful, and fruitful, to the eventual script of the film. I am very glad we met, so soon after making an option contract, because I am well aware as anyone of the kind of types that abound in the 'Film Business', and I wanted you to get a first-hand impression of not only Charles and myself, but the sort of things we were planning to do to your book and the sort of aims we have for the eventual film.
>
> Well having said all that, I'm looking forward to seeing you both again in the very near future, and I hope that the Abbey Theatre doesn't take too much of the stuffing out of you – or become too much of a drag. Next time you are in London, you must come down and visit us here in the country, as a change from London.
> With thanks again,
> Sincerely,
> Norman Spenser

Norman Spenser lived in Denham in Buckinghamshire.

The stress of coping with the workload in the Abbey Theatre and his dislocation from the west of Ireland and his peaceful life in Oughterard, all came to a head in June of 1966. Charles Crichton and Norman Spenser paid a second visit to discuss the script. In taking a break from the work, Norman, Charles, my father and mother decided to go out on Lough Corrib for a spot of fishing or boating. The two men were staying at Currarevagh House Hotel and my father brought the boat from its moorings in Derrymoyle over to the pier at Currarevagh Hotel. The two men got into the boat all right but my mother stumbled and fell into the lake. She was not in any danger but she got a terrible fright and my father of course jumped in and pulled her out. They went home, changed clothes and came back to have dinner with the two men in the hotel.

My father was shocked at what had happened and that night in bed, he had a very disturbed sleep and in the morning, he told my mother he had made a decision to leave his job with the Abbey Theatre. That morning he rang Ernest Blythe and resigned from his position, to take effect just after the official opening of the New Abbey in July. He spent the month preparing the official opening night show called *Recall the Years*, which featured extracts from plays that had become classics of the Abbey stage.

Meanwhile, Norman Spenser and Charles Crichton were still trying to put the film project together. Charles wrote in June, thanking him for bringing them fishing and telling him that he had been in contact with Pat McGoohan and he was interested in taking the part of Dualta in the film.

News also came about the Seven Arts production:

Gort na Ganiv.
Sept. 6th 1966

My dear Ultáin,

Just writing to tell you that Seven Arts came through on the option – so we'll be getting about £4,000. This, with what I have, should be enough to pay for Menlo and have a bit over to get the new car. If so, you can pick up the Viva – by October I hope – just in time for the winter.

We have to go to Dublin next Sunday the 11th, to see furniture, etc. We'll stay 2 nights and get home on Tuesday. We'll give you a ring on Friday to confirm. In the meantime, I'm enclosing £2 so that you can get yourself something for your birthday. You'd want a bit of time to think over how you will spend it!

Charles and Norman were here. We had a long hard session working on the script. I will tell you about it when I see you.

If you like you could take a bus out to the Lucan Spa Hotel on Sunday and meet us for lunch about 1.30. We will try and make it at that time.

All the best,
See you,
Your father

That same day, my father wrote to my brother:

Gort na Ganiv.
Sept. 6th 1966

My dear Wal,

Very pleased to hear from you and to know that things are going well. Can't wait to see you in glasses. I know they will improve your looks, but how about the intellect!!

See what they did for mine, I've been wearing them since I was twelve, and I'm as stupid as ever.

We just have had a very hard four days working on the script of 'The Scorching Wind'. Norman and Charles were here. We have finally got the script to the stage where it can be printed as a presentation script and sent around to the all the fat money cats of the film business. We should know in a month or two if they will be able to raise the money. It has turned into a good lively script with loads of excitement but any relation it bears to the original is a coincidence. Actually this is not so. There is quite a resemblance but it has a much different shape. It will be fun if they bring it off as they intend to shoot the whole thing in Galway and Connemara. Great excitement for the locals.

You will be glad to hear that Seven Arts are taking up the option on 'Seek the Fair Land'. This practically means that I will get about £4,000, which with what I have, will pay for the house in Menlo and take that worry off my back. So that means that we will really own Menlo, in partnership with the Income Tax Authorities.

The glass finally arrived for Menlo – 4 panes short – so now we have to wait another two months for these – but we will put in plain glass until they arrive but we hope to be in there before October 1st.

If I can scratch money from the leftovers I intend to get a new car and give Ultan the Viva. That means I have to give you the value of what I give him; so if you set a value on it, I will give you an IOU and the value in cash when we sell the house. This is only just – cannot treat my sons differently and I'm sure you need the money.

Nothing else much to report. I don't feel by now as if I was ever in the Abbey. It feels like a vague and disturbing dream. Certainly, no matter how hard I try, I feel no regrets. The only regret I have is that I should have said No where I said Yes. I didn't use the nut at the right time. However, I suppose I can write it down to experience and hope that somehow in the future, I will be able to use it.

Peggy is well,
All my love,
Your father

My mother wrote to me for my birthday as well:

Gort na Ganiv.
9th Sept. 1966

My dear Ultan,

A very happy birthday to you and many happy returns. I'll see you on
Sunday which is very pleasant and I must say I'm looking forward to
it. I imagine you're delighted that you're going to get the car – hope
you can manage to run it but I'm sure you'll be economical with
it. All is as ever here – Menlo is really nearly ready at last – hardly
believable! I think Daddy's tummy is still acting up alas but he's
looking much better, Thank God. I miss you sadly even if it was only
to have you telling me off. I hope you have managed to get a flat and
sure we'll help you to move if you get a flat.

There's not a sign of the place here going.
Lots of love,
My dear old son,
Always your loving,
Mammy

During the month of September, my mother put severe pressure
on the builder to finish and eventually they moved in at the
beginning of October. I think it was a huge psychological blow
to my father to leave Oughterard. My mother told me years later
that she was being practical and explained to my father that
they could not go on living in a large house so far away from
Galway. Before choosing the site at Menlo village, my father had
explored various places near Galway city. He travelled up the
Dyke Road and actually found a site over-looking Galway city,
but the landowner would not sell it to him. He continued up that
road and eventually came around a corner and found a beautiful
old Irish village, Menlo. At that time in 1965/66, there were only
about one hundred people living there, most of the families had

lived in the village for hundreds of years as tenant farmers of the Blake family who owned Menlo Castle.

My father made contact with a local woman, Mrs Martín McDonagh, and she agreed to sell my father a half acre site opposite where she and her husband lived. The site was bought for £100 and my father then planned the construction of a two-bedroom bungalow with an architect and the builder. Because my mother was fed up cleaning out fires, no fireplace was built into the house; it was heated with under-floor central heating. The living room was designed specifically to offer a wonderful view of the village and there were enormous windows from floor to ceiling.

While my father and mother moved into their new house in Menlo, I had moved into a flat in Pembroke Road in Dublin and within a week or so of their moving into the new house, I went down to visit them. I loved the house, and my father and I made some exploratory walks up the road from the house. They went to their daily mass in the New Cathedral.

My father wrote a letter to Rita Joyce a few weeks after they moved into the new house:

Menlo,
Galway.
Nov. 8th 1966

My dear Rita,

Just so that you will know we have finally moved into Menlo. We are here a few weeks now. Did I tell you I had left the Abbey Theatre? If I didn't, I'll let you know all about it the next time we meet. The spare room is there with a comfortable bed anytime at all that you want to come. We are gradually getting used to the place. Of course we miss Oughterard but the advantages of this place outweigh the nostalgia of the other.

We haven't sold it yet and so having paid for this place we are practically poverty-stricken which is good because it will make me want to work. I've finished a film script of 'The Scorching Wind' for an English film company. It turned out well and they will proceed to make it when they have raised the £1,500,000! I don't know if they will succeed but if they do we will have some fun for a few months.

Did we tell you that Ultan is now a journalist in the 'Irish Press', a Dublin newspaper, starting from scratch. That's where his science degree ended up, but he seems to love it.

We are both well, Peggy sends you her love. I think you will like Menlo when you see it. It's a real rural setting and yet it's only a few miles from Galway. I'm writing away, bits and pieces. Hope everything is going well with you and that we will meet soon.

All our love,

Walter

A letter came from Terese Sacco of Macmillan in London to say that the publisher was doing a hardback reprint of *Seek the Fair Land*. She had heard nothing from the two film men, Norman Spenser and Charles Crichton, about the filming of *The Scorching Wind*, other than that they had secured English actor David Warner to play the part of one of the brothers. BBC Radio had also broadcast *God Made Sunday*.

Brown Lord of the Mountain was published that autumn, possibly in September (in fact it might not have been published until 1967, as that is the date on my hardback edition. I think both my brother and I could have been given early editions of the book). Both my brother and I read it at the same time and Wally Óg wrote to my father and in reply my father spelled out what he saw the role of a writer as:

Menlo,
Galway.
Nov. 21st 1966

My dear Wal,

We just got back from Cork this Monday evening and were very pleased to get your letter. At least if it did nothing else the book seems to have stimulated you into a philosophical frame of thought in which you neatly tabulated – very for me – the philosophical aberrations (if I may call them that) of the last fifty years or so.

Basically, as Gilson says, since there is no such thing as an artistic creator since all artists use things already created to make-up their poems, paintings, books, statues, and they are really makers, they cannot set out to be philosophers. I suppose the literary people are makers of dreams, having the talent to put words into juxtaposition to make a pleasing whole; if all history before them had not happened to make the words they use, they would be dumb, so much do we owe to the millions of people who lived before us.

I have come to the conclusion that the art of the novelist or the playwright is merely the art of the storyteller. Their function is to tell a story in a cohesive form, attracting the attention of the listener; by various devices which is partly instinctive and partly learned over a long period; to hold the attention and when you feel that attention flagging you recall it dramatically with a shift of emphasis – the aim in short should be to hold your listener enthralled once you have got possession of him.

If one of your (readers) listeners starts to yawn, apart from what may be wrong with him – the storyteller is failing in his profession and should be pelted with refuse from the market place, after all the writers whose works have lived on for hundreds of years were essentially great story-tellers.

'Brown Lord' started off for me with savage indignation. There was a certain young girl in Oughterard who was simple. In the course of a few years, she was twice made pregnant. The thought of the sly, dirty minds of the men who did that thing is beyond my comprehension. The violent things one would like to do with them. But that's no answer of course and indignation doesn't get anywhere except to make a situation worse than it was if it is allowed to break into violence.

It was this aspect that I wanted to explore, joining with Donn [*the main character of 'Brown Lord'*], who in his way set the ball rolling and was the architect of most of what followed his original sin. This is the way life seems to be in fact, with a man bewailing everything except the confession of his own guilt, which he refuses to see.

Anyhow I wanted to tell a good story as well for the reader who won't bother to reflect but who might be caught up in a yarn. I don't want you to review the book. This doesn't matter at all. Reviews of men's work are merely an exposure of the intellect or lack of it in the reviewer himself. How does he know what was in the author's mind when the poor author is not sure himself? All the author thinks – and is sure of – is that he set out to say something and between the thought and the typewriter something is missing – which he has to find the next time; the next time; the next time.

I'm glad you got what you did get out of it. At least it is an assurance to me that I was on the right track even if it ended up a bit misty. I'm glad you like the ending. One expected it to end in a blaze of drama and yet it ends in gentle warmth, almost insouscience meaning more than it actually says. This was just the way it came out even if I expected myself that it would come out differently.

We enjoyed Cork. Saw Máirín O'Connor's triplets. They are ten months old now, very healthy. Gas to see the three of them, all slightly different and with their own personalities already. Like a gentle joke on the part of the Lord – and the bewilderment it brings to their parents.

We also saw Niall and Mary Porchess in Bunnyconnellan. We remembered the lovely holiday we all had there many years ago.

Again many thanks for your letter – looking forward to seeing you.

Much love,

Your father

Reading *Brown Lord of the Mountain* I see how my father used ordinary, everyday life experiences and incorporated them into his writing. The wedding in the novel was based on an experience we had when we attended a country wedding of one of our neighbours, who surprised us all when he announced that he was getting married. His bride to be had been working as a nurse in America. We were invited to the wedding, which was held at the house of the bride's family. My main contribution was to play guitar for the dancers to accompany an accordion player. Poitín was being served and this clear white liquid could be seen in everyone's glass as they sat outside in the sunshine. Word went around that the parish priest, Canon McCullagh was coming up the road and quick as a flash, the man of the house went around putting orange juice in all the glasses. My teetotal father was unaware of the sleight of hand and he went to drink one of the glasses and nearly choked.

In January 1967 he received a letter from a songwriter in England, Peter Hart:

Millbrook House,
Guildford,
Surrey.
January 2nd 1967

Dear Mr Macken,

I have recently returned from Co. Donegal after a motoring holiday in the west of Ireland. I am a writer of lyrics and music, and have for a long time been interested in writing a stage musical about life in the west of Ireland.

During my visit, I met Fr James McDyer of Glencolumbkille and I think his story would make a good basis for a musical. I am writing to ask whether you would be interested in writing the dialogue. I have read most of what you have written and it has given me great pleasure (especially 'Rain on the Wind' and 'Mungo's Mansion'.) I also believe that such a subject could only be written by an Irishman.

You will probably like to know what qualifications I have. I have written the score for a musical version of Charles Dicken's, 'A Christmas Carol', which ran for two Christmas seasons. I have also won two Ivor Novello awards for the film theme – 'The Wind Cannot Read' – and for a children's song, 'Nellie the Elephant' ...

I hope you will be interested in this project, if so I will gladly send you all the published information I have about Fr McDyer. I should add that Fr McDyer has given me permission to dramatise his story. I visualise a large production with a star of the calibre of Peter O'Toole in the lead. I do not think there has been a musical set in Ireland since 'Finian's Rainbow'. Looking forward to hearing from you.

Sincerely,

Peter Hart

My father replied positively to Peter Hart's suggestion, explaining that the musical he would write would have to be fictional and merely based on Fr McDyer's life. My father felt it was a new challenge to write a stage musical, although while working in the Taibhdhearc he would have written various musical pieces. He admired Fr McDyer enormously and he and my mother went to visit him. Peter Hart came to Menlo to discuss the project and my father began to work on it immediately. The title he gave to the musical was *God's Own Country*.

Tomás Mac Anna, the new Artistic Advisor in the Abbey Theatre, wrote to my father in January updating him on the plays they had on – *Tarry Flynn*, the dramatisation of the Patrick Kavanagh novel was a great success, and plans for the season included Brian Friel's *Cass Maguire*, Dion de Boucicault's *The*

Shaughraun and a dramatisation of the Brendan Behan novel, *Borstal Boy*. Mac Anna also told my father that the new Peacock Theatre would be opening on 1 May. But the most important piece of news he had to tell him was that an American TV company was planning to record a version of his script for the opening night of 1966 – *Recall the Years*. The Abbey needed my father's help to cut it down to the sixty minutes required by the American TV company. They planned to film it between 20–25 March.

A lot of what was happening in the early months of 1967 was speculative: Norman Spenser wrote that they needed to get another celebrity name attached to *The Scorching Wind*. Pat McGoohan was not free in 1967, so they sent to the script to Richard Harris who was looking at it. They also tried Paul Newman but while he liked the script he was wary of taking a part that required an Irish accent.

One of my mother's letters to me in February had a worrying paragraph:

Daddy's tummy is not really better at all but at least it's improved – he also says that he will have to have that operation done some time soon, when he can manage it, horrible thought but there you are.

Despite all the disruption, moving house and so on, my father continued writing and probably from August or September 1966, he wrote his second children's novel, *Flight of the Doves*. It took him about three to four months to write a children's book, so I imagine he started it in Oughterard and finished it in Menlo. It was a very contemporary story about two young orphan children, Finn and Derval, who are living with their cruel Uncle Toby in

England. One night they escape and make their way to Ireland on a ferry. They arrive in Dublin and succeed in making their way across Ireland to their Grandmother O'Flaherty who lives in Connemara. By early March of 1967, he still had had no response from the publishers about this new book. He refers to it in this letter to my brother:

Menlo,
Galway.
March 2nd 1967

My dear Wal,

Thanks for your letter. Now that Peggy has a typewriter, she'll keep you on your toes. Macken modesty is merely the exposition of Macken truth – it's just that, the rest of the world won't face it. In the midst of your news we were pleased to note that there is a possibility of you being here April 1 and 2. Hope this transpires. In case it does, I gave orders for the boat to be painted today so that it should be ready in a few weeks. Up to this the lake was no place to be with all the high cold winds. I had a nice letter to day from a an Irishman living in Fife, Scotland, saying how much he enjoyed 'Brown Lord of the Mountain'. He is an Irishman who works as a caddy on St Andrew's Golf Course in the summer, a bachelor, 55 years old, who would love to go back to Ireland but the booze has got hold of him – it was a nice vivid letter – and is one of the real rewards of writing.

My poor typewriter gave up the ghost today so I have brought it in to be fixed. It will take a few days. I've been bashing it pretty hard latterly anyhow. I'm struggling with the musical play. It's all very subtle. You just want to entertain people, not shove messages down their throats. If there is to be a message it mustn't be obvious or you'll hear the click of the seats as they all go home. Anyhow it's a change from the usual and I hope it turns out all right. I'll keep you informed.

We have heard nothing since about the film so it's looking a bit dicey. We haven't sold Gort na Ganiv yet. We haven't heard what Macmillans think of 'The Flight of the Doves', so there are a few swords hanging over our heads. The best thing to do is to keep working and that's what we are at. I don't know what we would do if we made a million and didn't have to work. Get rid of it fast would be the answer so you would have to keep working.

Had a nice week-end with Ultan here. Weather bad but it gave him a chance for some extra sleeping. Talk about the Mackens being thin in modesty, they are sure heavy in sleep. We'll have to get into the garden one of these days and dig some more.

All the best. Hope things work out well for you.

Love,

Your Father

He still was nervous about the publishers' reaction to the second children's book – but they loved it. Macmillan in New York said:

13 March 1967

Dear Walter,

You are incredible! When did you do it? Why didn't you mention that you were doing it? Not that I don't dearly love surprises! Anyway all that matters is that you did do it and it is just grand. We shall publish it in the spring of 1968, which sounds far away and is really almost tomorrow. Thank you very much for another Macken book on our list.

Oh Walter, you are so good. I don't think there is anyone writing today who can capture the very essence of a child the way you can. As you will see when you see the manuscript, I kept writing 'great' in the margins. I think readers will be crazy about the book, and quite rightly! Me too!

During the month of March, news came from Terese Sacco

regarding the possibility of my father and mother going to Poland and Russia for a holiday. Terese was arranging the details with both the Polish publishers and with people in Russia where *God Made Sunday* had sold over 200,000 copies. My father was proud, and he told me there were two words in the title of his story which were normally banned in publications in Russia. His proposed trip to Poland and Russia brought him some publicity. A journalist from the *Sunday Independent*, Gus Smith visited him in Menlo and a substantial story appeared in the newspaper – 'Walter Macken to Visit Russia'. At my own newspaper the other journalists were disgusted with me for not having the story before our main rival Sunday newspaper. I had actually been at home with my parents the previous weekend in Menlo and they had talked about the trip, but I did not think of my father as a news story!

In a letter my father wrote to my brother at the beginning of April, he spelled out how difficult he felt it was for people to understand each other:

Menlo.
April 6th 1967

My dear Wal,

It was very nice having you here for a little while. It's good for you to see how ordinary people live! If Peggy heard me saying that, there would be murder! Anyhow it was very nice having you with us. Even if – as age advances – one is inclined to think back with wonder and some dismay at the time when you were a boy – nearly 29 years ago now – blimey.

The more life advances, the greater one's ignorance. How little we really know about another human being, even one's children After all you are our son. We watched you all the way from the first most wonderful and joyful moment when I heard you were born – all the way up to what you are now and we know no more about you in a way than you know about us – it's mostly a guessing game. This leaves true emotion and what genius we possess in the subconscious or the soul, I suppose, which is the only true plane where people can meet and recognise each other, almost fully. That'll be the day.

There's a cold north-easterly blowing today and I am trying to get into the garden to sow grass seed. This wind would just turn it inside out so I'll just have to sit and look out. What a country for wind. We haven't heard from Ultan since he was here last, but I suppose he has his own troubles. Mick Lohan and myself intend to bring the boat up to Menlo today, but with the wind on the river, it's not going to be very pleasant. Anyhow if you manage to reach Menlo in the future, the boat will be there and we can explore this part of the lake.

I'm banging away at the musical – 5 scenes left to do and I hope to get them finished before we go to Sligo on the 22nd. We had another photographer here yesterday. He took some terrible pictures of me and a lovely one of Peggy for the 'Sunday Independent'.

Fielder Cook is coming to Galway tomorrow to see us. You remember he was the man who directed the film of 'Home is the Hero'. He's a mixed-up kid, but he's a very intelligent man. It will be a change.

It's going to take us years to get the gardens in Menlo in to shape, but one day they will look nice, if we live long enough. It's a bit fatal in this room to be writing a letter and looking out at the same time. The only cure is to firmly put your back to the window and look at the wall. I'm trying hard these days to tranquillise myself. I hope I can succeed. I'm taking an occasional zombie pill in the hope that it will do the trick [*pills prescribed by a doctor for his stomach aches*].

It was beautiful, calm and sunny yesterday in Salthill, a bogus promise of spring, alas. How can you satisfy the heart of man, longing for so many things, not accepting what he has got.

I hope you will have a happy birthday. We will pray for you. I found the two toughest birthdays were 30 and 50, as I think I told you before, but all men are different, Thank God and maybe 30 for you will be a really good one. Next year you can let me know.

All good wishes & much love,

Your Father

My mother wrote me a very nice letter on 12 April, full of news:

My dear Ultan,

It was good to hear you this morning [*I presume I had phoned*]. Actually I would have written as usual yesterday only that I was feeling awful – funny throat, etc., but Thank God today it is much better. Now anyhow you have all the news – about Fielder who has not changed appreciably – still beautifully turned out, the only thing is that the hair has greyed a bit. He's the same as ever, likes those funny jokes with Daddy – he has two little girls, six and four respectively. It looks bad about the film, we had letters both from Charles and Norman saying that they had got Stanley Baker as well as David Warner but if they cannot get the money in ten days or so, which does not seem likely, they will have to postpone which means it's unlikely to come off.

Menlo garden is really beginning to look something – even tulips out – I'm just going out now to plant some things I got from Alma – she was here on Monday night and was asking for you.

You must try and get home if Wally Óg comes to say mass here. Daddy says he will write to you tomorrow, so that you will get an-other letter. God bless you old son, I miss you. I have no one here to give me pep talks.

With love always,

Mammy

Easter 1967 was special. We attended the ceremonies at the cathedral. Again my father and I did a lot of walking and on our long walk on Easter Sunday, I mentioned that I thought my mother was depressed – just a feeling that I had. Of course, after I returned to Dublin, my parents discussed together the things I had discussed with them. My father wrote me a wonderful letter, which unfortunately I have mislaid, but I remember one particular section off by heart:

> Your mother told me that you had told her that you felt that I might have given you an inferiority complex. I am really sorry if I have ever hurt you in this way. Someone asked me once what were the best days of my life and I told them when one son was ordained and when the other son was awarded his science degree. I am just as proud of you and your accomplishments as I am of my elder son.

Looking now at photographs the late Jimmy Walshe (of the *Connacht Tribune*) took of my father in April 1967, you would never believe that he was only fifty-one at the time – he looked a much older man. The stomach aches he had for months were a sign that his health was failing. Finally on Sunday 16 April, his doctor had him admitted to Calvary Hospital for tests. He had great fun in hospital, talking to the nurses and doctors about their lives and questioning the doctors about the tests they were doing. My mother's sister, the warm-hearted Auntie May, came to visit him every day, bringing in flowers.

Finally, on Friday 21 April, the hospital released him, telling him that he would possibly have to have a minor operation, as they thought he might have some kind of a blockage in his intestines. He was home by 4 p.m. and enjoyed a cup of tea and a piece of cake in the kitchen. He phoned both my brother and me.

He sounded in good form and told me that he would have to go into hospital to have this minor operation, but there was nothing seriously wrong with him.

That night, I went to the 95 Folk Club in Harcourt Street, as I often did. I arrived home about 1.30 a.m. and I could not sleep. At 4 a.m., one of the members of Opus Dei, living with my brother in the house in Harvieston in Dalkey, rang to say that my father was seriously ill and that my brother would be picking me up at 7 a.m. to drive to Galway. On the drive down that morning I asked my brother to turn on the RTÉ Radio News and the second item on the headlines stated baldly – 'Walter Macken, the author and playwright, died at his home in Galway this morning.'

That was how we found out that our father had died.

A relative thought that we had been told and so contacted RTÉ news. We drove to Galway and on the way into the city we stopped at Calvary Hospital and went in to see my father laid out in the morgue. We prayed over his body for about twenty minutes. Both my brother and I have strong faith, and did not feel that his spirit was present in the room.

We left the morgue, went to our cousins', the Lohans, house in Woodquay, and went upstairs to see my mother. I will never forget that look she gave us as we went into the bedroom to her. She wrapped her arms around us.

We learned that when they returned from their walk on the prom on the Friday evening, my father had had his usual fry and then they went to watch television. At 11 p.m. they went to bed, but my father could not sleep so he told my mother that he was going to go out into the living-room to try to sleep on the sofa (where he often took afternoon naps). At around 3 a.m., she heard him making a sound. She went out to him and he was dead. The doctors later determined that he had died from a massive heart attack.

POSTSCRIPT

THE WORD AFTER

Although he died on 22 April 1967, my father's work continued
to be published. In 1968, his children's book, *Flight of the Doves*
was published in both England and America. A year or so later,
a new book of short stories, *The Coll Doll and Other Stories*, was
published. *Island of the Great Yellow Ox* was made into a three
part television series in a joint BBC/RTÉ co-production and was
broadcast on BBC and RTÉ in 1971. In 1970, American film
director Ralph Nelson made a film of *Flight of the Doves*, which
was released world-wide in 1971.

My mother continued to live in Menlo and royalties from my
father's books continued to flow in for her annually. I had lived at
home with her for three years from 1967 to 1970, and then I moved
to Dublin to work at RTÉ. My brother Walter was re-assigned
to Galway from Dublin which meant that he was able to see her
regularly. I married and had three children, and we made regular
visits to my mother.

In 1990, when my wife and I agreed to separate, I left RTÉ,
taking an early retirement package and went back to live with my
mother. It was a special time and I learned so much about my
father while living with her in Menlo from 1990 to 1992. She was

a woman who loved routine and every night before she went to bed, she crossed off the day on her calendar. At Easter 1992, after morning mass, I said goodbye to my mother and went to Dublin to see my daughters. I rang her that night, but she did not answer the phone. I was surprised, but thought she might be out with friends. I rang her again on Monday night and Tuesday night. Finally, on Wednesday one of Walter's colleagues in the university residence phoned me to say that my mother had died.

I believe that she died on Easter Sunday night, as that was the last day marked off on the calendar – 19 April 1992. Her burial was the following week, on 22 April 1992, with my brother Walter celebrating mass, as he had done for my father twenty-five years earlier. Finally she was re-united with the love of her life. She was eighty-three when she died, was suffering from a mild form of alzheimer's disease and had begun to have difficulty walking.

After she died, we found out that a number of my father's novels were out of print with Macmillan and Pan Books (the paperback imprint of Macmillan) in London. Brandon Books of Kerry reprinted many of them and most of his novels are now in print along with two new books of short stories – *City of the Tribes* and *The Green Hills* have also been published.

There were four books that my father had planned to write at the time of his death. They included a sequel to *The Bogman* and a book called *Before I Die*. He had also planned to write a novel set in Dublin. Sadly, none of these projects came to fruition.

Walter Macken left a wonderful legacy. During his lifetime, he published ten novels, seven plays and three books of short stories. He also had two children's books published. What an amazing body of work he left behind. I remember mother asking him once, what legacy did he want to leave and he said: 'When people pick up my books in a hundred years time, they will read them and say, so that's how people lived then.' This is what he did in his work, he left a compelling record of how people in Ireland lived in the first half of the twentieth century. Hopefully generations of people from all over the world will continue to read him for years to come.

PUBLISHED WORKS BY WALTER MACKEN

PLAYS:

Oighreacht na Mhara (Inherit The Sea), published by Kennys Bookshop (1946)

An Fear Ón Spidéil (The Man From Spiddal), published by An Gúm (Government Publishing Company, 1952)

An Cailín Aimsire Abú (Salute the Servant), published by An Gúm (1953)

Mungo's Mansion, published by Macmillan (London, 1946)

Vacant Possession, published by Macmillan (London, 1948)

NOVELS:

Quench The Moon, published by Macmillan (London, 1948)

I Am Alone, published by Macmillan (London, 1949)

Rain On The Wind, published by Macmillan (London, 1950)

The Bogman, published by Macmillan (London, 1952)

Sunset on the Window Panes, published by Macmillan (London, 1954)

Sullivan, published by Macmillan (London, 1957)

Seek The Fair Land, published by Macmillan (London, 1959)

The Silent People, published by Macmillan (London, 1962)

The Scorching Wind, published by Macmillan (London, 1964)

Brown Lord of the Mountain, published by Macmillan (London, 1967)

COLLECTIONS OF SHORT STORIES :

The Green Hills and Other Stories, published by Macmillan (London, 1956)

God Made Sunday and Other Stories, published by Macmillan (London, 1962)

The Coll Doll and Other Stories, published by Macmillan (London, 1969)

City of the Tribes, published by Brandon Books (Kerry, 1997)

The Grass of the People, published by Brandon Books (Kerry, 1998)

CHILDREN'S BOOKS:

Island of the Great Yellow Ox, published by Macmillan (London, 1966)

Flight of the Doves, published by Macmillan (London, 1968)

ARTICLES:

The Presentation Convent Annual 1965

The Patrician Annual 1965